MODERN LANGUAGE STUDIES

General Editors:
PROFESSORS J. BOYD AND J. SEZNEC

MODERN LANGUAGE STUDIES

RILKE'S CRAFTSMANSHIP

An Analysis of his Poetic Style

By H. W. BELMORE

Analysis cannot extend knowledge. True: but it can clarify apprehension, and clarified apprehension should surely mean a sharpened enjoyment.

(Lascelles Abercrombie)

La poésie se fait avec des mots.

(Mallarmé)

... mein festes Lied ist nicht gerissen.

(Rilke)

BASIL BLACKWELL
OXFORD
1954

Printed in Great Britain for Basil Blackwell & Mott, Limited
by A. R. Mowbray & Co. Limited in the City of Oxford
and bound at the Kemp Hall Bindery

TO

MY WIFE

FOREWORD

THIS study was originally a thesis submitted to the University of London for the degree of M.A.; it has been considerably revised for publication.

My gratitude is due to Miss G. Loewenstein, Capetown, for generous assistance in financing the publication of this work, and to the Research Committee of the University of Southampton for their contribution. I also wish to thank the editors and publishers for inclusion of my book in their series Modern Language Studies, and my wife for the great help she has given me in checking the numerous quotations.

The nature of the subject requires that all quotations be made in German. Rilke is quoted from his *Gesammelte Werke*, 6 vols., Leipzig, Inselverlag, 1930. The volume number is given in roman numerals, the page number in arabic numerals. *Späte Gedichte*, Leipzig, Inselverlag, 1935, is abbreviated S.G.

CONTENTS

RILKE'S CRAFTSMANSHIP

INTRODUCTION

ALTHOUGH his virtuosity is often admired, Rilke, unlike some of his contemporaries, has rarely been hailed as a master of form. In the great number of publications on the poet, interest is generally centred on his message and on his life, while literary histories stress his importance as a great mystic poet. Yet Rilke was undoubtedly one of the greatest stylists and artists among German lyric poets.

Since he published no critical writings apart from art criticism, we have only his letters as a source of information on what Rilke himself thought of style and technique. His utterances on the subject, measured by what he poured out on other matters, are not numerous, but from what we have, we can establish with certainty that he was very conscious of the paramount importance of crafts-manship in poetry. From an early period he speaks of '*Handwerk*', or *métier* as he liked to call it, and from what he has to say in this connection it is clear that he considered it the premise of his art; without a sure mastery of all his artistic means he could not, in his central period, imagine himself as a poet.

His early gropings for this '*Handwerk*' are somewhat pathetic; at a certain period (in 1903) it was almost a moral issue for him:

... darum tut es mir so furchtbar not, das Werkzeug meiner Kunst zu finden, den Hammer, meinen Hammer. . . . Es muss ein Handwerk stehen auch unter dieser Kunst; eine treue, tägliche Arbeit . . . muss doch auch hier möglich sein! Irgendwie muss doch auch ich dazu kommen, Dinge zu machen; nicht plastische, geschriebene Dinge — Wirklichkeiten, die aus dem Handwerk hervorgehen.[1]

At that time Rilke was convinced that a technical foundation, such as the plastic arts and music possess, would mean salvation for his undirected efforts. In fact, such a foundation hardly exists for the lyrical poet: while young sculptors, painters and musicians have to spend years in acquiring the technique of their art, all the young poet needs is a mastery of metre or metres, and an intimate know-ledge of the language he is writing in, in the sense that he must be thoroughly at home in it; with this equipment and no other, young

[1] *Briefe*, 1902–06, Inselverlag 1930. Brief 46, Aug. 10, 1903.

poets have written masterpieces. Rilke had this equipment too,
but for him it was somehow not sufficient—for reasons that have
nothing to do with technical skill.

Liegt das Handwerk vielleicht in der Sprache selbst, in einem besseren Erkennen
ihres inneren Lebens und Wollens, ihrer Entwicklung und Vergangenheit?
(Das grosse Grimmsche Wörterbuch, welches ich einmal in Paris sah, brachte
mich auf diese Möglichkeit . . .) Liegt es in irgendeinem bestimmten Studium, in
der genaueren Kenntnis einer Sache? . . . Oder liegt es in einer gewissen, gut
ererbten und gut vermehrten Kultur? (Hofmannsthal spräche dafür.) Aber bei
mir ist es anders; . . . ich bin fast ohne Kultur.[1]

Has ever a great poet been so unsure of himself and his craft
as to ask such utterly helpless questions? It seems doubtful whether
a poet can derive much benefit from the study of a dictionary.
In Grimm's excellent dictionary, which Rilke often consulted, he
would find much useful information on the history, etymology
and use of words, together with many suggestive examples—but
where are the poets whose strength goes back to such studies?

Rilke's last question, where he suspects that the lack of a 'well-
inherited and well-enhanced culture' may be at the root of his
deficiency, comes nearer the mark. Yet the military school he
attended was the equivalent of a secondary school, and afterwards
he spent more than two years at the universities of Prague and
Munich. What he lacked most of all, and what a better education
and more cultured background might have provided, was assurance
and taste: they would have given him some balance and direction
at a time when he was stifled by his earnestness and sentimentality.

Yet the problem goes deeper than that: the young Rilke, so
earnest and clumsy in everything he did, was nevertheless not
sincere; groping in the dark and imitating others, he lacked that
maturity that has nothing to do with years, but comes from an
integrated personality. His grip on the technical means of his craft
was really better than he himself knew; what was lacking was an
inner assurance, the flame that destroys all impurities, of which his
youthful poetry is so full. In later years, Rilke disowned his early
work, and we cannot blame him for doing so:

Jene leider vorhandenen Proben meiner Frühzeit sind in der Tat für *nichts*
heranziehbar, sie sind nicht, in keiner, keiner Weise, der Anfang meiner Arbeit,
vielmehr das höchst private Ende meiner kindlichen und jugendlichen Ratlosig-
keit.[2]

This repudiation is strongly worded: Rilke speaks of 'those un-

---

[1] Ibid.   [2] *Briefe*, Bd. 2, 1914–26, 1950. Brief 332, Dec. 24, 1921, pp. 276–7.

fortunately still existing samples of my early period' and passionately stresses 'his youthful helplessness' and the words *in keiner, keiner Weise*.

Technical mastery, the '*Handwerk*' so longed for by Rilke in his youth, is but the foundation of style, and style a thing that cannot be acquired by work or study, although work and study may perhaps improve it. Later, when he wrote his *Neue Gedichte*, Rilke was at last 'in the possession of his means', as he calls it—but as soon as that collection was completed, a new period of stress set in. '*Handwerk*' had indeed set Rilke on his feet; laboriously sought for with much self-discipline and at last triumphantly attained, it had made possible his great achievement in *Neue Gedichte*. Now it could no longer help him to reach the next stage on the road he was to travel.

Analysis of style is a fascinating and rewarding study, especially in a case like that of Rilke, whose style is an unfolding one. From insignificant beginnings, Rilke the man and poet grows to an astounding maturity, propelled by his earnestness, his intensity, all the time absorbing '*Bildung*' while progressing in depth; and his style progresses in step with the growth of his personality. If we had no dates we could, by a close analysis of style, chronologically reconstruct Rilke's opus, collection by collection, in many cases poem by poem. Moreover, we can distinguish in his style what belongs to his original equipment, what to his early surroundings, what to his various '*Bildungserlebnisse*', what to the final mystic maturing of his personality.

Anyone attempting an analysis of style will, in the course of his work, experience enthusiasm and a feeling of awe as ever new secrets of language are revealed, as the power of language shows itself ever more impressively, as the interplay of various linguistic forms in style becomes ever clearer. Yet enthusiasm and devotion to the task should not overbear a certain detachment and that firmness of scrutiny that enables the observer to discover lapses of style. A 'holy soberness' will best do justice to the task and its matter.[1]

Rilke was a conscious moulder of his style, working at it assiduously, improving it with conscientious care until he could at least feel he was a master in his own right. And what a master! Seen in perspective from the height of *Neue Gedichte*, his youthful gropings can hardly be believed. Yet he must have known that even more important than his efforts were the unconscious contributions that cannot be commanded, flowing from the innermost depths of the author's personality, and shaping his personal style,

[1] Wolfgang Kayser, *Das sprachliche Kunstwerk*, 2 Aufl., 1951, p. 330.

i.e. that manner which inalienably belongs to him alone, and by which he can always be recognized.

However personal an author's style, it rests on several foundations, among which are the style of his period, moving in a given direction while at the same time resting on tradition and convention, and the national style, embracing both the genius and the limitations of a particular people.

In dealing with Rilke's poetic style, the personal elements will undoubtedly appear as the most interesting and important, especially in his case, so unlike that of most other poets: a thwarted youth (*Frühe Gedichte*), a late flowering (*Stundenbuch*), a sharp turning away from his ideas and ideals, new apprenticeship crowned by the achievement of *Neue Gedichte*, then a long barren period and final triumph at the age of forty-seven (*Duino Elegies* and *Sonnets to Orpheus*).

The part technique played in this process of maturing is considerable and must attract a good deal of attention; while the background of period and nation cannot be neglected if we are fully to understand and appreciate Rilke's achievement. Our main concern must be with form, i.e. with the sum total of all the elements and processes used in translating poetical thought into language. Each element is to be examined separately in a documented analysis, while concluding chapters will trace the general development of the poet's style, and attempt to assess its importance for German language and literature.

VERSE FORMS

EVER since the controversy about free verse died down, verse
forms have ceased to occupy a central place of interest in the
discussion of poetry. We have become used to the simultaneous
existence of more or less severe traditional forms based on classical
or national models, with less well defined and less pretentious forms,
and even with free verse. This was the situation Rilke found when
he began writing poetry, and in conformity with the usage of his
period, he took it for granted. Finding a number of verse forms at
his disposal, he was only following the trend of his age when choosing from them freely and without bias (except for certain preferences), and perhaps even without much deliberation, at least in his
early production. In one of the rare passages in his letters that deal
with problems of form, he warns a young poet:

. . . weichen Sie zuerst denjenigen Formen aus, die zu geläufig und zu gewöhn-
lich sind: sie sind die schwersten, denn es gehört eine grosse, ausgereifte Kraft dazu,
Eigenes zu geben, wo sich gute und zum Teil glänzende Überlieferungen in Menge
einstellen.[1]

Though we may find some interesting variations by Rilke of existing verse forms, we must not expect that an examination of this
subject will carry us near a sphere of vital formal interest for his
poetry—this sphere lies elsewhere.

In his early poems, Rilke employs the forms in general use in
German poetry of the nineteenth century, with the exception of all
classical forms and metres, such as the ode, the sonnet, hexameters
and the like. The poems are generally short, of the kind made so
popular by Heine: two to three stanzas are the rule, four the exception. It is not difficult to trace other influences: Lenau and Storm
in a general way in many poems, while quite a number seem
to be modelled on Conrad Ferdinand Meyer. Thus 'Feuerlilie', in
Larenopfer, stands out with the compressed wealth of its concise
rhythm:

> Winters, als die Äste krachten,
> keine Bäche konnten frieren,
> weil die Fluten Blutes ihren
> Pulsschlag immer neu entfachten.   (I, 87)

[1] *Briefe an einen jungen Dichter*, Inselverlag, 1929, pp. 10–11.

We find a close model for this in Meyer's *Psyche*:

> Wo von alter Schönheit Trümmern
> marmorhell die Säle schimmern
> windet blass und lieblich eine
> Psyche sich im Marmelsteine.

And who would not think of C. F. Meyer when reading the opening lines of *Am Kirchhof zu Königsaal*, in the same collection:

> Auf schloss das Erztor der Kustode.
> Du sahst vor Blüten keine Gruft.
> Der Lenz verschleierte dem Tode
> das Angesicht mit Blust und Duft; . . .   (I, 74)

Another strong influence, admitted by Rilke himself, is Liliencron. Some early poems read as if they were actually by the older poet:

> Das flügellahme Kindchen flösste
> mir Mitleid ein, — das arme Ding . . .
> Da, sieh! Von seinen Lippen löste
> sich leicht ein kleiner Schmetterling. —   (I, 36)

and again:

> Der Wasserfall ist eingefroren,
> die Dohlen hocken hart am Teich,
> mein schönes Lieb hat rote Ohren
> und sinnt auf einen Schelmenstreich.   (I, 42)

It is remarkable that Hofmannsthal's influence is not so obvious. There are traces of it here and there in Rilke's early production, but it is not possible to point to a single poem where it is concentrated. This is probably due to the fact, stated by Rilke in a letter to Hermann Pongs,[1] that as a young man, he had not had the opportunity of reading many of Hofmannsthal's poems.

In *Advent* and *Frühe Gedichte*, and later in *Buch der Bilder*, Rilke is beginning to show a preference for a short poem with double or triple consecutive rhymes, a type that occurs again and again in the *Stundenbuch*. This short poem, containing one to three stanzas, is the first vehicle of expression of Rilke's personal melody and is typical of his early middle style, up to the *Stundenbuch*. In his *Form and Style in Poetry*, W. P. Ker quotes a similar stanza used by Swinburne, who, he says, may have got it from Victor Hugo, and adds that 'an abstract form, a ghost of this stanza seems to be moving in strange ways and in many countries'. It is possible that Rilke may have first encountered it in poems by Heinrich von Morungen

---

[1] *Dichtung und Volkstum*, Bd. 37, Heft 1, 1936.

and Walther von der Vogelweide, more probable that he got it from
Brentano and Mörike. There do not seem to be any other significant
models for it in German poetry. This is from Mörike's *Gesang zu Zweien in der Nacht*:

> Wie ein Gewebe zuckt die Luft manchmal,
> Durchsichtiger und heller aufzuwehen,
> Dazwischen hört man weiche Töne gehen
> Von sel'gen Feen, die im blauen Saal
> Zum Sphärenklang,
> Und fleissig mit Gesang,
> Silberne Spindeln hin und wieder drehen.

The very harmonious scheme here is a b b a c c b; 'b' rhyming
three times, though not together. In the next poem by Mörike,
the three rhymes are consecutive, as so often employed by Rilke:

> Im Nebel ruhet noch die Welt,
> Noch träumen Wald und Wiesen:
> Bald siehst du, wenn der Schleier fällt,
> Den blauen Himmel unverstellt,
> Herbstkräftig die gedämpfte Welt
> Im warmem Golde fliessen.
>
> *(Septembermorgen)*

Compare this with Rilke's

> Und manche stehn und schaun nach einem Haus,
> darin die Pilger, welche krank sind, wohnen;
> denn eben wand sich dort ein Mönch heraus,
> die Haare schlaff und die Soutane kraus,
> das schattige Gesicht voll kranker Blaus
> und ganz verdunkelt von Dämonen. (II, 260)

The somewhat unusual rhyming scheme corresponds exactly.
In spite of obvious differences in tone and style, a certain rhythmical
resemblance to Mörike is unmistakable in many of Rilke's stanzas,
supplied by the hammering, yet melodious urgency of the three
consecutive rhymes:

> Und sieh, wie ihrer Füsse Leben geht:
> wie das der Tiere, hundertfach verschlungen,
> mit jedem Wege: voll Erinnerungen
> an Stein und Schnee und an die leichten, jungen
> gekühlten Wiesen, über die es weht. (II, 285)

The urgency is enhanced by four rhymes:

> Wenn es nur einmal so ganz stille wäre.
> Wenn das Zufällige und Ungefähre

B

> verstummte und das nachbarliche Lachen,
> wenn das Geräusch, das meine Sinne machen
> mich nicht so sehr verhinderte am Wachen —
> dann könnte ich in einem tausendfachen
> Gedanken bis an deinen Rand dich denken.   (II, 178)

The *Stundenbuch* closes a period in Rilke's development; after its completion, he abandons most of the verse forms used in it, and turns to the sonnet and tripartite poem. Yet the multiple rhyming scheme was so dear to him, and with its repetitions so expressive of his urgency to exhaust an idea or an image to the last, that we find it recurring, again and again, in the longer poems of *Neue Gedichte*. Here are two examples from that collection:

> Die andern fühlen alles an sich rauh
> und ohne Anteil: Eisen, Zeug und Leder.
> Zwar manchmal schmeichelt eine weiche Feder,
> doch sehr allein und lieblos ist ein jeder,
> er aber trägt — als trüg er eine Frau —
> die Fahne in dem feierlichen Kleide.   (III, 73)

> Und das geht hin und eilt sich, dass es endet,
> und kreist und dreht sich nur und hat kein Ziel.
> Ein Rot, ein Grün, ein Grau vorbeigesendet,
> ein kleines kaum begonnenes Profil.
> Und manchesmal ein Lächeln, hergewendet,
> ein seliges, das blendet und verschwendet
> an dieses atemlose blinde Spiel.   (III, 81)

A word remains to be said on the form of the *Stundenbuch* as a whole. It is a conglomeration of short and longer poems, none of them of great length, strung together rather loosely by dominating motives and the ideas inspiring them, and divided into three separate books distinguished by their general themes. As in a book of hours prayer follows upon prayer in a traditional sequence, so in Rilke's *Stundenbuch* one poem is attached to the next by its theme, which modulates from poem to poem. If the theme links each poem to the next, it is the general tone that binds them all together into one whole. This tone is rhapsodic, sustained at varying degrees of intensity, yet always strong enough to make the reader feel the *Stundenbuch* as a whole, not just as a collection of related poems with a super-imposed title.

The sonnet is perhaps the most sharply defined form in European poetry, with a record of ever-recurring popularity unparalleled by any other definite form. It is easily the most articulate, the most 'formal' of the existing forms of poetry, with the possible exception of a few rare, somewhat playful oriental schemes. The classical, i.e. the Italian renaissance sonnet, is a short poem of fourteen lines, generally with five feet to the line; the first eight, called the quatrain, rhyme together to the scheme a b b a a b b a, while the rule for the last six, the sextet, is less rigid: they may have two or three rhymes in a variety of combinations, as cdc dcd, or cde cde, or ccd eed, etc. The sonnet thus contains two unequal groups, with a well defined and distinctly felt caesura between them. The Romance origin of the form is responsible for the architectural style of the sonnet: with its sparing outline and marvellous economy, it may be compared to columns carrying an entablature; the first two stanzas, longer by two lines and weighted with their repeated rhymes, are heavier than the following six lines with their freer and more varied rhyming scheme, which seem to be supported by the former. The caesura dividing the two groups has, at all times and by all poets, been made use of either for an epigrammatic condensation, in the last lines, of what preceded them, or for a sharp contrast, a dramatic conclusion, a brief summing up, a pointed epilogue.

In exchange for its forbiddingly severe form, the classical sonnet offers great dramatic possibilities within a small space, a clear architectural outline, and of all existing forms of short poems, it has the most harmonious and pleasing proportions. It is so short that beginning and end have a definite relation to each other: when the first line starts the last is, as it were, in sight, and the first line is well remembered when the last is being read.

Although handled with considerable skill, and sometimes with admirable art, by Goethe, Mörike, Rückert, Platen and others, the sonnet has always been felt as a somewhat foreign form-element in German poetry. This may well have been one of the motives that influenced Rilke in favouring the form after his *Stundenbuch* period. He was then open to Romance influence, searching, after the stressed '*Innerlichkeit*' of the *Stundenbuch*, from which no development in the same direction seemed possible, for a way out into a wider and more open field. It may seem paradoxical that he should find such liberation in one of the most artificial and restricted poetical forms, but it would not be the first instance of limitation leading to freedom. The sonnet compelled Rilke to condense the roaming looseness of his modulating *Stundenbuch* pieces into individual poems, each complete in itself, sharply outlined and forcefully concentrated.

Rilke did not adopt the strictly classical Italian sonnet, but the more pliable later form with four rhymes instead of the prescribed two in the first eight lines, a form already used by Shakespeare, and with preference by nineteenth-century poets, notably by Baudelaire. Enjambment, of which more will be said later on, further loosens the classical form, and tampering with the length of line almost destroys it. If Rilke's sonnet thereby loses something in architectural severity, it becomes more elastic, and the loss of outline is balanced by various devices, binding in their effect, such as alliteration, assonance, vowel cadence and occasional interior rhymes. It is as if the façade of a building were turned inside, as occurs in Byzantine architecture when the rich, mysteriously glittering interior takes the accent from the stern exterior. In Rilke's hands the sonnet is no longer an almost archaic, 'classical' form. As a form, it did not interest him at all, only as a vehicle for his poetic thought; he had no use for form as such, Platen's and Rückert's way of handling it was alien to his nature, and since his contemporary mind could not feel at home in any form with an even remotely archaic flavour, he did not hesitate to handle the sonnet in his own, very personal manner.

Slightly longer than most poems in his earlier collections, the sonnet seems just right for that something more than *'Stimmung'* Rilke now seeks to express. He has much to say, and the sonnet-form, imposing a limit on his poetic material, compresses his wealth of thought and experience, and helps him in condensing it. The rhymes call for further concentration, and bind the whole securely and satisfactorily together. Moreover, the last group of lines, with the pause, as for breath-taking, that precedes them, leads up to the conclusion Rilke needs: it compresses into a climax what has gone before. Rilke here loves to introduce characteristic words and phrases like

> plötzlich . . . auf einmal . . . da aber . . . nur manchmal . . . während er . . .
> dann erst . . . als wäre . . . doch gerade da . . .

and many more, all indicating a climax, or underlining a conclusion. The earlier poems, especially those preceding the *Stundenbuch*, were of a lighter texture, expressive of delicate moods; their ending was not so deliberate, and some could break off almost anywhere. *Neue Gedichte*, on the other hand, are densely concentrated experiences, compressed into a narrow form; it is natural that each poem should

move, more or less pointedly, to a more definite conclusion summarizing its essence. Conclusions like these:

> Auf einmal kreischt ein Neid durch die Volière;
> sie aber haben sich erstaunt gestreckt
> und schreiten einzeln ins Imaginäre. (III, 236)

> Doch plötzlich scheint das Blau sich zu verneuen
> in einer von den Dolden, und man sieht
> ein rührend Blaues sich vor Grünem freuen. (III, 65)

> Doch da sie den Mann entschlossen fand,
> ging sie mit ihm, nach dem Tode trachtend,
> und sie hatte Gott noch kaum gekannt. (III, 162)

The reader of *Neue Gedichte* gathers the impression that, with
the exception of a dozen or so longer poems and a few quite short
ones, most of the pieces in this collection are sonnets. Yet of the
191 poems that form the two parts, only fifty are genuine sonnets;
a great number are tripartite poems of twelve lines, and many of
the remainder are near-sonnets, that is to say they contain thirteen
or fifteen lines, and resemble Rilke's real sonnets so much in length
of line, metre and general structure that they do not stand out as
markedly different forms. We might say that the sonnet, although
not actually in the majority, marks the key tonality in these collections. Thus '*Die ägyptische Maria*' (III, 156) would be a sonnet
but for an interpolated, bracketed line (the twelfth), and in '*Selbstbildnis aus dem Jahre 1906*' (III, 70), the classical two-ryhme scheme
embraces the first nine, instead of eight lines, welding them into a
group, and leaving only five for the conclusion. In '*Römische
Fontäne*' (III, 79) the end-word '*Schale*' in the ninth line is left isolated
without a rhyme. Such instances show Rilke's independence in
handling a given form, his freedom from conventions. Without
scorning them, he did not hesitate to introduce small variations
when he felt the poem called for them. The objective rule of form:
so many lines, so many feet, so many rhymes, is substituted by the
poet's subjective rule which accepts the other one as a guide only,
without following it closely and minutely in every particular.
Such deviations might be dangerous were they due to indifference,
carelessness, laziness or haste; but they are, on the contrary, moti-
vated by the artist's formal conscience, which bids him transgress
the rule occasionally for the sake of a particular need of expression
or form. In view of Rilke's painstaking filing and 'modelling' of
each poem in *Neue Gedichte*, it would be absurd to speak of any

violation of form: his form is elastic, not rigid, and tolerates minor variations without breaking up the model. Moreover, most of these modifications, although of interest to the student of Rilke's style, do not stand out sufficiently to be noticed by the reader of the poems.

The form of the long poems in *Neue Gedichte* constitutes a real innovation, and is perhaps Rilke's most independent contribution to a new type of poem. The pieces in question are *Hetärengräber*, *Orpheus-Eurydike-Hermes*, *Alkestis*, *Geburt der Venus* and *Die Rosenschale*, all grouped together at the end of the first part of *Neue Gedichte*. Two of these poems, *Orpheus-Eurydike-Hermes* and *Alkestis*, might be called ballads, or rather lyrical ballads, not in the Wordsworthian meaning, but in the sense that the lyrical elements penetrate and at times overshadow the narrative content. The other three poems are predominantly lyrical, and there seems to be no model, with the exception perhaps of some pieces in Heine's *Harzreise*, for purely lyrical pieces of such length in blank verse in the German tradition, nor, for that matter, in that of other literatures. These poems vibrate with a peculiar tension produced by the contrast between the easy flow and comparative looseness of the blank verse and the compact density of Rilke's mature style, with its interplay of personal syntax, similes, sound effects and enjambment, a density matched only by the similar fullness in G. M. Hopkins' poems. Although he must have considered it successful, Rilke did not take up this form again; the longer poems of later periods are written in the elegy or near-elegy form, or in free verse like *Seele im Raum*, *Der Reisende* and other pieces in *Letzte Gedichte*. The two elegies in blank verse are hardly comparable with these flowery lyrical poems, since with their heavy, philosophical thought-content, they belong to a different category.

Length of line is another element modified by Rilke, especially in his *Sonnets to Orpheus*. Holthusen[1] has counted no fewer than eight different metres in this collection. We need not here be concerned with their names which are mostly artificial, i.e. combinations invented to designate these irregular metric schemes. Rilke either shortens the customary sonnet line throughout, or introduces shorter lines among those of normal length; occasionally, he lengthens it. Only eight of the fifty-five sonnets have the five-foot line that generally goes with the form. His modification of the rhyming scheme, often previously adopted by other poets,

[1] H. E. Holthusen, *Rilkes Sonette an Orpheus*, 1937.

does not alter the character of the sonnet so much as changing the length of line, which affects the structure of the form to such an extent that it becomes difficult for us to accept some of these poems as sonnets at all. They are, however, not without precedent: Mallarmé's sonnet *Salut*, which precedes his *Poésies* of 1898, has four feet only, while Valéry's *Poésies*, first published in 1921, one year before the birth of *Sonnets to Orpheus*, contains *Le Sylphe*, a sonnet with two feet only, shorter in line than anything Rilke has written in this form:

> Ni vu ni connu
> Je suis le parfum
> Vivant et défunt
> Dans le vent venu!

In *Sonnets to Orpheus* we have, side by side, lines as different as these:

> Hörst du das Neue, Herr,
> dröhnen und beben?
> Kommen Verkündiger,
> die es erheben.   (III, 330)

and

> Wo, in welchen immer selig bewässerten Gärten, an welchen
> Bäumen, aus welchen zärtlich entblätterten Blütenkelchen . . .
>   (III, 360)

In the first example, the line contains two feet (dactylic feet, longer than Valéry's), in the second seven trisyllabic feet! Neither resembles the classical sonnet line any more; the first is like the line used in many short poems, the second, with its dactyls and trochees, recalls an elegy or ode. We also encounter lines of five feet alternating with two feet in the same poem:

> Wie viele von diesen Stellen der Räume waren schon
> innen in mir. Manche Winde
> sind wie mein Sohn.   (III, 341)

Such arbitrary inequalities to some extent break the sonnet up; in these examples, it retains only the prescribed number of lines and a modified rhyming scheme as remnants of the original form.

The *Duino Elegies* have forerunners in Rilke's production in the three *Requiems* and the five *Gesänge* of August, 1914. The former, being iambic, and one of them rhymed, are rather different in form, but there is a close connection of form and tone between the five *Hymns* and the *Elegies*. The *Gesänge* were written, like some of the *Elegies*, in a sudden rush of productivity, spurred by an outside event: the warlike mood of sacrifice, greatness, triumph and sorrow that possessed German youth, for a brief moment, at the outbreak of war in 1914. To a great extent these Hymns are, in matter as well as form, the outcome of Rilke's readings of Hölderlin at that period. Rilke himself speaks of Hölderlin's 'great and generous influence'. In the circumstances, it is surprising how little there is of imitation or of a more direct influence; obviously, at that time, Rilke was already too independent, too individual an artist to be able to absorb a great deal from another poet's work. Yet two elements are undoubtedly owed to Hölderlin's influence: the great hymnic form, and the partial adoption of classical metres. (The first Elegy dates from 1912, and it is difficult to believe that a similar influence was not working at its origin.) The *Requiems* have the elegiac tone, but their slow, pensive movement lacks the spontaneity so characteristic of the *Gesänge* as well as of the *Elegies*. A comparison of passages will be interesting in this connection:

> Wer zeigt ein Kind, so wie es steht? Wer stellt
> es ins Gestirn und gibt das Maass des Abstands
> ihm in die Hand? Wer macht den Kindertod
> aus grauem Brot, das hart wird . . .   (III, 277)

That is from the Fourth Elegy; and this from *Requiem für eine Freundin*:

> Sag, soll ich reisen? Hast du irgendwo
> ein Ding zurückgelassen das sich quält
> und das dir nachwill? Soll ich in ein Land
> das du nicht sahst . . .   (II, 324)

Between the two passages, there is a slight difference in tone, none whatever in form. Let us now compare a piece from the Seventh Elegy,

> War es nicht Wunder? O staune, Engel, denn wir sinds,
> wir, o du Grosser, erzähls, dass wir solches vermochten, mein Atem
> reicht für die Rühmung nicht aus. So haben wir dennoch
> nicht die Räume versäumt . . .   (III, 291)

with a quotation from the Fourth Hymn:

> Aber im Rühmen, o Freunde, rühmet den Schmerz auch,
> rühmt ohne Wehleid den Schmerz, dass wir die Künftigen nicht
> waren, sondern verwandter
> allem Vergangenen noch: rühmt es und klagt.   (III, 395)

Again, a (very slight) difference in tone, none in the poetical form.

What is an elegy? Originally, a poem of indeterminate length, written in the so-called elegiac metre, i.e. in distichs: an hexameter followed by a pentameter. In German usage, the metre ceased to be strictly observed, and Rilke uses the name elegy in the widely accepted, somewhat vague designation for a longer poem of a mournful or heroic character, generally in classical metre. Of his *Duino Elegies*, the Fourth and the Eighth are in blank verse, the rest in a free, somewhat irregular metre, mostly of five feet with occasional hexameters and pentameters, and with shorter lines frequently thrown in. Although not written in a strictly classical metre, the elegies are nevertheless based on it, and always recall it to the reader's mind. C. M. Bowra suggests that the *Elegies* 'are written in "vers libre". The rhythm is predominantly, though by no means invariably, dactylic, and this gives a more regular tone than is usual in "vers libre".'[1]

I would consider this statement true only for the Fifth Elegy; the others are too regular, especially as regards length of line, to be styled free verse. Rilke needed these sweeping lines with their dactyls, spondees and trochees for the long breath of his pent-up emotional thought, released after many years of silence, and there can be no doubt that he sought the solemnity imparted by the form and metre of the elegy which, as usual, he modified to suit his own ends. Once more we see the poet seize upon a classical form at hand and transform it, by the impact of his personality, into a living, vibrating thing. For these forms and metres were not alive in the sense that a contemporary voice might wish to use them as a medium of expression. They recall the metres used in similar poems by Klopstock, Goethe, Schiller, Hölderlin and their followers, yet how distinctly do we feel Rilke's elegies as modern, close and contemporary! Their form connects them with tradition, but it does not bind them to the past.

If Rilke's *Letzte Gedichte* were really his last poems, it would be easier to consider their style in this study; but they are mostly those pieces, written at various periods, that were not included in any of the poet's collections during his lifetime, and were printed by his publisher in his Collected Works under the title *Letzte Gedichte und Fragmentarisches*, and partly in a separate publication with the title *Späte Gedichte*. As long as the date of each of these poems is not known, it will be difficult, though not impossible, to give them their proper place in an analysis of Rilke's style; many of them, however, are interesting enough formally to be considered here.

[1] *The Heritage of Symbolism*, p. 74.

The poem entitled *Die grosse Nacht* reveals, more perhaps than any other, the influence of Hölderlin, on whose *Brod und Wein* it seems to be modelled. Rilke keeps the five-feet dactylic metre with great regularity in this poem, and although it is shorter by one foot than Hölderlin's metre, the tone of the two poems is often similar:

> Oder es sang eine Stimme und reichte ein Stück weit
> aus der Erwartung heraus, oder es hustete unten
> voller Vorwurf ein Alter, als ob sein Körper im Recht sei
> wider die mildere Welt . . .   (III, 406)

and Hölderlin:

> Aber das Saitenspiel tönt fern aus Gärten; vielleicht dass
> Dort ein Liebendes spielt oder ein einsamer Mann
> Ferner Freunde gedenkt und der Jugendzeit . . .

Of the poem *Winterliche Stanzen* we know that it was written during the winter of 1913–14, and published anonymously in the *Inselalmanach* for 1917. It is an interesting instance of Rilke adopting a verse form he has only used here: the stanza of Goethe's *Zueignung*, six lines with alternating rhymes, concluded by two lines rhyming together. It must have been an experiment the poet could not repeat in spite of its success; his poetic material would not comply with the formality of this classical structure. Rilke had a liking for this isolated piece in his production, a liking we may well share: the thought dissolves without a break in the lines of the stanza which evoke memories of a different kind of poetry, and there is the stimulating contrast of such memories with the actual poem. Besides, Rilke's art of condensation fills the severe form so closely that we get the effect of a particular, happy fullness.

In some of the pieces in these collections, the form of the elegy is loosened to such an extent that something like free verse results; this refers to *Seele im Raum* (III, 402), *Man muss sterben* (III, 411), *Der Reisende* (III, 425), *Wendung* (III, 460), *Musik* (III, 472) and a few others; but these poems are too isolated in Rilke's production to carry weight in an analysis of his style. The same is true of *Ex Voto* (III, 423) and *Tränenkrüglein* (III, 424), two poems that surprise by their echoing, with the metre, the idyllic tone of Catullus, while others—*Die Tauben* (III, 410), *Narziss* (III, 415)—are closely modelled, in form and content, on Paul Valéry.

RHYME

WE have already dealt with the rhyming schemes in Rilke's poetry, i.e. with rhyme as an element in the general form of his poems. There is yet another aspect of rhyme: a poet's particular way of treating it, his preferences and manners, and the sound value it has within the poem. Rilke has written both rhymed and unrhymed poetry; in a general way we may say that not only is the greater part of his poetry rhymed, but that rhyme is a central feature of his style. With a few notable exceptions in *Buch der Bilder*, all his longer poems (i.e. those of more than forty lines), are without rhymes, while all the shorter ones, which form the bulk of his production, are rhymed. Of his three *Requiems*, two are in blank verse, and so are the long poems in *Neue Gedichte*. The poems in classical and semi-classical metre, i.e. the five *Gesänge*, the *Duino Elegies* and longer pieces in *Späte Gedichte*, are, of course, without rhymes. The rest: early poems, *Buch der Bilder*, *Stundenbuch*, *Neue Gedichte*, *Sonnets to Orpheus*, are all rhymed.

Rilke was a born rhymester, with a natural talent for and naïve delight in precise and resounding rhymes that found a first outlet in his early poems. It is obvious that difficult, sonorous, even slightly eccentric rhymes had a great attraction for the young Rilke. In *Erste Gedichte* and *Frühe Gedichte* we encounter quaint rhymes like

Menschenmühn dann—Mosgyn dann—Grünspan, Lichtgeglänz—Andersens, Gequalme wankt—Halme hangt, lehn ich—silbersträhnig.

This youthful exuberance is soon dropped, to be replaced by a more mature art of rhyming, though still a virtuosity. Rhyme is at an early phase established as one of the leading features in Rilke's poetry, not only because of its frequent occurrence, but also for the important part it has in the structure of the individual poem. '*Der Einklang zweier Worte*', as he calls it in one of his sonnets, means more to him than the knitting together of lines in an harmonious pattern. Paul Zech says:[1]

Bei Rilke ist der Reim der Unterbau des ganzen Gedichts. . . . Er ist nicht Schmuck, sondern Zweckmässigkeit. Er verziert nicht, sondern bindet.

Zech may go too far in asserting that Rilke's rhyme 'does not adorn'. It certainly is ornamental too, which need not preclude

[1] *Rainer Maria Rilke*, 1930, pp. 132–3.

18   Rilke's Craftsmanship

that its main function is to bind; his rhymes can be decorative as well as intense:

. . .

> er verneigte sich. Derselbe Baum,
> dessen Kränze toten Pharaonen
> für das Ewige die Stirnen schonen,
> neigte sich. Er fühlte neue Kronen
> blühen. Und sie sassen wie im Traum.   (II, 309)

We have already noted the poet's preference for two or three lines rhyming together. The frequent repetition of the rhyming word is very characteristic for Rilke's middle period, but at all times he loved the word harmony created by rhymes, lingered over it, adorned it, caressed and intensified it. Never is there the least trace of strain in Rilke's elaborate art of rhyming: the words, simple or sophisticated, fall into line with the greatest ease and naturalness, joining, as it were, of their own accord, as if to illustrate J. L. Lowes'[1] saying that

One of the curious phenomena of language is the uncanny way in which sound and sense have the trick of playing into each other's hands. The disclosure of a sort of Leibniz pre-established harmony between rhyme and reason is one of the prerogatives of the poetic gift. And some of the most felicitous turns of thought and phrase in poetry are the result of a flash of inspiration under the happy guidance of a rhyme.

It is difficult to point out significant examples of 'this happy guidance of a rhyme' in Rilke's work, for we encounter it almost everywhere. Rilke almost seems to make a rule of what Lowes regards as an exception under a 'flash of inspiration'.

Rhyme, together with alliteration, may be called the main technical feature of the poems in the *Stundenbuch*, and like alliteration it sometimes becomes tiresome and obtrusive, as in lines like

> Denn nur dem Einsamen wird offenbart,
> und vielen Einsamen der gleichen Art
> wird mehr gegeben als dem schmalen Einen.
> Doch jedem wird ein andrer Gott erscheinen,
> bis sie erkennen, nah am Weinen,
> dass durch ihr meilenweites Meinen,
> durch ihr Vernehmen und Verneinen
> verschieden nur in hundert Seinen
> ein Gott wie eine Welle geht.   (II, 197)

This is an instance of unbalanced preponderance of rhyme: the rhyming sound, '*einen*', is too harsh to tolerate so many repetitions,

---

[1] *Convention and Revolt in Poetry*, 1930, p. 163.

some of which, like '*nah am Weinen*', have evidently been thrown in more for the sake of rhyme than of meaning. In this and other passages the rhyme assumes an undue importance; we feel that from servant it has become master, and that some lines were written only to display their author's art. Yet the instances of an harmonious solution, even with frequent repetition of the rhyming word, are much more numerous:

> Des Armen Haus ist wie des Kindes Hand.
> Sie nimmt nicht, was Erwachsene verlangen;
> nur einen Käfer mit verzierten Zangen,
> den runden Stein, der durch den Bach gegangen,
> den Sand, der rann, und Muscheln, welche klangen;
> sie ist wie eine Wage aufgehangen
> und sagt das allerleiseste Empfangen
> langschwankend an mit ihrer Schalen Stand.
> Des Armen Haus ist wie des Kindes Hand.   (II, 289)

In this passage the rhyme occurs six times, as in the previous one, yet we feel it as organic and beautiful: the syllables '*angen*' are pleasant to the ear and will bear repetition which, moreover, never overrides the meaning. The lines acquire, through the rhymes, a sonorous fullness, and with exquisite art the poet lets the assonance of '*angen*' ebb away in the words '*langschwankend an*'.

Rilke likes his rhymes full, precise, on the most sonorous word, which frequently is a non-German one:

> Und ihre Menschen dienen in Kulturen
> und fallen tief aus Gleichgewicht und Maass,
> und nennen Fortschritt ihre Schneckenspuren
> unf fahren rascher, wo sie langsam fuhren,
> und fühlen sich und funkeln wie die Huren
> und lärmen lauter mit Metall und Glas.   (II, 290)

> Einfach steht sie an der Kathedrale
> grossem Aufstieg, nah der Fensterrose,
> mit dem Apfel in der Apfelpose,
> schuldlos-schuldig ein für alle Male . . .   (III, 162)

> Im Auge Traum. Die Stirn wie in Berührung
> Mit etwas Fernem. Um den Mund enorm
> viel Jugend, ungelächelte Verführung,
> und vor der vollen schmückenden Verschnürung
> der schlanken adeligen Uniform . . .   (III, 69)

Often, however, Rilke's rhymes do not fall on the most sonorous words, but on the most significant:

> Bei Tag bist du das Hörensagen,
> das flüsternd um die vielen fliesst;

> die Stille nach dem Stundenschlagen,
> welche sich langsam wieder schliesst.
> Je mehr der Tag mit immer schwächern
> Gebärden sich nach Abend neigt,
> je mehr bist du, mein Gott. Es steigt
> dein Reich wie Rauch aus allen Dächern.   (II, 258)

> Der Mund als Mund gemacht, gross und genau,
> nicht überredend, aber ein Gerechtes
> Aussagendes. Die Stirne ohne Schlechtes
> und gern im Schatten stiller Niederschau.
> Das, als Zusammenhang, erst nur geahnt;
> noch nie im Leiden oder im Gelingen
> zusammgefasst zu dauerndem Durchdringen,
> doch so, als wäre mit zerstreuten Dingen
> von fern ein Ernstes, Wirkliches geplant.   (III, 70)

Rilke's ease in rhyming, his perfect mastery, was assisted by the standard of pure rhyming attained in the modern German lyric. It is interesting to compare this standard with that ruling in the classical and romantic periods, where we frequently encounter, with Goethe, Schiller, Uhland, Heine, Lenau, Droste and others, rhymes such as

> beugen—zeigen, viel—will, acht't—macht, hin—grün, Wesen—bösen, Haymarket—Poet, Bürde—Begierde, Nähe—Höhe, untertänig—König, kunnt'—Grund, Brücke—zurücke, Blüt—Lied, Ketten—Raketen, dräut—Scheid'.

Such rhymes are impure either because the sound is not identical (*Nähe—Höhe, stehn—schön*), or because a long syllable is made to rhyme with a short one (*viel—will*), or because a word has been more or less arbitrarily shortened or lengthened to obtain the rhyme (*Kron'—Lohn, Brücke—zurücke*), or a vowel sound has been altered (*kunnt'—Grund*), or a hard consonant rhymes with a soft one (*Getose—Schoosse*). Mörike is somewhat more fastidious with his rhymes, but the greater purity really begins with Rückert, Platen and C. F. Meyer, and the new standard is fairly constantly maintained by later generations of poets.

This statement does not imply a criticism; pure rhymes cannot be said to constitute technical values *per se*, while impure rhymes need not be, indeed very often are not, the result of a poet's inability of making pure ones; they may even be more expressive or more appropriate than meticulously pure ones, and such irregularities in rhyming may substantially contribute to the charm of a poem. In modern German usage, slightly impure sounds like

Götter—Retter are still found and tolerated, but some of the older usages, like the custom of shortening words by arbitrary elision, have been discontinued: *Knab'—hinab*, or *zwei Grenadier—Quartier* are hardly encountered in the modern German lyric. Moreover, there is a considerable difference in the way such devices are handled: when Chamisso says '*Ich träum als Kind mich zurücke*', the line has its own charm, and '*zurücke*' (which by the way does not rhyme and has been lengthened for the sake of scansion), sounds natural; but when the fastidious Platen starts one of his sonnets *Mein Auge liess das hohe Meer zurücke* (to rhyme with *Tücke*), the lengthened word is slightly out of place in the solemn sonnet.

It was more than word-harmony Rilke sought in his rhymes: his need for precision in a poem is partly expressed in the sharp exactness, the sometimes almost machine-like clicking of his rhymes; the device of tampering with words in order to make them conform to a rhyme becomes unthinkable for such a craftsman. Absolute, flawless identity of sound is his aim, and in order to achieve it he, in his turn, overrules all considerations concerning the grammatical similarity of rhyming words. There is, indeed, no rule prescribing that such forms ought to be alike, but too great a discrepancy had generally been avoided. It was not usual either to rhyme words of foreign origin with homely German ones. Rilke has no prejudice in either respect and will rhyme

> betrat—Josaphat, Schneckenspuren—fuhren, vollster—Gepolster, Pfeilern—steilern, ersannst—kannst, Golds—zerschmolz, verzerrts—Herz, schluckten—Aquädukten, Rosenstocks—Phlox, Gesetz—Estaminets

—all pure as far as sound is concerned, but rhyming the past tense of a word with a noun, the comparative or superlative of an adjective with a noun, the past tense of a verb with the present, the genitive of a noun with the past tense of a verb, the contraction of a verb and pronoun with a noun, the nominative of a noun with the genitive of another. He displays the same insouciance in rhymes like

> trüb—Daguerrotyp, Gequäl—Kapitäl, berühme—Kostüme, Klosterhofe— Strophe, gross—Embryos, Lichte mehr—Luzifer, Mosaik—Stieg, Verhör— Monseigneur, Ohrs—Picadors

—again all perfectly identical in sound, but rather novel as rhyming words in the German tradition. This technique is very similar to that adopted in English poetry by G. M. Hopkins.

In their context, however, and when heard within the poem,

such rhymes, often so startling in isolation, seem natural enough,
so cleverly are they woven into the texture:

> In Spiegelbildern wie von Fragonard
> ist doch von ihrem Weiss und ihrer Röte
> nicht mehr gegeben, als dir einer böte,
> wenn er von seiner Freundin sagt: sie war
> noch sanft von Schlaf. Denn steigen sie ins Grüne
> und stehn, auf rosa Stielen leicht gedreht,
> beisammen, blühend, wie in einem Beet,
> verführen sie verführender als Phryne
> sich selber . . .   (III, 236)

> Wie sind sie alle um uns, diese Herrn
> in Kammerherrentrachten und Jabots,
> wie eine Nacht um ihren Ordensstern
> sich immer mehr verdunkelnd, rücksichtslos,
> und diese Damen, zart, fragile, doch gross
> von ihren Kleidern, eine Hand im Schooss,
> klein wie ein Halsband für den Bologneser;
> wie sind sie da um jeden: um den Leser,
> um den Betrachter dieser Bibelots,
> darunter manches ihnen noch gehört.   (III, 67)

It has been noted how Rilke's rhymes often fall on the most
significant words, yet with the subtle ingenuousness that sometimes
distinguished him in such matters, Rilke does not shrink from using
quite trivial, unimportant or casual words to hang his rhymes on.
We have a model for this technique in many of Verlaine's poems
and in verses like C. F. Meyer's *windet blass und lieblich eine/Psyche
sich im Marmelsteine.* Rilke carries the precedent further:

> meine Hand hat nur noch eine
> Gebärde, mit der sie verscheucht;
> auf die alten Steine
> fällt es aus Felsen feucht.   (III, 42)

While Meyer's *eine-Marmelsteine* is just a rhyme without a meaning,
Rilke's intention is to lift *eine* significantly from the line, giving it
stress by means of the rhyme: *nur noch eine*, thus stressed, becomes
eine einzige. In his frequent enjambments, Rilke also rhymes on
insignificant words like *und, er, wer, sie, als*, often with subtle art.
Take these lines from *Die Gazelle*:

> um dich zu sehen: hingetragen, als
> wäre mit Sprüngen jeder Lauf geladen
> und schösse nur nicht ab, solang der Hals
> das Haupt ins Horchen hält . . .   (III, 45)

Als as rhyming word lifts the line at the end, thereby increasing the intended tension, and the fuller echo of *Hals* gives significance to that word in turn, rendering it more visible.

Some of Rilke's poems seem to be stepping on their rhymes in a sonorous or more subdued rhythm. After the examples of the former kind, here is a more delicate one:

> Venedigs Sonne wird in meinem Haar
> ein Gold bereiten, aller Alchemie
> erlauchten Ausgang. Meine Brauen, die
> den Brücken gleichen, siehst du sie
> hinführen ob der lautlosen Gefahr
> der Augen, die ein heimlicher Verkehr
> an die Kanäle schliesst, so dass das Meer
> in ihnen steigt und fällt und wechselt. Wer
> mich einmal sah . . . (III, 75)

Haar stands out significantly and is taken up, after an interval of three lines, by *Gefahr*. *Alchemie* is almost silently echoed by the inconspicuous word *die*, and with a slightly fuller sound by *sie*. *Verkehr* and *Meer* are equally accentuated, the following *wer* much less. On the other hand, the rhymes used by Rilke in his enjambments sometimes not only are without any significance, but cannot even be sufficiently stressed to be heard as rhymes at all; they become submerged:

> Doch vor dem Apostel Thomas, der
> kam, da es zu spät war, trat der schnelle
> längst darauf gefasste Engel her . . . (II, 317)

> Gemieden von dem Frühherbstmorgen, der
> misstrauisch war, lag hinter den versengten
> Hauslinden, die das Heidehaus beengten,
> ein Neues, Leeres. Eine Stelle mehr, . . . (III, 177)

In the sonnet *Papageienpark*, the first two stanzas have only one rhyme each, an unusual scheme with Rilke; in the sestet, he introduces two rhymes, very closely related in sound, so as to form a strange harmony:

> Unten klauben die duffen Tauben, was sie nicht mögen,
> während sich oben die höhnischen Vögel verbeugen
> zwischen den beiden fast leeren vergeudeten Trögen.
> Aber dann wiegen sie wieder und und schläfern und äugen,
> spielen mit dunkelen Zungen, die gerne lögen,
> zerstreut an den Fussfesselringen. Warten auf Zeugen. (III, 193-4)

C

These are almost half-rhymes, differentiated only by the similar vowels (*ö* and *äu*); moreover, the *ö* in *mögen* is echoed by the rich vowel sounds in *höhnischen Vögel* in the following line, while *verbeugen* has its assonance in *vergeudeten*—a most intricate play on sonorous sounds, tones and modulating half-tones, rhyming and almost rhyming, delicately painting the gay, exotic remoteness of the captive parrots. Sometimes Rilke differentiates his rhymes by a single short syllable, as in

> Er sass sehr still. Sein grosses Schauen hing
> an ihrer Hand, die ganz gebeugt vom Ringe,
> als ob sie schwer in Schneewehn ginge,
> über die weissen Tasten ging.   (II, 31)

where the words *hing—Ringe—ginge—ging* form a strange harmony of their own, as in intervals of quarter-tones.

Still another kind of rhyme is encountered in *Sonnets to Orpheus*:

> Wir sind die Treibenden.
> Aber den Schritt der Zeit,
> nehmt ihn als Kleinigkeit
> im immer Bleibenden.
> Alles das Eilende
> wird schon vorüber sein;
> denn das Verweilende
> erst weiht uns ein.   (III, 334)

These rhymes somehow recall those in the second part of *Faust*:

> Alles Vergängliche
> Ist nur ein Gleichnis;
> Das Unzulängliche
> Hier wird's Ereignis;
> Das Unbeschreibliche
> Hier ist's getan;
> Das Ewig-Weibliche
> Zieht uns hinan.

The likeness lies in the fact that these rhymes are all present participles used as nouns, a form typical of the German language; such participles can, in their generalization, almost acquire the significance of philosophical conceptions. Rilke stresses the metaphysical character of such rhymes still further by making them pairs of antithetical notions. It may well be the first time that rhymes have been thus used to express the meaning of a poem, and a subtler way of using them can hardly be imagined.

Rilke's interior rhymes deserve special consideration. At times

these are not much more than supernumerary rhymes, an overflow
of fullness that found no outlet at the end of the line:

> der Freund und der Feind und das Mahl im Saal   (II, 11)
>
> und alle die Verschollenen erscheinen
> in welken Leinen, brüchigen Gebeinen   (II, 80)

More often, interior rhymes have the subtler mission of underlining or dramatizing a meaning:

> die vielleicht unbewohnt ist wie ein Mond   (II, 44)
>
> beschämte und veraltete Gewalten   (II, 99)
>
> zu roten Stücken von Toten   (III, 139)
>
> um die Nacht auf den Wiesen allein zu sein   (III, 332)
>
> und im Bangen des langen Jahrs   (III, 348)
>
> Unten klauben die duffen Tauben, was sie nicht mögen
>   (III, 193–4)

By printing the last quoted line differently, we may see how an
interior rhyme can create its own rhythm within the poem:

> Unten klauben
> die duffen Tauben,
> was sie nicht mögen . . .

Sometimes, such rhymes follow each other immediately, a more
insistent method of underlining, the most significant instance of
which is found in *Der Panther*:

> ihm ist, als ob es tausend Stäbe gäbe   (III, 44)

where the repetition assists in expressing the endless procession of
bars in front of the captive animal's eyes. There are other examples
of this technique in *Neue Gedichte*:

>   . . . in dem alten
> Faltenmantel ihrer Contreforts   (III, 33)
>
> in kurzen schnellen Wellen   (III, 97)
>
> gehn wie an Gift an meinem Mund zugrund   (III, 75)
>
>   . . . die schwache
> wache Jungfrau . . .   (III, 217)

In a line in *Sonnets to Orpheus*, even three rhyming words follow
each other:

> sein rein eingetauschter Weltraum   (III, 341)

Rilke also places rhymes at the beginning and end of one line, framing it, as it were, within rhymes:

> Nichte, deren nur auf ihn erpichte ...   (III, 148)
>
> Warte, ein Härtestes warnt aus der Ferne das Harte   (III, 354)

Interior rhymes may also act indirectly as suppressed rhymes that found no place at the end of the line, to make their presence felt in an oblique and hidden way:

> Der Abdruck meiner kleinsten Bewegung
> bleibt in der seidenen Stille sichtbar;
> unvernichtbar drückt die geringste Erregung ...   (II, 21)

Sichtbar has no direct rhyme in the poem, its only echo being *unvernichtbar* at the beginning of the following line. Other instances of such 'concealed' rhymes come from the *Stundenbuch*:

> wo ihnen alles Zorn ist und verworren
> und wo sie in den Tagen aus Tumult
> verdorren mit verwundeter Geduld,   (II, 288)

and from *Buch der Bilder*:

> liegen sie nicht wie Werkzeug da und Ding?
> Ist nicht der Ring selbst schlicht
> an meiner Hand ...   (II, 56)

Ding has no other rhyme: the lifting of *Ring* by indirect rhyming creates a hidden connection and links the two words more intimately than end rhymes would. A similar scheme occurs in *Späte Gedichte*:

> ... welches schon Verzicht getan
> auf einen Teil der in den Lebensplan
> der dumpfen Einfalt eingeweihten Beine ...
> Nur dass wir einmal in das Eine hineingehörten!   (S.G., 83)

Beine rhymes only with *Eine* in the next line, and the rhyme is surrounded and fortified by the vowel assonance of *Teil, Einfalt, eingeweihten, einmal, hinein.*

Rilke has still another use for interior rhymes: with their help, he stresses a relation of causality or even of antithesis between words. Examples of this technique are found in the *Stundenbuch* only:

> Alle, welche dich suchen, versuchen dich.
> Und die so dich finden, binden dich
> an Bild und Gebärde.   (II, 244)

Dir liegt an den Fragenden nichts.
Sanften Gesichts
siehst du den Tragenden zu.   (II, 244)

Nirgends will ich gebogen bleiben,
denn dort bin ich gelogen, wo ich gebogen bin.   (II, 182)

Finally, an example from *Späte Gedichte* may show how organically beautiful an interior rhyme can be, lighting up a poem with the echo of the end rhyme in the middle of a line, giving a second and different stress to a word already stressed:

Wann war ein Mensch je so wach
wie der Morgen von heut?
Nicht nur Blume und Bach,
auch das Dach ist erfreut.   (S.G., 102)

RHYTHM

METRE confines a poet's rhythm as little as measure does a composer's. Both are limitations imposed not only to allow true freedom, but rather to make it possible, and to facilitate its expression. 'In the hands of the artist, the rhythmic cadences determined by the thought, or by the breath, or both, flow around and through and in the beat of the lines, but the beat of the lines is *there*, like time in music.'[1] Poets rarely invent new metres, yet they may use the existing schemes in such a manner as to make them express and carry their personal rhythm. There are various ways of obtaining this result: the poet's personality may bend and override the metre, as a storm bends a tree; he may show a preference for certain metres and gently fill them with his personal melody; he may use the 'hard' or the 'sleek' way of fitting words to a given metre; certain characteristics of syntax or deviation from the metre belonging to the adopted verse scheme may make for individual expression, and simplification or complication can help in the process. Generally all or several of these methods will be found combined in a poet's style, and analysis shows this to be the case with the rhythm that makes Rilke's cadence and melody. Syntax and enjambment are such important features in this connection that they require separate chapters; deviation from a given scheme will mainly occupy our attention here.

Metre is hardly ever strictly observed, not even in the most formal poetry of classical epochs; deviations from the rigid rule, obvious or recondite, make it alive. In Rilke's earlier work, the change of rhythm is often brusque, as in the poem *Einsamkeit*, which after eleven iambic lines, tails off into the vague prose line

Dann geht die Einsamkeit mit den Flüssen . . .   (II, 50)

In the next poem in the collection (*Buch der Bilder*), the last line interrupts the iambic flow of the preceding ones with an abrupt dactyl:

unruhig wandern, wenn die Blätter treiben,   (II, 51)

thus effectively stressing the word *unruhig*. It is interesting to note, in this connection, how this particular word, whenever it appears

---

[1] J. L. Lowes, *Convention and Revolt in Poetry*, 1930, p. 151.

in Rilke's poetry, becomes the cause for some rhythmic refinement. The *un* is a supernumerary syllable in *Der Knabe*:

> Dunkel, aber mit einem Helm von Gold,
> der unruhig glänzt. Und hinter mir gereiht . . .   (II, 32)

If it ran: *der ruhig glänzt*, the line would be regular; the word *unruhig* jerks it up. The same occurs in *Leichenwäsche*, where the poet, by means of this word, destroys the regularity of the second line and thus achieves his intention of giving, by an altered rhythm, the effect of a flickering lamp:

> Sie hatten sich an ihn gewöhnt. Doch als
> die Küchenlampe kam und unruhig brannte
> im dunkeln Luftzug, war der Unbekannte
> ganz unbekannt.   (III, 171)

The poem *Sappho an Eranna* begins with the heavy spondee

> Unruh will ich über dich bringen   (III, 11)

Again, in the Third Elegy,

> . . . und in die Falten des Vorhangs
> passte, die leicht sich verschob, seine unruhige Zukunft,   (III, 271)

the odd syllable *un* shatters the regular flow of the line, creating the same restlessness as in the previous examples.

The sudden interruption of the rhythmical flow is still more obvious in *Das Lied des Blinden*, where despair cries out with something like a shriek, brought about by a change of rhythm as well as by the shift of accent through enjambment:

> und ich weiss nicht, schreit mir mein
> Herz oder meine Gedärme.   (II, 123)

In the *Stundenbuch*, the rhythm changes more evenly from one poem to another, hardly ever brusquely within the poem itself. One of such variations may be illustrated by an example where the lengthening of the line acts as a brake and severely slows down the tempo, in order to emphasize the angels' inability to fly:

> Eins muss er wieder können: fallen,
> geduldig in der Schwere ruhn,
> der sich vermass, den Vögeln allen
> im Fliegen es zuvorzutun.
> (Denn auch die Engel fliegen nicht mehr.
> Schweren Vögeln gleichen die Seraphim . . .).   (II, 246)

Some of the poems in the *Stundenbuch* have the fresh and simple rhythm of folk songs, and since they are often preceded or followed by slower or more involved rhythms, the effect by contrast is strong. Thus, the solemn lines

> Wem du das Buch gibst, welches die umfasst,
> der wird gebückt über den Blättern bleiben.
> Es sei denn, dass du ihn in Händen hast,
> um selbst zu schreiben,

are followed by the refreshing *allegro cantabile* of

> So bin ich nur als Kind erwacht,
> so sicher im Vertraun,
> nach jeder Angst und jeder Nacht
> dich wieder anzuschaun. (II, 221)

In many instances, rhythm and rhyme combine to give life to a stanza:

> Und über sie, wie Nächte blau,
> von Angesichte blass,
> schwebt, die dich freuete, die Frau:
> die Pförtnerin, der Morgentau,
> die dich umblüht wie eine Au
> und ohne Unterlass. (II, 216)

The *Stundenbuch* is full of such varied rhythmical movements, necessary in a collection where the slow unfolding of a few themes would be wearying without them; and, in fact, the few passages where the poet fails to provide these rhythmical variations are felt as slightly monotonous. On the whole, the rhythmical movement follows the modulation of themes closely and harmoniously, avoiding too abrupt changes. Here is a last example, showing Rilke's gentle art in changing a rhythm:

> Er ging in Mänteln und Metamophosen
> durch alle steigenden Stimmen der Zeit.
>
> Da ward auch die zur Frucht Erweckte,
> die schüchterne und schönerschreckte,
> die heimgesuchte Magd geliebt.
> Die Blühende, die Unentdeckte,
> in der es hundert Wege gibt. (II, 195)

The quickening is notable in the line *Da ward auch die zur Frucht erweckte*, and it proceeds line by line till the last, which slows it down again.

It is fascinating to study the subtlety of Rilke's rhythmical skill in *Neue Gedichte*. The well-known and rightly famous *Das Karussell*

owes its expressive movement to the alternation of very regularly
scanning lines with irregular ones:

> Und dann und wann eine weisser Elephant.
> Sogar ein Hirsch ist da ganz wie im Wald,
> nut dass er einen Sattel trägt und drüber
> ein kleines blaues Mädchen aufgeschnallt.
> Und auf dem Löwen reitet weiss ein Junge
> und hält sich mit der kleinen heissen Hand. (III, 80)

The first two lines of this passage are perfectly regular; in the third,
the first four words must be blurred over, and there are only two
full accents, on *Sattel* and *drüber*, with half an accent on *trägt*. The
next line is regular again, while the fifth shows the same characteristics as the third: stress on *Löwen* and *Junge*, half-stress on *weiss*.
Later in the poem, two lines are even trochaic in the otherwise
iambic scheme:

> . . . diesem Pferdesprunge
> fast schon entwachsen; mitten in dem Schwunge
> schauen sie auf, irgendwohin, herüber . . . (III, 80–1)

The refrain-like repetition of the line *Und dann und wann ein weisser
Elephant* articulates the poem in a musical way, suggesting the perpetual gay circling of the merry-go-round, *dieses atemlose blinde
Spiel*. The effect of the whole is one of utmost lightness, speed and
colourful giddiness.

A perfect identity of mood and rhythm is achieved in many
poems of *Neue Gedichte*. Thus, *Eine Welke* begins

> Leicht, wie nach ihrem Tode,
> trägt sie die Handschuh, das Tuch.
> Ein Duft aus ihrer Kommode,
> verdrängte den lieben Geruch . . . (III, 175)

Two accents mark the first line, *leicht* and *Tode*, with the subdued, all
but inaudible, beat of the iambic rhythm in its other words. The
next line consists of two regular dactylic feet. The third line is
iambic, with one dactyl, and the fourth corresponds with the
second, with its two dactyls. The words flow very delicately on
this rhythm, suggesting the lightness the poet wishes to express.
A similar effect is achieved in *Tanagra*:

> Ein wenig gebrannter Erde
> wie von grosser Sonne gebrannt.
> Als wäre die Gebärde
> einer Mädchenhand
> auf einmal nicht mehr vergangen . . . (III, 59)

The line *einer Mädchenhand* stands isolated with its trochees that have

no relation to the iambs and anapaests of the rest and lift it significantly out, leaving it, as it were, suspended in their midst. A
humorous effect is intended in Auferstehung (III, 72) with its
limping rhythm, and the impossibility of getting the stress right in
the line *im Erbbegräbnis*—it must needs fall upon the unaccented
and rhyming last syllable. *Lied vom Meer* (III, 190), with its short,
irregular lines, is trochaic, with a slight tension in some lines,
caused by artificial stresses, as in *du kommst zu keinem her*, and *so
muss er sehn wie er*. By this scheme, the jerky gusts of the night
wind are reproduced in a magnificent simplicity of utterance.

Neue Gedichte are not devoid of the *cantabile* rhythms we met in
the *Stundenbuch*. Note the singing melody in the first lines of *Die
Genesende*:

> Wie ein Singen kommt und geht in Gassen
> und sich nähert und sich wieder scheut . . .,   (III, 57)

the subdued rush in *Endymion*:

> In ihm ist Jagd noch. Durch sein Geäder
> bricht wie durch Gebüsche das Tier.
> Täler bilden sich, waldige Bäder
> spiegeln die Hindin, und hinter ihr . . .,   (III, 119)

the silent singing in *Die Liebende*:

> Das ist mein Fenster. Eben
> bin ich so sanft erwacht.
> Ich dachte, ich würde schweben.
> Bis wohin reicht mein Leben,
> und wo beginnt die Nacht —?   (III, 223)

The majority of Rilke's poems have a quiet, even flow, sustained
throughout, only occasionally interrupted by the subtle variations
that make them alive: shifts from iambic to trochaic metre, different
lengths of line, irregular stresses. All these changes occur likewise
in the *Duino Elegies*, yet their heavy, majestic flow, as that of flowing
lava, suffers a deeper disturbance: irregular accelerations nervously
interrupt it when emotion breaks through and overpowers thought.
All through the *Elegies* we encounter these explosive eruptions,
this sudden intensification of rhythm and language. In the Second
Elegy, after a relatively quiet beginning, the poet breaks into the
tumultuous lines with their rhythmical variations:

> Frühe Geglückte, ihr Verwöhnten der Schöpfung,
> Höhenzüge, morgenrötliche Grate
> aller Erschaffung — Pollen der blühenden Gottheit,
> Gelenke des Lichtes, Gänge, Treppen, Throne,

Räume aus Wesen, Schilde aus Wonne, Tumulte
stürmisch entzückten Gefühls und plötzlich, einzeln,
Spiegel, die die entströmte eigene Schönheit
wiederschöpfen zurück in das eigene Antlitz.   (III, 264-5)

It is remarkable how efficiently and elegantly Rilke checks this
passionate outburst by means of the word *plötzlich*, followed by
the still more retarding *einzeln*, after which the initial tempo is
quietly resumed. The Fifth Elegy, the last to be composed, and
probably written in a shorter time than any of the others, is the
most irregular, with shorter lines frequently interpolated:

Und dennoch, blindlings,
das Lächeln . . .
Engel! o nimm, pflücks, das kleinblütige Heilkraut.
Schaff eine Vase, verwahrs! Stells unter jene, uns noch nicht
offenen Freuden . . .,   (III, 280-1)

and again:

Du, auf alle des Gleichgewichts schwankende Wagen
immerfort anders
hingelegte Marktfrucht des Gleichmuts,
öffentlich unter den Schultern.   (III, 281)

Note the heavy stress the line *immerfort anders* acquires by its isolation.
In the Seventh Elegy, intensity is markedly strong from the very
beginning, and grows until it reaches a climax in the passage

sondern die Nächte! Sondern die hohen, des Sommers,
Nächte, sondern die Sterne, die Sterne der Erde.
O einst tot sein und sie wissen unendlich,
alle die Sterne: denn wie, wie, wie sie vergessen!   (III, 288)

After this acceleration, the elegy subsides again until, towards the
end, there comes another eruption:

War es nicht Wunder? O staune, Engel, denn wir sinds,
wir, o du Grosser, erzähls, dass wir solches vermochten, mein Atem
reicht für die Rühmung nicht aus. So haben wir dennoch
nicht die Räume versäumt, diese gewährenden, diese unsere Räume.
                                                (III, 291)

Sometimes the interpolation of shorter lines serves to create a quiet
interval, as in the Ninth Elegy:

Zwischen den Hämmern besteht
unser Herz, wie die Zunge
zwischen den Zähnen, die doch,
dennoch die preisende bleibt.   (III, 299)

This is really a hexameter followed by a pentameter; Rilke's
shortening of the metre by distributing it over four lines shows

that he wanted a slightly different intonation for them. After these lines, which in addition stress the thought by means of alliteration on the main words (*Hämmer* and *Herz*, *Zunge* and *Zähne*), the forcefulness of the following long lines stands out with sharper relief:

> Preise dem Engel die Welt, nicht die unsägliche, ihm
> kannst du nicht grosstun mit herrlich Erfühltem . . .   (III, 299)

Not all the rhythmical changes in the *Elegies* will be considered successful. Minor irregularities at times become irritating, when they interrupt the flow of the poem too much and make it hard to read:

> Wo immer du eintratst, redete nicht in Kirchen
> zu Rom und Neapel ruhig ihr Schicksal dich an?   (III, 262)

It looks as if in the last line, Rilke wished to avoid the too obvious rhythm of the pentameter (*zu Neapel und Rom ruhig ihr Schicksal dich an*), with the pause of the caesura in the middle; but the resulting line sounds somewhat flat. The two following lines are alike in this respect:

> Oder es trug eine Inschrift sich erhaben dir auf,
> wie neulich die Tafel in Santa Maria Formosa   (III, 262)

Again, Rilke goes out of his way to avoid the hexameter (*wie die Tafel neulich in Santa Maria Formosa*), which, however, would have left the slightly colloquial *neulich* less isolated, and been more in keeping with the rest of the poem. In the *Elegies*, the rhythm is often a sure indication that a thought or image has not been wholly transformed, or is not harmoniously incorporated in the poem:

> O, nicht, weil Glück ist,
> dieser voreilige Vorteil eines nahen Verlusts.   (III, 297)

There is something harsh, almost prosy about the last line, residing in the words, but shown up by the rhythm. The same may be said of the next example, from the Fourth Elegy:

> Und waren doch in unserem Alleingehn
> mit Dauerndem vergnügt . . .   (III, 277)

Such rare blemishes, however, can hardly be more than a foil to the strong, convincing rhythm of the *Elegies*, flowing, and uneven, like a living stream.

In the *Sonnets to Orpheus*, Rilke's rhythm and tempo are still less retarded, and become more evenly spontaneous; never before have we known him so unimpeded, so direct in his utterance, in such a free and singing mood. There are dark rhythms of an irresistible urgency:

> Rufe mich zu jener deiner Stunden,
> die dir unaufhörlich widersteht:
> flehend nah wie das Gesicht von Hunden,
> aber immer wieder weggedreht . . .,   (III, 368)

and direct utterances like this:

> Da stieg ein Baum. O reine Übersteigung!
> O Orpheus singt! O hoher Baum im Ohr! (III, 313)

or like this:

> Tanzt die Orange. Die wärmere Landschaft
> werft sie aus euch, dass die reife erstrahle
> in Lüften der Heimat! Erglühte, enthüllt
> Düfte um Düfte!   (III, 327)

The first of these rhythms is achieved by trochees, the second by iambs, the third by dactyls; all three are simple, direct, compelling.

If it was rarely given to Rilke to express his ego in an accelerated rhythm, he could admirably recapture a dumb creature's blood-beat:

> Herüber vom Dorf kam der Schimmel allein,
> an der vorderen Fessel den Pflock,
> um die Nacht auf den Wiesen allein zu sein;
> wie schlug seiner Mähne Gelock
> an den Hals im Takte des Übermuts,
> bei dem grob gehemmten Galopp.
> Wie sprangen die Quellen des Rossebluts!   (III, 332)

How vividly the rhythm, with its strong emphasis on the stressed syllables, expresses the lonely animal's roaming into the night, with the regular clop-clop of the hooves as an underlying melody!

TEMPO

FOLLOWING a study of Rilke's rhythm, a short note on his tempo will not be out of place. If verse forms are among the most objective elements of poetic style, a poet's tempo, on the other hand, is much more difficult to define. For its statement and description, we have to rely mostly on our feeling; but if this our sensitiveness is schooled and experienced, we shall not be completely without a guide in judging poetic tempo. Most readers will readily agree that on the whole, Rilke's tempo is rather slow. The pulse of simple, direct passion does not accelerate his diction; thus he will rarely have any rhythm comparable to young Goethe's

> Es schlug mein Herz, geschwind zu Pferde!
> Es war getan fast eh' gedacht . . .,

or his

> Wie herrlich leuchtet
> Mir die Natur!
> Wie glänzt die Sonne!
> Wie lacht die Flur!

These are fast rhythms, and so is Schiller's

> Nehmt hin die Welt! rief Zeus von seinen Höhen
> Den Menschen zu. Nehmt, sie soll euer sein!

These poets have, of course, written many slow-moving poems, with every gradation of tempo between such extremes, and the lines above are quoted only to point out fast tempos as they are hardly found in Rilke's poems, with the exception, perhaps, of a few accelerated passages in the *Elegies* and in some of the *Sonnets to Orpheus*. Rilke can occasionally accelerate, but his normal tempo is slow, at times extremely so. His usual rhythm is halting, retarded, and even when he drives on to a faster beat, the tempo is soon slowed down again, curbed by his pensive mood. Here is a typical example from his early middle period, taken from the *Stundenbuch*:

> Mach, dass er seine Kindheit wieder weiss;
> das Unbewusste und das Wunderbare
> und seiner ahnungsvollen Anfangsjahre
> unendlich dunkelreichen Sagenkreis.   (II, 276)

Compare this to a passage from Hölderlin:

> Nur einen Sommer gönnt, ihr Gewaltigen,
> Und einen Herbst zu reifem Gesange mir,
> Dass williger mein Herz, vom süssen
> Spiele gesättiget, dann mir sterbe!

Both passages have roughly the same initial speed, but Hölderlin's is sustained, while Rilke soon slows down. Already, the long words *ahnungsvollen Anfangsjahre* put a break on the tempo, and it will prove impossible to read a line like *unendlich dunkelreichen Sagenkreis*, with its heavy composite adjectives and noun, otherwise than *ritardando*.

Even in his most accelerated poems Rilke can rarely sustain a quicker tempo for long. *Der letzte Graf von Brederode entzieht sich türkischer Gefangenschaft* is a highly dramatic ballad, with its breathless start:

> Sie folgten furchtbar, ihren bunten Tod
> von ferne nach ihm werfend, während er
> verloren floh . . .,   (III, 74)

but as the poem proceeds, we come to lines like these:

> Ein Lächeln adeliger Frauen goss
> noch einmal Süssigkeit in sein verfrühtes
> vollendetes Gesicht . . .,

where the sequence *verfrühtes vollendetes Gesicht* considerably diminishes the initial tempo. Rilke can be extremely slow, as in lines like these:

> Denn du bist der Boden. Dir sind nur wie Sommer die Zeiten,
> und du denkst an die nahen nicht anders als an die entfernten
> und ob sie dich tiefer besamen und besser bebauen lernten:
> du fühlst dich nur leise berührt von den ähnlichen Ernten
> und hörst weder Säer noch Schnitter die über dich schreiten.
> (II, 219–20)

The slow rhythm here is mostly due to the extreme length of line, but Rilke can be just as halting in shorter ones:

> Einst, vor Zeiten, nannte man sie alt.
> Doch sie kam dieselbe Strasse
> täglich. Und man änderte die Maasse . . .   (III, 137)

This is a typical tempo from *Neue Gedichte*, while the following is more in the nature of an exception; it shows how effectively Rilke

could write fast flowing lines on the rare occasions when it suited
his purpose:

> ordnet der Zufall hastig die Gesichter,
> lockert sie auf und drückt sie wieder dichter,
> ergreift zwei ferne, lässt ein nahes aus,
> tauscht das mit dem, bläst irgendeines frisch,
> wirft einen Hund, wie Kraut, aus dem Gemisch . . . (III, 178)

This is indeed *hastig*, with its flickering rhythm, partly due to the
many short words, and still more so may seem the following
passage:

> Denk, dass einer heiss und glühend flüchte
> und die Sieger wären hinterher,
> und auf einmal machte der
> Flüchtende kurz, unerwartet, kehr
> gegen Hunderte: — so sehr
> warf sich das Erglühende der Früchte
> immer wieder an das blaue Meer . . .   (III, 186)

On closer examination, however, it will be found that these lines
are not as fast as they at first appear. Rilke suggests a sustained
intensity; characteristically, he begins with the word *denk*, imagine,
and the first part of the passage is a sequence of subjunctive clauses:
*dass einer flüchte, die Sieger wären hinterher, der Flüchtende machte
kehr.* All this in indirect, and although a breathless flight is effectively
suggested, the lines in question, in order to be understood with
their involved thought, must be read slowly.

The tempo of the *Elegies*, following their rhythm, is very uneven; emotionally it is, throughout the collection, faster than that of
Neue Gedichte, but heavy thought often retards it. Thus we have
hectic, forward rushing passages alternating with others that are
more static. The Seventh Elegy begins emphatically

> Werbung nicht mehr, nicht Werbung, entwachsene Stimme
> sei deines Schreies Natur . . .;   (III, 287)

in a later passage, this has calmed down to

>   Sichtbar
> wollen wirs heben, wo doch das sichtbarste Glück uns
> erst zu erkennen sich gibt, wenn wir es innen verwandeln.
>   (III, 289)

The *Elegies* are full of such lively contrasts. The short poems in
Neue Gedichte needed a steadier tempo and did not offer opportunities for such diversity. On the other hand, the swelling and ebbing
in the longer Elegies is not felt as arbitrary, it becomes a natural

rhythm that enlivens the wide spaces they cover and contributes to the grandeur of their tone.

Tempo in the *Sonnets to Orpheus* is more stable again, generally conditioned by the length of line in each poem: the shorter the line, the quicker, as a rule, the rhythm:

> Wandelt sich rasch auch die Welt
> wie Wolkengestalten,
> alles Vollendete fällt
> heim zum Uralten, (III, 331)

against

> Alles Erworbene bedroht die Maschine, solange
> sie sich erdreistet im Geist, statt im Gehorchen, zu sein. (III, 350)

On the whole, speed is much advanced in the *Sonnets to Orpheus* as against *Neue Gedichte*, and since each poem carries, as it were, its own tempo, the different speeds are naturally and harmoniously balanced.

D

VOLUME

IF it is difficult to ascertain a poet's speed, recording his volume is perhaps still more open to controversy. Since in poetry we have not, as in music, conventional signs for loud and soft, we must rely almost entirely on our discretion. But here again, the difficulty may appear greater in theory than it is in reality, and there will be agreement among most readers that, just as Rilke's tempo is usually slow, so his tone is usually soft. From a 'piano espressivo' it rises to 'mezzoforte', while any louder notes are the exception. Comparison alone will render this clearer, and it may be best to compare Rilke's voice with that of contemporary poets. Let us listen to Werfel:

> Tötet euch mit Dämpfen und mit Messern,
> Schleudert Schrecken, hohe Heimatworte,
> Werft dahin um Erde euer Leben!
>
> ———
>
> Ihr Keuchenden auf Strassen und auf Flüssen!!
> Gibt es ein Gleichgewicht in Welt und Leben,
> Wie werd' ich diese Schuld bezahlen müssen!?

This may well be the loudest contemporary voice. But Stefan George, too, can be much more sonorous than Rilke:

> Glanz und Ruhm! So erwacht unsere Welt.
> Heldengleich bannen wir Berg und Belt.
> Jung und gross schaut der Geist ohne Vogt
> Auf die Flur, auf die Flut die umwogt . . .,

and even in more intimate lines like these:

> Erfinder rollenden Gesangs und sprühend
> Gewandter Zwiegespräche . . .
>   nie wieder werden
> Der Knaben Preis und Jubel so mir schmeicheln,
> Nie wieder Strophen so im Ohr dir donnern!

Some poets have command over a wide range of emotion and experience, and therefore of style; they will sing to us fast and slow, loud and soft; others are contained, for their poetic expression, within a narrower circle. In Rilke's case, however, the greater uniformity of style is not due to any paucity of experience, but rather to the intensity with which he assimilated all experience before giving it shape and expression in a poem. In this often lengthy process, everything became imbued with the poet's own temper and tone, with his slow, soft intensity. It was not in Rilke's nature to raise his voice to a loud pitch. *Wer, wenn ich schriee, hörte mich denn aus der Engel / Ordnungen?* are the opening words of the First Duino Elegy. The *Elegies*, however, more than any of his previous poetry, contain evocations or temperamental outbursts where his tone has a broad and sonorous ring, while the *Sonnets to Orpheus*, with all their joyous elation, sing in a high and clear, yet slightly more subdued, voice.

In one of the sonnets in *Neue Gedichte* (*Persisches Heliotrop*), Rilke says:

> Es könnte sein, dass dir der Rose Lob
> zu laut erscheint für deine Freundin. Nimm
> das schön gestickte Kraut und überstimm
> mit dringend flüsterndem Heliotrop
> den Bülbül . . .   (III, 237)

That was Rilke's own case: to drown louder voices with his 'urgent whisper'. Within its limited volume, far from being monotonous, this voice is rich in gradations of tone; but volume defies closer analysis and can only be hinted at in this connection. Nor will many examples make the understanding clearer. Instead, a single one may suffice, a passage from *Der Marmorkarren*, with its beautiful crescendos and decrescendos:

> . . .
>
> so kommt es durch den stauenden Verlauf
> des Tages, kommt in seinem ganzen Staate,
> als ob ein grosser Triumphator nahte,
> langsam zuletzt; und langsam vor ihm her
> Gefangene, von seiner Schwere schwer.
> Und naht noch immer und hält alles auf.   (III, 77)

ALLITERATION

ALLITERATION, considerably older than rhyme, has led an unobtrusive, almost undefined, existence in European poetry ever since, in the north, rhyme superseded it as an aid to the structure of a poem. If we are to believe certain critics, the only restriction to its use now is indicated by the unwritten laws of good taste:

Perhaps it pleases most when used as an undermelody, to be discerned only by attentive ears, occurring at the beginning of the second half of a word, or in even less prominent places. Some highly musical passages in our best poets seem to owe some of their melodiousness to such subtle and recondite use of alliteration.[1]

And Percival Gurrey says:

Two of the less important resources of language are alliteration and vowel cadence. In most text-books on poetry there is a great deal said about alliteration and vowel music, usually with the implication that poets should be praised (and wondered at) for their skill in introducing alliteration and vowel music into their poems. Though, obviously, if the poet shows too much concern about the sounds and rhythms of his words, he will not be expressing anything intellectually or imaginatively of any real value. . . . And it is obvious that if he has something vital or distinctive to express, he will choose the most expressive words at his command—and the alliteration and vowel music will look after themselves.[2]

If there were not more to alliteration (and vowelling) than such quotations allow us to suppose, it would be hard to understand why, at all times, great poets have so persistently used these devices in their finest works. Alliteration is as old as poetry, and probably much older: it goes back to the very creation of language, when words were being formed by doubling a syllable, as is still the case to-day in baby-talk, as ma-ma, pa-pa, gee-gee, or, in the language of primitive peoples: noah-noah, wal-wal, tse-tse, etc. Significant, too, in this connection, are onomatopoetic words like 'murmur', or the Latin 'turtur'. In the most effective alliteration, a syllable, or part of a syllable, is still being doubled: 'I am a very fo-olish, fo-nd old man, / Fo-urscore and upwards' (King Lear); 'heaven's baffling ban bars', 'braid or brace, lace, latch or catch or key to keep' (G. M. Hopkins); 'den traurigen Traum' (Hölderlin); 'in unermüdlich gleichen Gleisen' (C. F. Meyer); 'Silber sintern, Windes Schwinge' (Rilke). There is no doubt something mysterious in the origin as well as in the effect of alliteration, something leading us

---

[1] T. S. Omond, *Some Thoughts about Verse*, 1923, p. 18.
[2] *The Appreciation of Poetry*, 1935, p. 67.

back not to the nursery only, but to the infancy of peoples, to the cradle of language, to primitive poetry, bards, singers and minstrels, when poetry was sung and heard, not read. The ancient doubling of syllables has now given way to the mere repetition of consonants or groups of consonants and vowels, yet our delight persists as of old, inexplicable and profound. It is true, nevertheless, that alliteration occupies different planes in poetry: it may indeed be mainly decorative, in the service of mere virtuosity and prettiness, like most other poetic devices:

In verse after verse, words beginning with the same letter hurry to Swinburne's demand; and all that can really be felt about them is that they do begin with the same letter.[1]

On the other hand, alliteration may be profoundly, mystically linked to the inner meaning of language and to the age-old bloodstream of poetry itself.

Rilke had no rich tradition of alliterative verse in the more recent German poetry to lean upon. While never totally absent, alliteration was not, like rhyme and the various metres, a regular feature of German poetics; where we encounter it, it seems to belong to the language almost as much as to poetry. Classic as well as romantic poets have made a sparing use of it, but the student in search of examples will have no difficulty in finding many an interesting and beautiful one, as Goethe's

> Ein Blick, der mich an jenes Meer entzückte,
> Das flutend strömt gesteigerte Gestalten,

or Matthias Claudius:

> Der Wald steht schwarz und schweiget
> Und aus den Wiesen steiget
> Der weisse Nebel wunderbar.

The last lines are an example of the 'subtle and recondite use of alliteration', which, hardly noticed by the reader, is yet responsible, together and in close harmony with vowel music, for much of the loveliness in the simple poem. The fourfold repetition of 'w', coupled with two 'schw' and the two 'st', achieves a marvellous, if almost hidden, effect of balanced fullness. Where, on the other hand, lack of taste may lead, can be seen in Schiller's *Wollust ward dem Wurm gegeben*.

There are further models for alliteration in French nineteenth-century poetry, and the Viennese origins of Rilke's art with their

[1] Charles Williams, Introduction to the Second Edition of *The Poems of G. M. Hopkins*, 1933, p. x.

accent on the sensuous and beautifying elements in poetry, have contributed not a little to his skilful mastery of the device. Moreover, Stefan George and his school made a liberal use of alliteration. Yet Rilke, more than any other modern poet, with the exception perhaps of G. M. Hopkins, uses it in every poem, often in every line. We encounter it in his earliest work, and he never ceased perfecting it. The way he uses it is quite his own, and differs considerably from the style of contemporary German poets. Stefan George, basing himself on ancient German idiom and tradition, employs it with preference in phrases like

> Berg und Belt, Sünde oder Sitte, Freund und Führer dir und Ferge, Haupt und Hand, Wunder der Welt, stark und stolz, Wald der Wunder —

i.e. in coupled groups of words. Rilke often makes a similar use of alliteration, but he prefers to let it pervade a whole line or sequence of lines, emanating not from the key words only, but from unimportant words or syllables as well.

Alliteration came to Rilke as easily as rhyme, and this natural profusion brought with it the danger of an uncritical use of the device. Although occasionally very felicitous, in the early work it is not infrequently obtrusive, not yet blended into harmony with the rest of the poem. As with the art of rhyming, Rilke's natural virtuosity in alliteration had to be toned down and balanced before it reached its final perfection. Here are examples from his early work:

> Senke dich, du segnendes Serale,
> das aus feierlichen Fernen fliesst!
> Ich empfange dich, ich bin die Schale,
> schimmernd wie aus einem Goldpokale,
> die dich schön und scheu umschliesst.

This is from the original version in *Mir zur Feier*. Note the three alliterating 's', followed in the next line by three 'f', and by no less than five 'sch' distributed over the last three lines. We cannot help feeling that the poem is overloaded with purely ornamental alliteration. Characteristically, in a later revision (1909), Rilke changed the poem to

> Senke dich, du langsames Serale,
> das aus feierlichen Fernen fliesst.
> Ich empfange dich, ich bin die Schale,
> die dich fasst und hält und nichts vergiesst.   (I, 355)

Segnendes has now become *langsames*, with the 's' in the middle of the word only just noticeable as alliteration; the redundant fourth

line has been dropped altogether, and in the new fourth line, made
from the fifth in the original version, the ornamental alliterating
words have been replaced by others expressing a firmer meaning.
Here is another example from the early work:

> Jeder Schimmer ist scheu
> und kein Klang ist noch zahm,
> und die Nacht ist zu neu,
> und die Schönheit ist Scham.   (I, 291)

Here, the symmetry of two alliterating words to every line is felt
as too intentional and gives an effect of stiffness. Nor is the following quite integrated in the poem as a whole:

> Du wacher Wald, inmitten wehen Wintern
> hast du ein Frühlingsfühlen dir erkühnt,
> und leise lässest du dein Silber sintern,
> damit ich seh, wie deine Sehnsucht grünt.   (I, 268)

Four 'w' overload the first line, but the consecutive two 'l', two 'd'
and two 's' in the third line foreshadow the poet's later skill in the
unobtrusive as well as melodious use of alliteration for enriching
a line and emphasizing a meaning. If adjectives or nouns alliterate,
the effect will be both stronger and more monotonous than in this
instance, where the alliterating words are an adjective and a verb,
a personal and a possessive pronoun, a noun and a verb. The two
pronouns and the first verb are submerged, almost silent, and the
repeated 'si' in the last two words of the line adds two discreet
reflexes, while the whole line, borne along by the rhythm and
supported by the alliterating words, achieves a soft and silvery
musical effect.

In *Buch der Bilder* we still encounter instances of a superficial use
of alliteration, together with others where the device is mastered
as a means of giving beauty and expression to the poem.

> Dann bin auch ich an das rasende Rennen
> eines rauchenden Rückens gebunden.   (II, 59)

This, if skilful, is not altogether convincing in its hard profusion.

> Sie haben alle müde Münde
> und helle Seelen ohne Saum.   (II, 23)

Another instance of decorative alliteration: we feel the words have
been chosen for their initial letters only and have no justification
otherwise, like the suppressed line in the poem from *Mir zur Feier*
quoted above. The last line of *Der Knabe*:

> und unsere Rosse rauschen wie ein Regen,   (II, 32)

avoids this mistake. The double 's' in *Rosse* is effectively increased by the 'sch' in *rauschen*, and the rush of rain dramatically, though perhaps a little obviously, suggested by the combination of words beginning with an '*r*'.

Sometimes the poet attempts too much, and such audacious and interesting experiments must fail, as

> und (wie ein Schuss die Vögel aus den Schoten
> scheucht) scheucht er ihre Hände aus den Broten.   (II, 35)

This is experimental in more than one respect: a rather novel simile, placed in parenthesis and pressed into a daring enjambment, the unlovely word *scheucht* repeated in immediate sequence, and in addition the unusual four alliterating 'sch'—an effect perhaps more original than convincing. As a contrast, how expressive in its simplicity is a passage from the preceding poem:

> und draussen war ein Tag aus Blau und Grün
> mit einem Ruf von Rot an hellen Stellen.   (II, 34)

The sound of *Ruf* and *Rot*, the two alliterating words placed exactly right in the line to evoke the colour with their clarion-like vowel sounds, followed by the suggestive internal rhyme *hellen Stellen*—this shows what the masterly handling of the various devices by a poet can achieve, and how firm and immovable such a line will stand in the poem.

The Rilke of the *Stundenbuch*, in the rush of youthful inspiration, does not stop to cut down the luxuriant shoots of his exuberant art. He is now approaching a state of full command over his poetic means, but has not yet learnt to husband his wealth. As rhyme submits to his will and touch, so alliteration comes to him easily and naturally. It is a question of selection and integration, of deciding when the device is to be modified or rejected altogether. Not only the frequency of alliteration, but also its varying character is of importance: whether the alliterating letters are slight or heavy, whether they belong to stressed or unstressed, significant or unimportant words or syllables, how they combine with the sounds following them, and whether they occur at the beginning of or inside a word. Of the very great number found in the *Stundenbuch*, we will examine a few alliterations for these qualities. When Rilke writes

> ihnen die Stirnen an die Steine stiess,   (II, 101)

and

> und stossen mit den Stirnen nach den Sternen,   (II, 193)

the effect of the repeated heavy 'st', as will be noted when reading
the lines aloud, is harsh and unpleasant, because each 'st' is followed
by a vowel. It is interesting to compare the effect of the three 'st'
in Goethe's

> strömt gesteigerte Gestalten,

where it is harmonious, because the following 'r' in *strömt* softens
the sound which, moreover, in the last two words occurs not at the
beginning, but in the middle of the word. In the passage

> Ihre Hände, die sich lautlos lösten

and

> Ihm reifte sie aus allen Rätseln reiner,   (II, 196)

alliteration—the soft, listless 'l', the round, clear 'r'—contributes
not a little to the expressive rendering of the meaning, although
too frequent repetition, like that of rhymes, has an irritating effect.
In the line

> du bist der raunende Verrusste,   (II, 199)

the dark, quaint expressiveness of the metaphor is increased by
sparing alliteration. The same can be said of

> Sei du der Hüter mit dem Horne,   (II, 205),

where, in addition to the two 'h', we have three almost voiceless
alliterating 'd' in unimportant words. The following passage shows
how the effect of alliteration is dependent on the rhythm as well as on
length of line:

> Ich war bei den ältesten Mönchen, den Malern und Mythenmeldern,
> die schrieben ruhig Geschichten und zeichneten Runen des Ruhms.
> Und ich seh dich in meinen Gesichten mit Winden, Wassern und Wäldern
> rauschend am Rande des Christentums,
> du Land, nicht zu lichten.   (II, 219)

Here, the accumulation of alliterating sounds that would be hardly
bearable in shorter lines is borne along on the flowing, majestic
rhythm of the six-feet metre, enhancing its effect with their sonorous
weight.

Alliteration can be an aid to graphic expression, especially when
combined with vowel sounds and supported by the rhythm:

> und mach sie duftender als die Syringe
> und wiegender denn deines Windes Schwinge
> und jubelnder als Josaphat.   (II, 276)

In the second line of this passage, a combination of 'w' and 'd'
culminates in the repetition of the syllable 'win' in *Windes*

and *Schwinge* (assonance), reminiscent of *Silber sintern*, slightly
modified by the preceding '*sch*' and the different pronunciation;
the two '*j*' in the last line, both preceding vowels, are convincing
in their simplicity. Similarly, in

> Denn dein ist nichts, so wenig wie des Windes,   (II, 283)

the same combination of '*d*' and '*w*' achieves, by its simple harmony,
a quiet beauty.

> und werden wachsen wie des Waldes Beeren,
> den Boden bergend unter Süssigkeit.   (II, 287)

Here we have three '*w*' followed by three '*b*', consonants that with
their softness naturally and effortlessly support the meaning of
growth and sweetness in the context.

In *Neue Gedichte* alliteration, although still present in almost
every poem, is far less conspicuous than in the earlier poems.
The device is now fully integrated, it gives a poem colour and
occasionally underlines a passage with exquisite art, generally with
discretion and restraint. A line like

> Er ging wie Hagel nieder über Halmen   (III, 23)

is forceful in its simplicity.

> und legte seine Stirne voller Staub
> tief in das Staubigsein der heissen Hände.   (III, 26)

Here, again, nothing seems forced, alliteration unobtrusively
accompanies and supports the meaning.

> Die, so ihn leben sahen, wussten nicht,
> wie sehr er e i n e s war mit allem diesen,
> denn dieses: diese Tiefen, diese Wiesen
> und diese Wasser waren sein Gesicht.
> O sein Gesicht war diese ganze Weite,
> die jetzt noch zu ihm will und um ihn wirbt . . . (III, 30)

These six lines contain no less than ten '*w*', artfully combined with
'*d*' and long vowel sounds on '*ie*', giving a rich, yet quiet, effect of
softness. The following passage, again, owes its beauty to a combination of five '*t*' with particularly sonorous vowels:

> so tritt das Dunkel dieses Tores handelnd
> auf seiner Tiefe tragisches Theater.   (III, 36)

Die Fensterrose begins with the line

> Da drin: das träge Treten ihrer Tatzen . . .,   (III, 38)

where '*dr*' is followed by two '*tr*' and by '*ta*', the great effect of

the line entrusted to alliteration alone. Such effects can be extraordinary, as in the simple line from *Die Gazelle*:

> Aus deiner Stirne steigen Laub und Leier, (III, 45)

an unusually happy combination of the apt words with very sym-
metric alliteration. A similar result, if possible still finer, is obtained
by a subtle combination of modulation on vowels with alliteration:

> und ein gestirnter stiller Himmel ging,
> ein Klage-Himmel mit entstellten Sternen —. (III, 101)

The passage contains six short '*i*' sounds (*gestirnter, stiller, Himmel,
ging, Klage-Himmel, mit*) followed by five short '*e*' sounds (*ent-
stellten Sternen*), combined with two '*st*', two '*h*', and again two '*st*':
modulation from '*i*' to '*e*' is facilitated by the alliterating sounds.
The exquisite perfection of such lines is characteristic of Rilke's
mature art.

In the process of this maturing, alliteration ceases to be a device
the poet may use or discard at will, it is now most intimately
connected with the very texture of the poem, deeply woven into
the warp of his language. We may point it out without always
being able to separate it from the whole as a distinctive device.
The vibrating life of lines like the following is centred in their
repeated '*f*', '*zu*', and '*w*', which are not superimposed on them,
but belong to the poem from its conception:

> froh, als fühlte sie die Fluten glänzend:
> Warme, Zugetane, deren Zug,
> wie mit Zuversicht die Fahrt bekränzend . . .; (III, 121)

and later, in the same poem, we have:

> selig, sorglos, sicher vor Verwundung . . .

How perfectly the meaning is translated into sound in the first
line of *Übung am Klavier*, by the close combination of '*s*', '*mm*' and
'*m*':

> Der Sommer summt. Der Nachmittag macht müde . . ., (III, 222)

yet no effort is visible: the line reads smoothly, naturally, and the
supreme art that went into its making is concealed. What use Rilke
can make of the rare letter '*z*' may be shown by two examples:

> dieweil der Löwe Zähne zeigt und Zunge . . . (III, 80)
> . . . nach allen Seiten
> zuckende Zungen streckt — beginnt im Kreis
> naher Beschauer, hastig, hell und heiss
> ihr runder Tanz sich zuckend auszubreiten. (III, 82)

'*H*' is sometimes used to express a tension:

> ... solang der Hals
> das Haupt ins Horchen hält ...,   (III, 45)

and, combined with '*w*':

> und dann scheint er wartend wen zu wählen:
> hingegeben hebt er seine Hand ...   (III, 174)

In *Die Anfahrt*, the unusual sequence of three '*gl*' is so skilfully placed that we do not feel it as too pronounced:

> ... denn da war das Tor,
> das nun, als hätte es sie angerufen,
> die lange Fahrt zu einer Schwenkung zwang,
> nach der sie stand. Aufglänzend ging ein Gleiten
> die Glastür abwärts ...   (III, 233)

The first, most felicitous line of the same poem is tuned on '*w*':

> War in des Wagens Wendung dieser Schwung?

Here, added to the obvious alliteration, we have the not so obvious relation between the '*gen*' in *Wagens* to the '*wen*' in *Wendung*, as well as the repetition of this world's last syllable '*ung*' in *Schwung*— a complex and delicate interplay of sounds. How natural and final is the first line of *Der Platz*, with its three painting '*w*':

> Willkürlich von Gewesnem ausgeweitet ...   (III, 85)

And finally, two examples showing the use of '*f*':

> das Fliegende, Entfliehende, Entfernte ...   (III, 88)

Here again, alliteration is only the most obvious means of binding words together; in addition, the middle word *Entfliehende* is linked to the preceding word by the syllable '*flie*' and to the following by their common prefix '*ent*': such connections give Rilke's language its inimitable fullness and firm texture. The melancholy concluding lines of *In einem fremden Park* contain four '*f*' sounds:

> und warum siehst du schliesslich, wie verloren,
> die Falter flimmern um den hohen Phlox?   (III, 61)

In the *Duino Elegies*, Rilke's use of alliteration is somewhat different from that in his previous poems. It is more unevenly distributed within the individual poem: long stretches are almost without it, alternating with others where it is massed in a few lines. It is now never in the least decorative, always full of an often sombre expressiveness. Combination with vowel sounds is very close, as in the lines

> ... und verschlucke den Lockruf
> dunkelen Schluchzens ...   (III, 259)

or in these

> Wenigen steigt so stark der Andrang des Handelns,
> dass sie schon anstehn und glühn in der Fülle des Herzens
> wenn die Verführung zum Blühn wie gelinderte Nachtluft . . .
> (III, 284)

Alliteration may underline a particularly apt adjective:

> . . . die ganze
> lautlose Landschaft . . ., (III, 273)
> und fallen ein auf teilnahmlosen Teich . . ., (III, 274)
> . . . in den milden
> muldigen Bildern von Karnak den siegenden König.
> (III, 285)

Sometimes, alliteration helps to stress an unusual thought or expression:

> und niemals Nirgends ohne Nicht. (III, 293)

Finally, there are many instances of complete integration, of a simple force achieved as the result of stressing, with the help of alliteration, the final and exhaustive expression:

> . . . wenn der Wind voller Weltraum . . . (III, 260)
> . . . hochauf -
> schlagend erschlüg uns das eigene Herz (III, 264)
> Ihn rührt ihre Haltung. Die Schulter, der Hals, vielleicht
> ist sie von herrlicher Herkunft. (II, 304–5)
> Und sie leitet ihn leicht durch die weite Landschaft der Klagen.
> (III, 305)

We encounter alliteration in each of the *Sonnets to Orpheus* in various degrees of intensity; in every instance it is part of the poem from its very conception, inseparable from the whole. There is not the slightest too-much, not even the almost imperceptible strain felt in some of the pieces of *Neue Gedichte*. The result is a diaphanous beauty, very harmonious, and comparable to the quiet perfection of lines like those of Matthias Claudius quoted earlier (*Der Wald steht schwarz und schweiget . . .*), with the difference that Rilke's style is more spiritual and has far more involved processes to express. The connection of alliteration with vowel sounds is very intimate, in many instances the two are inseparable, mutually enhancing their effectiveness, as may be studied in the lines

> Kundiger böge die Zweige der Weiden,
> wer die Wurzeln der Weiden erfuhr. (III, 318)

The combination here is 'w' and 'ei'. In the first line, the syllable '*wei*' is repeated, varied only by the '*z*' of *Zweige*; in the second line, there is a relation between the initial '*w*' of *Wurzeln* and the '*z*' in the same word, which is reminiscent of the '*z*' in the first line; the modulation from '*ei*' back to '*u*' is achieved in *erfuhr*; *Weiden* is repeated as a word and binds the two lines more closely together.

Have all these involved relations been planned and executed with an almost superhuman skill and more than usual felicity? No, they have been poetically conceived: we need only repeat the two lines, speaking them aloud, to feel that these relations are the chemistry of the crystal, not those of the synthetic compound. They resemble some of nature's works in that they are complex in essence, simple in appearance. It is interesting to note that these lines have a forerunner in Rilke's earlier poetry, in *Buch der Bilder*:

> Doch ohne Zeichen blieb der Zweig der Weide,   (II, 28)

which shows that the combination of words had been stored in the poet's mind for many years.

Alliterating '*t*' is combined with the vowel '*o*' in

> trat in das trostlos offene Tor,   (III, 337)

and of '*w*' and '*o*', followed by '*t*', in

> Irgendwo wohnt das Gold in der verwöhnenden Bank
> und mit Tausenden tut es vertraulich,   (III, 363)

where the repeated syllable '*wo*' modulates to '*wö*' in the first line. Another example of this art of intertwining is

> Schon, horch, hörst du der ersten Harken
> Arbeit.   (III, 370)

—the syllable '*hor*' becomes '*hör*', then '*har*' in *Harken*, which immediately modulates to '*ar*' in *Arbeit*.

Frequent in the *Sonnets* is the alliterating combination of a group of two or more words, as *Weg und Wendung, Sternbild unserer Stimme, das Lied überm Land, Raum der Rühmung, die Stimme am Staube, vom Mädchen zum Manne, / wenn es ihn meidet und meint.* Such combinations are in keeping with the somewhat stylized simplification of the *Sonnets* which, as we have seen, is akin to the simplification in nature, though often based on most involved processes.

VOWEL SOUNDS

MUCH that has been said of alliteration is equally true of vowel sounds, and in the case of repeated syllables it may not even be possible always to differentiate between the two. As a rule, however, vowel music is not based, like alliteration, on repetition; or rather, the effect of repeated vowels lies more in their intensification by accumulation than in their being repeated. Eduard Scherrer has shed some light on the nature of sounds in poetry; he says:[1]

Es ist allgemein üblich, von hellen und dunklen Tönen zu sprechen. Gemeint damit ist jene schwer zu beschreibende Verwandtschaft, wie sie besteht zwischen hohen und tiefen Tönen einerseits, und dunklen und hellen Farben andererseits. Tiefe Töne sind dunkel, . . . hohe Töne sind hell . . . Aber noch Anderes. Den einzelnen Tonempfindungen kommt Räumlichkeit zu in ganz eigenem Sinn. Tiefe Töne haben etwas Voluminöses, Volles, räumlich Ausgedehntes. Hohe Töne erscheinen dünn, spitzig, gleichsam punktförmig. Sie sind 'kleiner' als tiefe Töne. Andere Unterschiede gehen damit parallel. Dunkle Töne erscheinen auch leicht massig, dick, dumpf, schwer, diffus und weich . . . Auch hier zeigen hohe Töne gegensätzlichen Character. Sie sind eher spitzig, scharf, stechend, leicht.

[2] Die gehobene Sprechweise der Lyrik hebt einzelne Worte durch Akzent und Dehnung hervor. Die betreffenden Vorstellungen haben so eher Gelegenheit, voll bewusst zu werden.

And A. R. Orage says:[3]

Vowels play a very large part in the magical effect of sound in general. They are more primitive than consonants, and probably express, or at least reveal, a deeper layer of consciousness. One object, therefore, . . . of every writer is to select such vowel sounds as will induce in his reader the mood appropriate to the nature of his subject and favourable to its reception.

It is clear, from the foregoing, that the clever use of vowelling provides great opportunities for 'painting' with sounds, opportunities which poets of all periods and climes have eagerly seized upon. We must be careful, however, not to assign too positively certain qualities to certain sounds, that is not to assert, e.g., that the vowel 'u' is invariably dark and voluminous, 'e' always pointed and light. Too many other factors have to be taken into account to allow for such generalizations; in the same way as every painting creates a new and individual system of colour values, so each poem creates, to a certain extent, its own world of sound. Vowel music

---

[1] 'Das Problem der anschaulichen Gestaltung in der Lyrik', *Archiv für die Gesamte Psychologie*, Bd. 39, 1920, p. 162.
[2] Ibid., p. 191.   [3] *Select Essays and Critical Writings*, 1935, p. 38.

in poetry, moreover, is never pure sound, it is inseparable, to a large extent, from the meaning of words, and dependent also on the consonants that accompany the vowels. This explains why certain vowel combinations can be used to express widely contrasting sensations. Compare the softness of

Du meines Leidens leiser Zweiter,   (II, 233)

with the harshness of

unter kreissendem Gekreisch,   (III, 148)

both based on '*ei*': in the first instance, the consonants '*m*', '*l*' and '*w*' are softening, in the second the repeated '*kr*', as well as '*ss*' and '*sch*' hardening factors; furthermore, the rhythm plays a part, the different tempo, the influence of the gentle *du* at the beginning of the line.

Rilke's ear for the sounds of language, their subtle variations and relations to each other, was almost miraculously fine. In a letter to his publisher[1] on account of a misprint which had altered, in his *Klage um Jonathan* (III, 127), his *löhren* to *röhren*, he states that the two words have not the same '*ö*'-sound. This sounds at first somewhat perplexing: why should two words, distinguished only by their first letters, but otherwise perfectly rhyming, have a different vowel sound? Only when we pronounce each word, the difference becomes noticeable: the sound '*ö*' can follow on '*l*' with hardly a change of tongue or lips, while the position of the tongue after forming '*r*' affects also the lips and therefore the sound, making it ever so slightly deeper. Very few people, we might perhaps add few poets even, would notice the almost imperceptible difference. Again, as with rhymes and alliteration, Rilke's natural talent in the handling of vowel sounds, improved by careful study, is astounding. Utterances by the poet regarding his style are very rare: the observation addressed to his publisher was provoked by a typographical error. Hidden away in one of his sonnets (*Persische Heliotrop*), we find, in a surprising simile, an expression of the delight he felt at the sound-harmony produced by vowels: the dense starry texture of the flower is compared to 'sweet words':

... wie süsse Worte nachts in Sätzen
beisammenstehn ganz dicht, durch nichts getrennt,
aus der Vokale wachem Violett
hindüftend durch das stille Himmelbett ...   (III, 237)

The danger of a superficial and merely decorative use of thi

---

[1] *Briefe an seinen Verleger*, 1934; Letter dated Nov. 8, 1908.

device is not so great as with certain others: vowel sounds are more intimately connected with meaning and expression, do not lend themselves quite so easily to empty effects and pretty patterns as do rhyme and alliteration. There is hardly a better aid in the poet's arsenal to modelling a thought, a sensation, than vowel sounds: they underline it most effectively, give it shape and colour.

The use of vowels for their sonorous effect was, of course, not new to German poetry, yet the technique of the device remained for a long time in a dormant state and was, moreover, not a regular feature of the German lyric. Vowels were often massed in a kind of careless rapture, sometimes with remarkable results, though their potentialities were by no means fully exhausted. In the following examples, Goethe and Mörike use full-sounding vowels in profusion, yet they make no attempt at grouping them:

> Sogleich umsäuselt Abendwindes Kühle,
> Umhaucht euch Blumenwürzgeruch und Duft.
> Es schweigt das Wehen banger Erdgefühle,
> Zum Wolkenbette wandelt sich die Gruft...
>> (Goethe, *Zueignung*)
> Der Kuckuck nur ruft sein einförmig Grüssen
> Versteckt aus unerforschter Wildnis Grüne —
> Jetzt kracht die Wölbung und verhallte lange,
> Das wundervolle Schauspiel ist im Gange!
>> (Mörike, *Besuch in Urach*)
> Ihr Auge sieht die goldne Wage nun
> Der Zeit in gleichen Schalen stille ruhn...
>> (Mörike, *Um Mitternacht*)

Droste-Hülshoff has her own way of handling vowels to great advantage; by repeating full-vowelled words, she achieves intensity:

> Jetzt möcht ich schlafen, schlafen gleich,
> Entschlafen unterm Mondeshauch,
> Umspielt von flüsterndem Gezweig,
> Im Blute Funken, Funk im Strauch,
> Und mir im Ohre Melodei; —
>> (*Durchwachte Nacht*)

After the romantic poets, the first perhaps to arrange words in homogeneous groups and thus to play consistently on one sound was Mörike, and his great art makes the effective device so natural that it is hardly noticeable. Here he uses the vowel *a* in this manner:

> Am langsamsten von allen Göttern wandeln wir
> . . . .
> Und machen mannigfaltig ihm den langen Tag.
>> (*Inschrift auf einne Uhr mit den drei Horen*)

E

C. F. Meyer closely follows Mörike in this technique. He models a passage, very effectively and unobtrusively, on *au*:

> es glaubt, es glaubt an die barmherzge Lüge
> des Traums. Es lauscht dem Hauch der Hirtenflöte ...
>
> (*Die sterbende Meduse*)

His poem *Nachtgeräusche* is effectively tuned on the 'dark' vowel '*u*' which occurs sixteen times in its eleven lines, mostly with assonance in the non-rhyming end words:

> wie das Atmen eines jungen Busens,
> wie das Murmeln eines tiefen Brunnens,
> wie das Schlagen eines dumpfen Ruders,
> dann der ungehörte Tritt des Schlummers.

Stefan George, following and developing this technique, has created majestic lines, as

> Jung und gross schaut der Geist ohne Vogt
> auf die Flur auf die Flut die umwogt,

or

> Nie wieder Strophen so im Ohr dir donnern!

Hofmannsthal can play on single sounds in the manner of C. F. Meyer:

> Der tiefe Brunnen weiss es wohl,
> Einst waren alle tief und stumm,
> Und alle wussten drum.

but more often, he gives a melodious mixture of vowels in the older style:

> Mir war's, als ginge durch die blaue Nacht,
> Die atmende, ein rätselhaftes Rufen.

Rilke surpasses all these models by the frequency with which he uses vowel sounds, which become a regular feature in his poems, and by the subtlety he develops in his technique of handling them. Vowelling is never absent from any of Rilke's different periods as an element of his style. Only Stefan George, in lines like those quoted above, is his equal in modelling a passage on a single vowel, but while Rilke's poems abound in this art, it is rarer, at least in this perfection, in George's work. Rilke improves and intensifies the technique either by grouping different vowels together until he has exhausted all the contrasts of a sound pattern, or by exploiting to the full the possibilities of a vowel or diphthong, extracting from them all the expressive qualities relevant to his theme, all the melodious softness or characteristic hardness they are capable of yielding. In the lines that follow, 'o', 'u' and 'e' are the predominant vowels:

> Sie folgten furchtbar, ihren bunten Tod
> von ferne nach ihm werfend, während er
> verloren floh, nichts weiter als: bedroht.
> Die Ferne seiner Väter schien nicht mehr
> für ihn zu gelten . . .,   (III, 74)

while the more sophisticated mixture in *Die Sonnenuhr* plays upon 'au', 'eu', 'a' and 'o':

> Selten reicht ein Schauer feuchter Fäule
> aus dem Gartenschatten, wo einander
> Tropfen fallen hören und ein Wander-
> vogel lautet, zu der Säule,
> die in Majoran und Koriander
> steht und Sommerstunden zeigt . . .   (III, 234)

Instead of following them chronologically through his production, it may be more instructive to show Rilke's handling of vowels by an arrangement according to the various sounds, for a progressive development in the use of the device is not so obvious as with others, and the juxtaposition of the different vowels is interesting in itself.

'E' is for Rilke the least expressive of the vowels, and the one he uses less frequently than the others.

> Fast bis zu den fernen Meeren
> kann ich den ernsten, schweren,
> verwehrenden Himmel sehn.   (II, 53)

This is typical for Rilke's earlier style; later he would have avoided the accumulation of adjectives in this example from *Buch der Bilder*. For his later manner, we may compare it to a line from *Sonnets to Orpheus*:

> Schwer sind die Berge, schwer sind die Meere. (III, 316)

How compact that is, how effective in its monumental simplicity!

> Die Einsamkeit ist wie ein Regen.
> Sie steigt vom Meer den Abenden entgegen;
> von Ebenen, die fern sind und entlegen,
> geht sie zum Himmel . . .   (II, 50)

Note how, in these lines, the 'e's' increase until they dominate the very effective third line entirely; but the clause *die fern sind und*

entlegen is mere padding for the sake of the e-sound. Here are a few
examples from the *Stundenbuch*:

über den Ebenen der Ewigkeit   (II, 252)
erst wenn er sterben muss auf diesem Stern,
sehn wir, dass er auf diesem Stern gelebt,   (II, 237)

and finally, the fine, simple line

Da leben Menschen, leben schlecht und schwer.   (II, 271)

Of the few examples in *Neue Gedichte*, the most felicitous perhaps is
this:

und die Gelenke lebten wie die Kehlen.   (III, 107)

In *Letzte Gedichte* we have the highly expressive

Aber im Stehn ist er herrlich,   (III, 448)

and, repeated refrain-like throughout the poem:

Ausgesetzt auf den Bergen des Herzens.   (III, 420)

From *Sonnets to Orpheus* comes

zehrende Lehrer,   (III, 357)

and the line, as remarkable for its rhythm as for the vowel music
in it:

Wer sich als Quelle ergiesst, den erkennt die Erkennung.   (III, 354)

The next vowel in frequency is '*a*', more sonorous than '*e*'
which becomes almost voiceless in short and unstressed syllables,
while '*a*' retains some of its sonority even in these. Rilke likes to
stress the contrast between long and short '*a*':

und wurden in dem Glanz der Ampeln klar   (II, 106)
und kalte Jahre ohne Kampf und Kraft   (II, 272)
in deren Adern Kraft und Adel schlief   (II, 97)
die Gassen haben einen sachten Gang.   (III, 86)

Sometimes, he uses the short vowel only to good effect:

arm wie die warme Armut eines Stalles,   (II, 289)

with the three repeated '*arm*', and, very elaborate and a trifle artificial, to fit the subject with its scented air:

fühlt man lang noch auf dem Rand des Dachs
jene Urnen stehen, kalt, zerspalten,
doch entschlossen, noch zusammzuhalten
um die Asche alter Achs.   (III, 240)

These four lines contain no fewer than eleven '*a*', all short, most of
them stressed, and the last three, in their close succession, very

effective. In the musical line that follows, there is some rivalry
between '*ie*', '*o*' and '*a*':

und diese hier, opalnes Porzellan,   (III, 112)

but '*a*' wins in carrying the most sonorous sound.

Numerous are the poet's uses for the '*a*'-sound in the *Duino
Elegies*:

rascher als Wasser   (III, 280)

(compare, in *Sonnets to Orpheus*:

zu dem raschen Wasser sprich   (III, 374))

> Nicht nur die Andacht dieser entfalteten Kräfte,
> nicht nur die Wege, nicht nur die Wiesen im Abend,
> nicht nur, nach späten Gewitter, das atmende Klarsein,
> nicht nur der nahende Schlaf und ein Ahnen, abends . . .
> (III, 288)
> streifend im langsamen Abstrich die Wange entlang,   (III, 307)

and the seven exquisite lines:

> Abends führt sie ihn zu den Gräbern der Alten
> aus dem Klage-Geschlecht, den Sibyllen und Warn-Herrn.
> Naht aber Nacht, so wandeln sie leiser, und bald
> mondets empor, das über alles
> wachende Grab-Mal. Brüderlich jenem am Nil,
> der erhabene Sphinx — : der verschwiegenen Kammer
> Antlitz.   (III, 306)

The *Sonnets to Orpheus* contain equally fine passages:

und im Bangen des langen Jahrs   (III, 348)

(compare this with the verbose

> und alternd nach und nach
> begriffen sie die Bangnis der Aprile   (II, 99));
> sein Wandeln, seine Haltung, seinen Hals   (III, 344)
> alles des wach oder schlafend atmenden Gelds   (III, 363)
> Wagt zu sagen, was ihr Apfel nennt   (III, 325)
> Bang verlangen wir nach einem Halte;   (III, 368)

and, with the predominating short '*a*':

> die auf dem Gartentisch oft von Kante zu Kante
> lagen, ermattet und sanft verletzt,
> wartend des Wassers . . .;   (III, 347)

the metallic line:

Warte, ein Härtestes warnt aus der Ferne das Harte,   (III, 354)

in which the combination of '*a*' and '*ä*' with the consonant '*r*'
makes for hardness; there are five '*a*' in this line, and five vowels

followed by '*r*'; the first word rhyming with the last contributes a severe frame—can hardness be more adequately or more beautifully expressed?

Lovely, too, are the contrasted lines

> ... vom Hang des Apennins
> tragen sie dir dein Sagen zu, das dann
> am schwarzen Altern deines Kinns ...;   (III, 358)

and finally, the line that expresses its meaning with such diaphanous clarity:

> klar zu werden, wach und transparent.   (III, 325)

In the first lines of *Winterliche Stanzen*, the sound is used in its full sonority:

> Nun sollen wir versagte Tage lange
> ertragen in des Widerstandes Rinde ...

while later lines, in the same poem, show that it can equally well suggest a subdued emotion:

> die Nacht ist stark, doch von so fernem Gange ...
> ein Vogelanklang, halb wie ein Verdacht ...   (III, 400)

> Gedanken der Nacht, aus geahnter Erfahrung gehoben,
> die schon das fragende Kind mit Schweigen durchdrang,
> langsam denk ich euch auf ...   (III, 417)

> ... schwankt abends
> in ihrem Flattern die Angst vor dem Anprall
> an die erkaltete Qual.   (III, 384)

'*Ä*', a comparatively rare sound in the language, is not frequent as a vowel cadence in Rilke's poems. We will limit our examples to two; in the first, from *Neue Gedichte*, a whole poem is pervaded by '*ä*', which colours eleven lines in it:

> Durch sein Geäder
> bricht wie durch Gebüsche das Tier.
> Täler bilden sich, waldige Bäder
> spiegeln die Hindin, und hinter ihr
> hurtigt das Blut des geschlossenen Schläfers,
> von des traumig wirren Gewäfers
> jähem Wiederzergehn gequält.   (III, 119)

The second passage comes from the Seventh Elegy:

> Aber nicht sie nur
> käme ... Es kämen aus schwächlichen Gräbern
> Mädchen und ständen ... Denn, wie beschränk ich,
> wie, den gerufenen Ruf?   (III, 289)

In German, '*i*' has the highest pitch of the vowels, characterized by E. Scherrer as 'pointed, sharp and light'. This description, however, is not exhaustive: '*i*' has a musical sound in long syllables, and can be very soft in short ones; it is also particularly penetrating when long. Some of Rilke's finest lines are modelled on '*i*', and the effects he could obtain through his skilful handling, especially of the short sound, are remarkable. Here is an example of the long quality:

> denn dieses: diese Tiefen, diese Wiesen   (III, 30)

and here some of the short:

> und der Gestirne stiller Mittelpunkt   (II, 43)
> und ein gestirnter stiller Himmel ging,   (III, 101)

and, perhaps the loveliest and most elaborate:

> und mischen, dass sie fast davon verschwimmt,
> die Stille mit Vanille und mit Zimt.   (III, 237)

Both lengths are often contrasted:

> wilder Gebilde, dass ein Schimmer ihre
> stillen Gesichter finde und verliere.   (II, 104)

> windiges Licht. Fast fliegend siehst du hier
> die Himmel wieder . . .   (III, 83)

> Wie er sich hingab —. Liebe.
> Liebe sein Inneres, seines Inneren Wildnis,
> diesen Urwald in ihm . . .   (III, 278)

A few more examples, from the *Duino Elegies*, mostly of the short vowel:

> Sondern er wringt sie,
> biegt sie, schlingt sie und schwingt sie,
> wirft sie . . .   (III, 272)
> mitten im Schicksal stands, im vernichtenden, mitten
> in Nichtwissen-Wohin . . .   (III, 291)

In close conjunction with alliteration:

> und niemals Nirgends ohne Nicht: (III, 293)
> dient als ein Ding, oder stirbt in ein Ding —   (III, 300)

and very beautiful in the line

> das sie ins Heitere wirft, in die innigen Himmel.   (III, 287)

Sometimes, '*i*' modulates to the related '*ü*':

> doch sieghaft, sicher und mit einen süssen
> grüssenden Lächeln . . .   (III, 82)

Sonnets to Orpheus, too, are full of interesting examples:

> wie sie, ertrinkend in sich, sich wehrt
> wider ihr Süss-sein . . .   (III, 327)
> Spiegel, noch nie hat man wissend beschrieben   (III, 343)
> und war im Silber-Spiegel und in ihr.   (III, 344)
> Nähme sie einer ins innige Schlafen und schliefe
> tief mit den Dingen . . .   (III, 357)

The finest examples in the *Sonnets* are probably these:

> bis in des stillen Blickes Licht — geliebt.   (III, 344)

Note how, after five short '*i*', the one long sound in *geliebt*, emphasized by the preceding pause, seals the sentence with its musical sound. Again, in

> allen den stillen Geschwistern im Winde der Wiesen,   (III, 357)

the long i-sound comes at the end of a string of short ones; in addition, the combination with the alliterating '*w*' is so perfect, and the line so natural and musical in its soft flow, that it becomes a triumph of poetical language.

In the sonnet, *Dame vor dem Spiegel*, the i-sound, long and short, occurs in almost every line, until the one that forms the climax of the poem is tuned exclusively on it:

> trinkt sie still aus ihrem Bild. Sie trinkt . . .   (III, 228)

So flawless is the technique that the reader, unless his attention is drawn to it, will hardly be conscious of the concentration which, however, is so important to the structure of the poem.

Sometimes, instead of being concentrated, the i-sounds are more loosely scattered over a number of lines, as in the ending of the last of the Orpheus sonnets:

> und wenn dich das Irdische vergass,
> zu der stillen Erde sag: Ich rinne.
> Zu dem raschen Wasser sprich: Ich bin.   (III, 374)

A few passages, even in the later poems, have an artificial ring, as this one from *Skizze zu einem Sankt Georg*:

> Während silberner über dem silbernen Tier,
> unberührt von der Kühle und Trübe
> sich der Helm, vergittert und spiegelnd, hübe,
> Frühwind in der schwingenden Zier.
> Und im steilen Abstieg würde der ganze
> Silberne sichtbar, klingend von lichtem Gerinn . . .
>   (III, 379)

This is decorative in a very sophisticated way, and the modulation from '*i*' to '*ü*' extremely skilful—but there is something experimental about it, it is one of the rare instances where Rilke's style is not integrated.

'*I*' used in conjunction with '*z*' produces a hissing sensation:

> huscht sie es an überm Spielen, das Kind, und zischelt
> Zwietracht ins Blut . . .   (III, 467)

Later on, in the same poem, the sound is used in a very different manner:

> Das innige Kindsein
> steht wie die Mitte in ihr.   (III, 467)

In *Vor-Ostern*, Rilke handles the vowel in a most interesting way: the half-line

> (wie in Fliessendem gespiegelt)   (III, 182)

expresses by sound, as closely as seems possible, the meaning of the words. The long '*i*' with their soft, yet penetrating sound, suggest the brightness of water and the glistening reflexes upon it, while the short '*e*' in *fliessendem* and *gespiegelt* seem to shake and slightly distort the sound, as reflected images are distorted in water; the rhythmical movement of the line contributes to the effect. Meaning and sound are perfectly parallel: the aim of all poetry.

'*O*' has a more sonorous sound than the three vowels analysed; it is the natural, spontaneous interjection which may express surprise, joy, admiration, dismay, pain, and grief; besides, it is an invocation, an address, a call, a supplication, a command. The difference between long and short '*o*' is very marked: long, the vowel is full, rich, sonorous; short, it has a dry, curt, hollow ring. In his early poems, Rilke indulges freely in the more sonorous sound:

> eine von den hohen, schlanken, roten
> Hochsommerblumen . . .   (II, 117)
> verkünden, dass im köstlichen Ikone
> die Königliche wie im Kloster wohne,
> die überfliessen wird von jenem Sohne,
> von jenem Tropfen, drinnen wolkenohne
> die niegehofften Himmel blaun.   (II, 104-5)

Such lines leave the impression that the poet could not stop, the sound carried him on and on, as it did Swinburne.

> Des Sommers Wochen standen still   (II, 229)

—this is another example of the felicitous combination of vowel sound with alliteration, which takes over with the repeated '*st*' where the repeated '*o*' leave off.

Some lines from *Neue Gedichte* are typical of the hollow, muffled sound of the short vowel:

> Noch ist die Welt voll Rollen, die wir spielen.
> Solang wir sorgen, ob wir auch gefielen,
> Spielt auch der Tod, obwohl er nicht gefällt.   (III, 63)

The nine 'o' in these three lines are discreet, hardly noticeable. The sound is more emphasized in the first lines of *Das jüngste Gericht*, an example of audacious artfulness, though we may feel that virtuosity is perhaps overshooting the mark:

> So erschrocken, wie sie nie erschraken,
> ohne Ordnung, oft durchlocht und locker,
> hocken sie in dem geborstnen Ocker ...   (III, 147)

It is difficult to accept *oft durchlocht und locker* as quite natural, while *der geborstne Ocker* provides a magnificently painting touch. With no less skill, Rilke plays on the hopeless sound of 'o' in *Das Auswandererschiff*, where it occurs sixteen times in six lines:

> als das langsame Orangenboot
> sie vorübertrug bis an das grosse
> graue Schiff, zu dem, von Stoss zu Stosse,
> andre Boote Fische hoben, Brot, —
> Während es voll Hohn in seinem Schosse
> Kohlen aufnahm, offen wie der Tod.   (III, 186)

The long poem, *Die Geburt der Venus*, ends, very effectively, with the deadly finality of the four-word line:

> Tot, rot und offen.   (III, 109)

We have an equally impressive last line, firm and final, in *Die Berufung*:

> und konnte und gehorchte und vollzog.   (III, 249)

Marienprozession contains a very successful and sonorous line based on 'o':

> dem Glockendonnern des grossoffnen Domes,   (III, 92)

and equally magnificent lines occur in *Corrida*:

> in die wiederhergerollte grosse
> Woge über dem verlornen Stosse ...   (III, 214)

The vowel can change to softness by a combination with 's':

> nun liegt es sorglos in den offnen Rosen.   (III, 113)
> dieser offenen Rosen,
> dieser sorglosen, sieh:
> wie sie lose im Losen
> liegen ...   (III, 225)

Invocation stands out with purity in the opening lines of the first
Orpheus sonnet:

> Da stieg ein Baum. O reine Übersteigung!
> O Orpheus singt! O hoher Baum im Ohr!   (III, 313)

and in passages like these:

> O du verlorener Gott!   (III, 338)
> Rose, du thronende . . .   (III, 346)
> Wo ist ihr Tod? O, wirst du dies Motiv . . .   (III, 314)
> O wie ein Golf hofft ins Offene . . .   (III, 470)

Fullness is expressed in

> Vorrat der vollen Natur,   (III, 356)

hopelessness in the sad lines

> aus dem tonlosen Los   (III, 308)
> nach schrecklichem Pochen
> trat in das trostlos offene Tor,   (III, 337)

a restrained longing in the lovely

> Ins reine, ins hohe, ins torig
> offene Herz träte er anders, der Gott.   (III, 349)

Finally, two examples of the vowel modified by *umlaut*, both very
effective sound-painting:

> . . . dass wir ihr ein Mal entrönnen
> und sie in stiller Fabrik ölend sich selber gehört. (III, 350)
> in dem gehöhlten Gewölb.   (III, 424)

'U' is the deepest among the German vowels—it is dark, and
therefore 'massive, thick, dull, heavy, diffuse, and soft'. We find
examples of all these qualities in Rilke's poetry. The heaviness of
the repeated sound is obvious in lines from the *Stundenbuch*, where
we find it in combination with '*au*':

> Du dunkelnder Grund, geduldig erträgst du die Mauern.
> Und vielleicht erlaubst du noch eine Stunde den Städten zu dauern . . .
> (II, 220)

Truly magnificent, in its variation and combination with others,
is the use of the vowel in *Der Platz*:

> Willkürlich von Gewesnem ausgeweitet:
> von Wut und Aufruhr, von dem Kunterbunt,
> das die Verurteilten zu Tod begleitet,
> von Buden, von der Jahrmarktsrufer Mund,
> und von dem Herzog, der vorüberreitet,
> und von dem Hochmut von Burgund . . .   (III, 85)

The dark sound of 'u' is for Rilke symbolic of the deep call of the blood, of primeval instinct, as shown in the beautifully impressive passage:

> anders als die stumme, stumpfgemute
> Zucht der Fische, Blut von ihrem Blute ...   (III, 121)

The Third Elegy, which deals with the primitive force of love, is particularly rich in this sound; no fewer than ten passages are tuned on 'u', of which here a few:

> jenen verborgenen schuldigen Flussgott des Bluts.
> O des Blutes Neptun, o sein furchtbarer Dreizack.
> O der dunkele Wind seiner Brust aus gewundener Muschel.
> Ruf ihn ... du rufst ihn nicht ganz aus dunkelem Umgang
> ... in das ältere Blut, in die Schluchten,
> wo das Furchtbare lag ...   (III, 269–73)

But the vowel could also become calm and soft in Rilke's hands, as in the idyllic concluding lines of *Der Turm*:

> ... bis er ganz im Hintergrunde
> beruhigt geht durch Buschwerk und Natur.   (III, 84).

Rilke's technique at its subtlest can be studied in the line

> huldvoll, prunkend, purpurn und pompös.   (III, 195)

Note the increase and decrease of the vowel sounds: first a 'u' in the first syllable of two words, then in both syllables, modulating in the last word of the line to short 'o' and long 'ö'; overlapped and supported by the movement of alliterating 'p', which again begins singly in *prunkend*, to be doubled in *purpurn* and *pompös*. Vowelling and alliteration combine in perfect symmetry, yet the line is not just playful virtuosity: the sound closely supports the meaning.

The earlier lines from the *Stundenbuch*: *Du dunkelnder Grund* ... are recalled in the invocation of the fountain sonnet:

> O Brunnen-Mund, du gebender, du Mund ...,   (III, 358)

with the three 'e' in the middle, which serve as a perfect foil to the dark 'u' sounds that dominate the line.

Dumpf is the key-word to the following passages:

> Zu dem gebrauchten sowohl, wie zum dumpfen und stummen
> Vorrat der vollen Natur ...   (III, 356)
> den dumpfen Mund zu jenem Ruf zu formen;   (III, 387)

dunkel for these:

> und dunkeln wie der Grund von einem Fluss   (III, 97)

und Wind und Regen und Geduld des Frühlings
und Schuld und Unruh und vermummtes Schicksal
und Dunkelheit der abendlichen Erde . . .   (III, 112)

Was Blut und Dunkel war in einem Tier
das wuchs in uns . . .   (III, 29)

Dunkel ruhlose Luft
entmutigte sich . . .   (III, 384)

But the sound could also suggest something lighter, if difficult to define and therefore dark:

Seit Jahrhunderten ruft uns dein Duft   (III, 346)
ein duftendes Vermuten   (III, 401)

While '*u*' is predominantly dark and massive, '*ü*' is more akin to the vowel '*i*', i.e. sharp and pointed. It is, however, more sonorous than '*i*', also more musical and expressive, and therefore a great favourite in Rilke's poems. With his preference for modulating half-tones, he sometimes uses the two vowels in combination:

viel zu glücklich, überstürzt gesiegelt   (III, 239)
und wie die kühle fühllos sich zurückzieht.   (III, 111)

Examples from the *Stundenbuch* still show a somewhat strained vowel music:

. . . mit Früchten gefüllt, verfrüht,
doch er wurde mitten im Blühen müd,
und er wird keine Früchte haben.   (II, 194)

Sie hielten diese müden Parke wach;
sie flüsterten wie Lüfte in den Büschen,
sie leuchteten in Pelzen und in Plüschen,
und ihrer Morgenkleider Seidenrüschen . . .   (II, 279)

In *Neue Gedichte*, this artificiality gives way to a more natural and assured technique in handling the vowel:

. . . dass ein Gefühl entsteht,
weil Blütenblätter Blütenblätter rühren?   (III, 111)

Aber selbst noch durch die Flügeltüren
mit dem grünen, regentrüben Glas . . .   (III, 239)

in den überfüllten Früchten   (III, 248)

verführen sie verführender als Phryne.   (III, 236)

In the *Duino Elegies* the use of '*ü*' is very conspicuous, and different again: it often serves to express turbulent feelings, impatient soaring, glowing enthusiasm:

. . . stürmisch entzückten Gefühls   (III, 265)
deinem erkühnten Gefühl die erglühte Gefühlin.
O und der Frühling begriffe . . .   (III, 287)

Frühe Geglückte . . . Pollen der blühenden Gottheit   (III, 264) uns rühmt es zu blühn   (III, 284)

die ewig gültigen Münzen des Glücks   (III, 283)

O Glück der Mücke, die noch innen hüpft   (III, 295)

Was müssen sie fürchterlich gross sein,
da sie Jahrtausende nicht unseres Fühlns überfülln.   (III, 291)

The treatment of '*ü*' in *Sonnets to Orpheus* is very similar:

in Lüften der Heimat! Erglühte, enthüllt
Düfte um Düfte!   (III, 327)

Sieh, um ihre stillen Schultern früht
das Gefühl, dass sie die jüngste wäre
unter den Geschwistern im Gemüt.   (III, 320)

Nicht in den Grüften der Könige Moder
straft ihn die Rühmung Lügen . . .   (III, 319)

. . . wie trübe ermüdende Sünden,
die das Gepflücktsein beging . . .   (III, 347)

Rilke makes still another use of the vowel, mostly in its short form,
to express artificial prettiness:

Und des behübschten Glücks figürliche Schiesstatt (III, 303)

Rüschen, Blumen, Kokarden, künstliche Früchte   (III, 282)

Der behübschende Irrtum,
die sie verschürzt und berüscht . . .   (III, 465)

The diphthong '*ei*' is ideally suited for vowel music; its tone is
rich and long and can, as we have seen, be made to sound soft or
harsh, according to the way it is used and combined with other
sounds. Unlike single vowels, it does not vary in length; nevertheless Rilke, by clever combination with consonants and by other
means, has been able to draw the most diverse music from it.
In his earlier work, he loves to dwell on the length of the diphthong,
combining it with softening consonants:

O immer mehr entweichendes Begreifen . . .
O Kindheit, o entgleitende Vergleiche   (II, 30)

Und nur ein Zeichen scheinen ganze Zeiten   (II, 109)

. . . die Preiser,
ihr Neigen nähert sich, sie schmeicheln heiser.   (II, 102)

In the *Stundenbuch*, this soft insistence sometimes gives way to a
profusion only as great a craftsman as Rilke could render acceptable:

Ich aber will dich begreifen,
wie dich die Erde begreift;
mit meinem Reifen
reift
dein Reich.

Ich will von dir keine Eitelkeit
die dich beweist.
Ich weiss, dass die Zeit
anders heisst
als du.   (II, 244-5)

Great is the variety in the use of '*ei*' in *Neue Gedichte*, ranging from
sweet tenderness to boldly painting colour:

der erste weisse Schleier, leise gleitend   (III, 58)

da er sie nahm von der seidenen Leiter
und sie weitertrug, weiter, weiter   (III, 241)

    Drum reichen sie sich schweigend
mit einem Neigen, Zeigende zu zeigend
Empfangenden, geweihtes Wasser . . .   (III, 88-9)

und die das Steife schmeichlerisch erweicht   (III, 179)

Mit einem Neigen seiner Stirne weist
er weit von sich . . .   (III, 49)

Auf einmal kreischt ein Neid . . .   (III, 236)

Only occasionally, such profusion makes a passage sound strained
and artificial:

den ihr Herz, ihr reines und bereites,
aus dem Licht des göttlichen Geleites
niederreisst. Zu seiten seines Streites
stand, wie Türme stehen, ihr Gebet.   (III, 218)

The poet's power of painting with vowels reaches a summit in
Totentanz:

Bald wird ihnen allen zu heiss,
sie sind zu reich gekleidet;
beissender Schweiss verleidet
ihnen Stirne und Steiss
und Schauben und Hauben und Steine.   (III, 145-6)

We can study Rilke's grace and felicity of expression, achieved by
the intimate combination of vowelling with alliteration, in a passage
like this:

und eine Greisin, weilend, hinterher —
zu ihren Häusern, die sie schnell verschweigen
und die sich durch die Ulmen hin von Zeit
zu Zeit ein wenig reine Einsamkeit,
in einer kleinen Scheibe schimmernd, zeigen.   (III, 89)

Here, the sound '*ei*' seems to swell and ebb in a pattern: it first
occurs three times, then once only in each of the following lines,
five times at the climax of the fourth line, and four times in the

last. The syllable *wei* repeats in *weilend* and *verschweigen*, *zei* in the two *Zeit* and in *zeigen*. The word *schimmernd*, taking the '*sch*' from *Scheibe*, modulates perfectly to *zeigen*, which again contains the '*ei*'; it is the key word of the passage, no other would do in its place.

In the *Duino Elegies*, '*ei*' cedes the place of preference to '*u*' and '*ü*'; it pervades some elegies, like the Tenth, with steady, if scattered, repetition, and is found concentrated in few significant passages only:

> keiner versage an weichen, zweifelnden oder
> reissenden Saiten. (III, 302)

> Weite Speicher der Kraft schafft sich der Zeitgeist. (III, 290)

The *Sonnets to Orpheus*, on the other hand, are rich in significant and beautiful lines based on the *ei*-sound:

> In deinem Reichtum scheinst du wie Kleidung um Kleidung
> um einen Leib aus nichts als Glanz;
> aber dein einzelnes Blatt ist zugleich die Vermeidung ... (III, 346)

This passage, in only three lines, contains the surprising number of eleven '*ei*', without striking us as being overloaded. The sound can be softly suggestive, as in

> Leise liess man dich ein, als wärst du ein Zeichen,
> Frieden zu feiern. (III, 352)

> Zeige, mein Herz, dass du sie niemals entbehrst.
> Dass sie dich meinen, ihre reifenden Feigen. (III, 366)

Here it is accurately painting:

> ... schneidet sie steifer den Stein (III, 350)

Finally, without losing anything of its fullness, the sound acquires an inimitable transparency:

> Ist er ein Hiesiger? Nein, aus beiden
> Reichen erwuchs seine weite Natur.
> Kundiger böge die Zweige der Weiden,
> wer die Wurzeln der Weiden erfuhr. (III, 318)

> Rein ist im heiteren Geist ... (III, 353)

> ...
> ist nicht entschleiert.
> Einzig das Lied überm Land
> heiligt und feiert. (III, 331)

More sonorous than either of its components '*a*' and '*u*', '*au*' is the heaviest and bulkiest of the German vowel sounds. Rilke rarely uses it in accumulation, and there are hardly any instances in his earlier work. Here are two from *Neue Gedichte*:

> Wie sich aus eines Traumes Ausgeburten
> Aufsteigend aus verwirrendem Gequäl,   (III, 39)

where the compact diphthongs stand for the heavy oppressiveness of a nightmare; and

> Kauen sie Graues, verschleudern es, finden es fade.
> Unten klauben die duffen Tauben . . .   (III, 193)

There is one significant line, based on '*au*' in combination with '*ei*', in the *Duino Elegies*:

> Schaukeln der Freiheit! Taucher und Gaukler des Eifers!   (III, 303)

while *Sonnets to Orpheus* yield the greatest number of lines with the diphthong:

> Und in dem Raume, klar und ausgespart,
> erhob es leicht sein Haupt und brauchte kaum
> zu sein.   (III, 344)
>
> . . . ihre Erscheinung in alles Geschaute;
> und der Zauber von Erdrauch und Raute . . .   (III, 318)
>
> . . . eine Handvoll von bleichen
> taumelnden Tauben ins Licht . . . Aber auch das ist im Recht.
> Fern von dem Schauenden sei jeglicher Hauch des Bedauerns, . . .
>   (III, 352)
>
> baut im unbrauchbaren Raum ihr vergöttlichtes Haus.   (III, 351)

F

ASSONANCE

ASSONANCE is really an impure, or half-rhyme: the vowel or vowels are identical, while the accompanying consonants are different, as in 'later—baker, winter—singer'. In medieval poetry, assonance was used for end-rhymes; later, we encounter it within the lines only, as a binding and reinforcing element. It has been widely used in German poetry, sometimes to great effect, as in Storm's line

> Die Kerzen brennen, und die Geigen schreien (*Hyazinthen*)

It is obvious that Rilke could not omit assonance from the number of devices he used to bind his words closely together and to create a dense relationship of sound affinity between them. In the lines, already quoted in the chapter on vowel sounds,

> Fast bis zu den fernen Meeren
> kann ich den ernsten, schweren,
> verwehrenden Himmel sehn, (II, 53)

we have assonance in the words preceding the rhymes, *fernen* and *ernsten*—a kind of doubling echo that considerably strengthens the effect of the rhyme. When expressed by a more sonorous vowel, the accompaniment to rhyme by assonance will be still more marked:

> mit einem Mund, gemacht aus hundert Munden,
> gewahrst du garnicht, wie dir unsre Stunden... (III, 32)

While in vowelling the effect resides in the accumulation of similar vowels, in assonance the sequence of vowels must be repeated:

> kamen zagen Falles (III, 97)
> mit flachem klaren Wasser (III, 98)
> wir raten nur und sagen alles fragend. (S. G., 82)

Rilke often uses assonance to connect words in an unobtrusive, as it were subterranean, manner, acting like a softer accompaniment to the more sonorous vowel music. There is a certain indirectness in the effect of assonance; it is vaguer than both alliteration and vowelling, and is often so discreet as to pass almost unnoticed. It adds some of those modulating half-tones that are so important to Rilke's palette. It can produce very delicate effects:

> ... immer wieder, wo ein Schimmer
> von Himmel trifft auf ein Gefühl von Flut. (III, 203)

The four nouns in this passage are intimately connected by their associative meanings: alliteration ('*f*' and '*l*' in *Gefühl* and *Flut*), internal rhyme and assonance (*immer, Schimmer, Himmel*), by translating this relationship into sound, bind the words closely together, revealing poetically the existing connection and giving it body. Likewise, in

> ... auf alle Fragen ihr
> nur eine Antwort vage wiedergebend.   (III, 58)

we note the delicate echo to *Fragen* in *vage*, preceded by a vaguer assonance in *alle*; in *tragische Klage* (III, 63), the half-rhyming assonance of the two consecutive words. Rilke's poems are pervaded by such assonances, fainter echoes of the more precise and obvious agreement of rhyme, alliteration and vowel music:

diese Tiefen, diese Wiesen	(III, 30)
das wache Nachten	
von unbewachten Gärten gärend	(III, 191)
Schauer feuchter Fäule	(III, 234)
das Schreien eines Steines	(III, 201)
auf der Tierstirn, auf der stillen, lichten	(III, 46)
in der Mitte ihrer Mythen	(III, 10)
sich geführt zu fühlen und zu führen.	(III, 221)

These examples come from *Neue Gedichte*; the *Elegies* also provide interesting assonances:

blumiger, schwungiger	(III, 281)
an zweifelnden oder reissenden Saiten	(III, 302)
Taucher und Gaukler	(III, 303)

A characteristic and particularly successful assonance occurs in the *Sonnets*:

> das fröhliche Wasser römischer Tage,   (III, 322)

where the dactylic rhythm very effectively underlines the assonance. Or take two lines like

> zu der stillen Erde sag: ich rinne,
> zu dem raschen Wasser sprich: ich bin.   (III, 374)

Here we have the assonance of *stillen* and *rinnen*, enhanced by the four additional short *i*-sounds of *ich, sprich, ich, bin,* and in the next line *raschen Wasser*—an example of the discreet harmonies that underlie Rilke's later poems everywhere. In the Sonnets, too, occurs one of his most beautiful, musical assonances:

> Frauen wie Lauten   (III, 329)

Finally, from *Letzte Gedichte*:

auf den Bergen des Herzens.   (III, 420)

These words with their mysteriously sad ring are repeated four times in the short poem of fifteen lines, pervading it with the strong assonance of *Bergen* and *Herzens*, to which must be added the parallel *der grosse geborgene Vogel* and the half-rhyming *Ortschaft der Worte*.

ENJAMBMENT

ENJAMBMENT, the running of a sentence from one verse into the next, is one of the most characteristic elements in Rilke's style. It is not a new device, and its use in the classical and romantic periods of German literature was more widespread than is generally supposed. Lessing employs it frequently, and so does Schiller, e.g. in *Don Carlos*. There is, however, a marked difference in the nature and effect of enjambment according to its use with rhymed or unrhymed verse. The Story of the Ring, in Lessing's *Nathan*, is written throughout with enjambment; the effect produced by the device in blank verse is to give Nathan's account a certain urbanity: the lines merge gently one into another, creating an atmosphere of distinguished worldliness. Such effects produced by enjambment have probably given rise to the prevalent opinion that it tends to blur the edges of verse by knitting the lines together without a break. Yet enjambment in combination with rhyme, as mainly used by Rilke and characteristic of a great deal of his poetry, does not invariably produce this result. Quite often, it gives the opposite effect: a tension between the last, rhyming word of a line and the first word on the next line, separating them by a longer or shorter pause which has the effect of isolating the rhyming word and stressing the next, while the end word in its turn is being stressed, in a manner peculiar to enjambment only, by the rhyme as well as by the pause. The rhyming word is, as it were, suspended for a moment before the reader dips down upon the next one, artificially separated from it by the beginning of the line. This tension varies a great deal, according to the rhythm, the importance or soundcharacter of the rhyming word, the degree of logical connection between the two words thus separated. In this example from Goethe, where the enjambment-effect is very discreet and harmonious, the tension is small:

> Ein zärtlich jugendlicher Kummer
> Führt mich ins öde Feld; es liegt
> in einem stillen Morgenschlummer
> Die Mutter Erde. Rauschend wiegt
> Ein kalter Wind die starren Äste. Schauernd
> Tönt er die Melodie ...

Rilke has other models for his technique, especially in French poetry. Verlaine used many a daring enjambment, e.g. the much quoted

> Et je m'en vais
> Au vent mauvais
>   Qui m'emporte
> Deçà, delà,
> Pareil à la
>   Feuille morte.

The separation, in these lines, of a noun from its article was rather unusual and gave cause for much comment. Noun and adjective are torn asunder in the next example, and another revolutionary trait is that the noun forms a line by itself:

> Un vaste et tendre
> Apaisement
> Semble descendre
> Du firmament
> Que l'astre irise . . .

We encounter similar enjambments in the poems of Valéry, Derème and others.

It is obvious that with Rilke, enjambment is not so much a device as part of his personal rhythm; far from being always expressive in a specific way, it often belongs to the poet's cadence, giving it its characteristic turn. In his earlier poems up to *Buch der Bilder* and *Stundenbuch*, he makes a moderate use of enjambment; it is not particularly frequent, hardly enough to be conspicuous or even noticeable, and when it occurs, it seems to be used in order to stress a word forming the end rhyme:

> Weinberg, Weide, alter Apfelgarten,
> Acker, der kein Frühjahr überschlägt,
> Feigenbaum, der auch im marmorharten
> Grunde hundert Früchte trägt . . .   (II, 217)

> Je mehr der Tag mit immer schwächern
> Gebärden sich nach Abend neigt,
> Je mehr bist du, mein Gott. Es steigt
> dein Reich wie Rauch aus allen Dächern.   (II, 258)

Enjambment with unstressed or unimportant words is an exception, as

> Denn, Herr, die grossen Städte sind
> Verlorene und Aufgelöste . . .,   (II, 271)

and so are strident interruptions, used by the poet with special
intent to express some extreme tension:

> und ich weiss nicht, schreit mir mein
> Herz oder meine Gedärme. (II, 123)
>
> Dass sie mir immer wieder den Strick
> zerschneiden. (II, 125)

With *Neue Gedichte*, enjambment becomes a definite element in
Rilke's style. Hardly a poem in this collection is without this
device, which tends to single out the rhyming end word or the word
following it, leaving them suspended in a tension very peculiar
to Rilke. This tension is weighted, to a varying degree, with expec-
tation, intensity, anxiety. If an adjective is thus separated from its
noun, it will become endowed with a stress that, even if it is not
particularly strong, has an inimitable quality:

> wie ein dunkler Sprung durch eine helle
> Tasse geht. (III, 174)
>
> das alte Standbild mit dem kleinen heissen
> Gesichte . . . (III, 92)
>
> sprich so, als sprächest du von einer reifen
> gewölbten Feige . . . (III, 207)

The effect is enhanced when the adjective is in the comparative or
superlative:

> vor dem Lichter-Vorgefühl beglänzter
> schimmert. (III, 183)
>
> und ihre Stimmen gehn den immer steilern
> Gesang hinan . . . (III, 88)
>
> wie ein Tobender, wenn er in vollster
> Raserei ins Schwarze stapft . . . (III, 181)

The separation may concern an adverb, with similar effect:

> Um den Mund enorm
> viel Jugend . . . (III, 69)
>
> Wie ein Liegender so steht er; ganz
> hingehalten . . . (III, 47)
>
> den unbeholfne Häuser manchmal nur
> verbergen . . . (III, 84)

(Compare with the last Goethe's milder:

> Ach, denkt das Veichen, wär ich nur
> die schönste Blume der Natur . . .)
>
> Denn seit es nicht mehr war, erschien es ihm so
> seltsam; phantastischer als Pharao. (III, 177)

The almost voiceless *so*, in the last example, can hardly be sufficiently stressed to make it rhyme with *Pharao*; the accent shifts with great weight to *seltsam* on the next line.

Nouns are affected in the same manner, i.e. either the rhyming word, or the one beginning the new line, or both, are lifted from their context and lit up with the peculiar, oblique stress of enjambment:

> die Asche ihres Grams und ihrer Plage
> Neige . . . (III, 140)

> Seit sie damals, bettheiss, als die Hure
> übern Jordan floh und, wie ein Grab
> gebend, stark und unvermischt das pure
> Herz der Ewigkeit zu trinken gab . . . (III, 156)

> wenn, auf meiner Brüste Hügeln
> stehend, mein Gefühl nach Flügeln
> oder einem Ende schreit. (III, 8)

> Du wusstest nicht, was den Haufen
> ausmacht. Ein Fremder fand
> Bettler darin. Sie verkaufen
> das Hohle aus ihrer Hand. (III, 169)

One characteristic feature of enjambment as used by Rilke is that it often affects conjunctions, pronouns, prepositions and even the definite and indefinite article, i.e. unimportant words. H. E. Holthusen asserts:[1]

Je schwächer das übergiffene Reimwort, desto grösser ist seine rhythmische Verantwortung, desto mehr akzentuierende Energie versammelt es auf sich.

This is frequently so, but not invariably. The following are examples of enjambment with so-called unimportant words:

> Es wäre gut, viel nachzudenken, um
> von so Verlornem etwas auszusagen . . . (III, 52)

> . . . hingetragen, als
> wäre mit Sprüngen jeder Lauf geladen . . . (III, 45) √

> Wüsste einer denn zu sagen, welche
> Dinge eingeschmolzen wurden . . . (III, 78)

> zu dem sein weitgeschwungenes Vertrauen
> zurück als Feuer fiel von ferne, und
> hatte er dann nicht Hunderte zerhauen . . . (III, 129)

> Nächte ohnegleichen von sich ab
> fallen lassend . . . (III, 250)

> . . . und beide Hände —, die
> abwarten . . . (III, 69)

> O wie fühlt dich ein
> treibender Feigenbaum . . . (III, 190)

[1] *Rilkes Sonette an Orpheus*, 1937, p. 64.

In the line

> unter Bäume wie von Dürer, die
> das Gewicht von hundert Arbeitstagen . . ., (III, 248)

the *die* is very slightly and delicately stressed, while the definite article on the next line is hardly affected; in

> und auf einmal machte der
> Flüchtende kurz, unerwartet, kehr . . . (III, 186)

the accelerated rhythm of the poem overrides the effect of enjambment, and neither the rhyming word nor the next are particularly stressed.

> Wie soll ich meine Seele halten, dass
> sie nicht an deine rührt? Wie soll ich sie
> hinheben über dich . . . (III, 9)

Here we have enjambment with two unimportant words in succession: *dass*, at the end of the first line, receives a stronger stress than the second *sie* on the next line; the energy gathers, instead, on the first syllable of *hinheben*.

Occasionally, Rilke lets enjambment cut right through an idiom:

> und die sich durch die Ulmen hin von Zeit
> zu Zeit ein wenig reine Einsamkeit
> in einer kleinen Scheibe schimmernd, zeigen. (III, 89)

Here, *von Zeit zu Zeit* is distributed over two lines. Enjambment may even cut into composite words:

> . . . wo einander
> Tropfen fallen hören und ein Wander-
> vogel lautet . . . (III, 234)

> . . . sind nicht wie die Zug-
> vögel verständigt (III, 274)

Employed throughout a poem, enjambment can have various effects: it may create a counter-rhythm running independently of the metre, or even against it, comparable to syncopic treatment in music, which shifts the accent from the first beat of the measure, or to counterpoint, which combines two melodies in a pattern. The ending of a sentence in the middle or at the beginning of a line instead of at the end is mainly responsible for this counter-rhythm. On the other hand, enjambment may serve to knit the lines together and thereby lengthen, as it were, the poet's breath, by doing away with the continuous interruptions due to the division into verse.

This intertwining tendency is modified to some extent by the increased stresses on rhyming words and those following them. There are many striking examples of this manner of handling enjambment in *Neue Gedichte*, with *Schlaflied* perhaps among the finest:

> Einmal, wenn ich dich verlier,
> wirst du schlafen können, ohne
> dass ich wie eine Lindenkrone
> mich verflüstre über dir?
>
> Ohne dass ich hier wache und
> Worte, beinah wie Augenlider,
> auf deine Brüste, auf deine Glieder
> niederlege, auf deinen Mund?   (III, 238)

Other instances of this style are encountered in *Die Kurtisane, Die Treppe der Orangerie, Archaischer Torso Apollos, Römische Fontäne, Die Insel der Sirenen.*

Das Roseninnere is perhaps the most characteristic example for Rilke's manner of running on verses that all but obliterates the structure of the poem. In this particular case, the intertwining movement is admirably suited to the poetic thought:

> Sie können sich selber kaum
> halten; viele liessen
> sich überfüllen und fliessen
> über von Innenraum
> in die Tage, die immer
> voller und voller sich schliessen,
> bis der ganze Sommer ein Zimmer
> wird, ein Zimmer in einem Traum: (III, 225)

enjambment here is the very soul of the poem, translating its thought into a vibrating rhythm that grows and grows until it overflows in the climax of the last lines. The sonnet *Die Fensterrose* ends with a sentence, distributed by means of enjambment, and without punctuation, over three lines, thus:

> so griffen einstmals aus dem Dunkelsein
> der Kathedralen grosse Fensterrosen
> ein Herz und rissen es in Gott hinein.   (III, 38)

In logical division, this would read: *So griffen einstmals | aus dem Dunkelsein der Kathedralen | grosse Fensterrosen ein Herz | und rissen es in Gott hinein.* The verse movement runs independent of the logical division and creates a strong counter-rhythm, yet the effectiveness of the lines seems to be enhanced by it. Taken by itself, each line is incomplete, and although, in order to convey a meaning, the lines must be read without a break, the verse structure still shines through them. Even a mutilated line like the last, *ein Herz und rissen es in Gott hinein*, acquires a certain force, that unaccountable expressive power bestowed by enjambment only. We meet a similar effect in the last line of Hölderlin's *Die Nacht*:

> über Gebirgeshöhn traurig und prächtig herauf.

On the other hand, enjambment, if employed in excess and without stylistic justification, can destroy the outline of a poem:

> Wenn sein Mund jetzt troff und prophezeite,
> war es nur, damit der Flüchtling weit
> flüchten könne. So war dieses zweite
> Mal. Doch einst: er hatte prophezeit ...   (III, 131)

The suspension of *weit*, although somewhat harsh, may be justified by the meaning (it stresses the word effectively), but the very brusque separation of *zweite* from its noun gives the impression of being pointless and arbitrary, and the isolated *Mal* on the next line, forming the end of the sentence, becomes almost meaningless. If the logical connection of words is thus constantly disregarded, a poem may be literally cut to pieces by enjambment:

> Doch man sah ihn ohne
> Helm an den bedrohten
> Orten die ärgsten Knoten
> zu roten Stücken von Toten
>   auseinanderhaun.
> Dann wusste lange keiner
> von ihm, bis plötzlich einer
> schrie: er hängt dort hinten
> an den Terebinthen
> mit hochgezognen Braun.   (III, 139)

Lines like *Orten die ärgsten Knoten*, and *von ihm, bis plötzlich einer*, are unbearable. Doubtless, it was the poet's intention to create a hacked and jerky rhythm, but he misjudged the limits of his means, and the result reads like a parody of Rilke's style.

In the *Duino Elegies* enjambment is frequent, but since they are unrhymed, its characteristics are not so marked, and it is of small account in connection with their style. On the other hand, the *Sonnets to Orpheus*, where the device is as general as in *Neue Gedichte*, supply many interesting examples of counter-rhythm produced by sentences ending at the beginning of a line:

> Schon, horch, hörst du der ersten Harken
> Arbeit; wieder den menschlichen Takt
> in der verhaltenen Stille der starken
> Vorfrühlingserde. Unabgeschmeckt
> scheint dir das Kommende . . .   (III, 370)
>
> ging er hervor wie das Erz aus des Steins
> Schweigen.   (III, 319)
>
>   . . . und heben die Hämmer, die immer
> grössern.   (III, 336)

The way in which the words *Arbeit, Vorfrühlingserde, Schweigen, grössern*, are not only given stress, but that peculiar heaviness that enjambment imparts, is highly characteristic. Frequent, too, is the separation of adjectives from their nouns:

> Nein, aus beiden
> Reichen erwuchs seine weite Natur.   (III, 318)
>
> An der Kreuzung zweier
> Herzwege steht kein Tempel . . .   (III, 315)
>
>   . . . weil sie der harte
> Stahl . . . nicht kennt, . . .   (III, 336)

The Fountain-sonnet in Part II is a fine example of Rilke's art of harmoniously knitting the lines together in a softly flowing rhythm:

> Und im Hintergrund
> der Aquädukte Herkunft. Weither an
> Gräbern vorbei, vom Hang des Apennins
> tragen sie dir dein Sagen zu, das dann
> am schwarzen Altern deines Kinns
> vorüberfliesst in das Gefäss davor.   (III, 358)

An interesting instance of the most precarious form of enjambment, the separation of a verb from its noun, occurs in the lines

> Nur im Raum der Rühmung darf die Klage
> gehn, die Nymphe des geweihten Quells . . .   (III, 320)

Such audacities, as we have seen, tend to destroy the structure and harmony of a poem; here, however, *Klage*, with its clear *a*-sound, benefits by the suspension, while *gehn* receives a deeper, more significant sound and is, moreover, slightly stretched. Rilke's handling of the delicate and difficult device has become assured.

SYNTAX

Clauses

THE analysis of a poet's style does not necessarily include syntax: it is not a poetic device in the sense that vowel music and alliteration are. But if his syntax has marked characteristics that distinguish it from common usage as well as from that of other poets, we have to consider it as part of a poet's style. This clearly is the case of Rilke's syntax which, of all the elements that make up his style, is perhaps the one that belongs to him most intimately as the direct expression of his artistic personality.

The intellectual shape of poetic matter—the coherent isolation of it into self-sufficient organism—to effect *that* is the affair of syntax in poetry.[1]

Rilke, largely concerned with 'the intellectual shape of poetic matter', needs a syntax of his own; its main features are the extensive use of clauses and questions, as well as a preference for the subjunctive mood: these elements give his middle style its characteristic allure, that carefully advancing deliberateness which accompanies, while guarding and restricting it, a considerable boldness of expression. The use of these syntactic forms is necessary to Rilke's at times laborious efforts to arrive at the accurate, fully satisfactory and exhaustive expression of his poetic truth.

The use of clauses in poetry is an exception rather than the rule. Owen Barfield goes so far as to assert that 'if we truly understand the normal processes of language, the poet's distaste for abstract words and his preference for the "concrete", his distaste for subordination and his love of main sentences fall equally smoothly into line'.[2]

Main sentences are indeed favoured by lyrical poets, and used by many almost to the exclusion of others. The reason for this preference is easy to understand: the main sentence, simple and direct, is the best vehicle for the expression of poetic feeling, while clauses interrupt the free flow of a poet's song, tend to make it heavy and intellectual. So strong is the poet's need for direct utterance that even the main sentence is often mutilated and replaced by grammatically incomplete forms like ejaculations, invocations, contractions and other syntactical ellipses. The same is true of the indicative mood which is the natural expression of plain and direct statement,

[1] Lascelles Abercrombie, *The Theory of Poetry*, 1926, p. 147.
[2] *Poetic Diction*, 1928, p. 165.

whereas the allusive, indirect subjunctive stands for doubt, supposition, uncertainty, unreality.

Judging from these contrasts we see how deeply Rilke's preference for what other poets shun must be rooted in a different way of feeling and thinking, of which his peculiar style is the expression. Often his poetry is not free and direct utterance: it does not give the result of emotional or intellectual processes only, but at the same time retreads the road that led up to them, i.e. it gives the process itself. Rilke makes us witnesses of the various stages of his poetic thought: many of his poems are like processes fixed by language, developments moving towards a conclusion while containing it, or part of it, at every moment. This, while not equally true of all his poetry, refers particularly to his central period, that of *Neue Gedichte*. It makes many of these poems akin to musical compositions unfolding toward a solution which, however, we are quite incapable of separating from them, as each phase is a part of it. Sometimes a poem in this collection consists of a single, long-drawn-out sentence, and very often of two or three sentences only. The movement of such poems is necessarily heavy and slow, accompanied as it is by doubt and uncertainty that have to be resolved or expressed.

This way of feeling, very much his own, is responsible for Rilke's characteristic syntax with its clauses, questions, parentheses, subjunctives and participles, forms that serve to express the poet's continuous questioning, his careful weighing of evidence, his striving for accuracy. While other poets avoid clauses because they interrupt and retard, Rilke needs and employs them for this very reason: for him, it is natural and vital to pause and reflect, and he is indifferent to any loss of spontaneity or tempo if it helps him to express an idea with greater clarity, a shade with more precision. He will stop in the middle of a poem to contradict himself:

> . . . etwas Ungewisses mitten
> im nassen Niederschlag der Gasse, das
> nach dir verlangte. Oder nicht nach dir.   (III, 170)

> . . . die ein Blau
> nicht auf sich tragen, nur von ferne spiegeln.   (III, 65)

> . . . als Gleichgewicht
> des Lichtes, das in allen seinen Dingen
> sich so vermehrte, dass sie fast vergingen.
> Und plötzlich zweifelst du: vergehn sie nicht?   (III, 205)

The clause in its various forms—adjective, relative, adverbial—

is a useful syntactic device to arrive at a clear, unambiguous statement, and therefore indispensable in prose, and more particularly
in philosophical and scientific prose. Clauses in poetry are, however,
not altogether an anomaly: we encounter them wherever a wealth
of qualities is to be expressed, or a state of mind to be described
with great accuracy and detail, as in these examples:

> Denn was der Mensch in seinen Erdeschranken
> Von hohem Glück mit Götternamen nennt:
> Die Harmonie der Treue, die kein Wanken,
> Der Freundschaft, die nicht Zweifelsorge kennt,
> Das Licht, das Weisen nur zu einsamen Gedanken,
> Das Dichtern nur in schönen Bildern brennt — :
> (Goethe)

> Wenn ich, von deinem Anschaun tief gestillt,
> Mich stumm an deinem heil'gen Wert vergnüge,
> Dann hör' ich recht die leisen Atemzüge
> Des Engels, welcher sich in dir verhüllt,
> Und ein erstaunt, ein fragend Lächeln quillt
> Auf meinem Mund, ob mich kein Traum betrüge,
> Dass nun in dir, zu ewiger Genüge,
> Mein kühnster Wunsch, mein einz'ger, sich erfüllt?
> (Mörike)

A passage like the last, rather in the nature of an exception in
Mörike's poetry, comes very close to Rilke's style in his central
period. His extensive use of clauses starts with *Buch der Bilder* and
goes on increasing until it reaches a climax in *Neue Gedichte*. It is
much less pronounced, although not quite absent, in Rilke's later
work. This example from *Buch der Bilder* is typical:

> Und seine Hände halten, wie erschlafft,
> sein braunes Haupt, das schwer ist von den Säften,
> die ungeduldig durch das Dunkel rollen,
> und sein Gewand, das faltig, voll und wollen,
> zu seinen Füssen fliesst, ist stramm gestrafft
> um seinen Armen, die, gleich starken Schäften,
> die Hände tragen, welche träumen sollen.　　(II, 77)

The weight of seven clauses impedes, like the fall of the full woollen
garment they describe, the flow of these seven lines. In the following passages, from the *Stundenbuch*, the position of the relative
clauses, in front of the verb, or cutting the sentence in two, is
characteristic:

> Auch du wirst gross sein. Grösser noch, als einer,
> der jetzt schon leben muss, dich sagen kann.　　(II, 255)

> Aber der Weg zu dir ist furchtbar weit
> und, weil ihn lange keiner ging, verweht.　　(II, 265)

But the intricate play of intertwining clauses, closely following
and expressing the poet's halting thought, is best seen in *Neue
Gedichte*:

> Sie sind im Gleichgewicht auf den Konsolen,
> in denen eine Welt, die sie nicht sehn,
> die Welt der Wirrnis, die sie nicht zertraten,
> Figur und Tier, wie um sie zu gefährden,
> sich krümmt und schüttelt und sie dennoch hält,   (III, 36-7)

and still more pronounced:

> Damals als wir mit den glatten Trabern
> (schwarzen, aus dem Orloffschen Gestüt) — ,
> während hinter hohen Kandelabern
> Stadtnachtfronten lagen, angefrüht
> stumm und keiner Stunde mehr gemäss — ,
> fuhren, nein: vergingen oder flogen
> und um lastende Paläste bogen
> in das Wehn der Neva-Quais
> hingerissen durch das wache Nachten,
> das nicht Himmel und nicht Erde hat, —
> als das Drängende von unbewachten
> Gärten gärend aus dem Ljetnij-Ssad
> aufstieg, während seine Steinfiguren
> schwindend mit ohnmächtigen Konturen
> hinter uns vergingen, wie wir fuhren — :
> damals hörte diese Stadt
> auf zu sein.   (III, 191)

This is one of those long-drawn-out periods in *Neue Gedichte*, with
their bewildering wealth of participles and clauses, and it is truly
remarkable how, in spite of the continuous interruptions, the poem
rushes to its conclusion like a strong flow of lava that has the force
to overcome such obstacles. Other poems of this type are *Corrida*,
Schlangenbeschwörung, *Der Auszug des verlorenen Sohnes*, *Die Insel
der Sirenen*, *Die Gruppe*, *Auswandererschiff*. It is difficult to limit
quotations from these constructions; here is another typical one:

> und wie dann plötzlich eine von den Katzen
> den Blick an ihr, der hin und wieder irrt,
> gewaltsam in ihr grosses Auge nimmt, —
> den Blick, der, wie von eines Wirbels Kreis
> ergriffen, eine kleine Weile schwimmt
> und dann versinkt und nichts mehr von sich weiss,
> wenn dieses Auge, welches scheinbar ruht,
> sich auftut und zusammenschlägt mit Tosen . . .   (III, 38)

The interruptions here compel Rilke to pick up the thread by
repeating the key words *den Blick* and *dieses Auge*; the word *der*,

isolated and enclosed by commas, preceded and followed by an involved system of clauses, causes a break: the language is almost seen modelling the thought as a sculptor models clay. A similar effect is obtained in *Die Gazelle*:

> und alles Deine geht schon im Vergleich
> durch Liebeslieder, deren Worte, weich
> wie Rosenblätter, dem, der nicht mehr liest,
> sich auf die Augen legen, die er schliesst,
> um dich zu sehen: hingetragen, als
> wäre mit Sprüngen jeder Lauf geladen
> und schösse nur nicht ab, solang der Hals
> das Haupt ins Horchen hält . . .   (III, 45)

The clauses here are helping to express the intricate movement of the wandering images as they leave the gazelle and return to it. In the poem *Der Turm* the entangling of clauses reaches a culmination:

> Als wäre dort, wohin
> du blindlings steigst, erst Erdenoberfläche,
> zu der du steigst im schrägen Bett der Bäche,
> die langsam aus dem suchenden Gerinn
> der Dunkelheit entsprungen sind, durch die
> sich dein Gesicht, wie auferstehend, drängt
> und die du plötzlich siehst, als fiele sie
> aus diesem Abgrund, der dich überhängt
> und den du, wie er riesig über dir
> sich umstürzt in dem dämmernden Gestühle,
> erkennst, erschreckt und fürchtend, im Gefühle:
> o wenn er steigt, behangen wie ein Stier — .   (III, 83)

These weird interlacings are meant to express, in a forceful manner, the oppressiveness of endlessly winding stairs inside the belfry, but the device is perhaps too strained to be fully successful (twelve clauses in twelve lines!). Yet even so, as an achievement of sheer technical ability, craftsmanship and mastery of language, how magnificent, how breath-taking it is! It is, besides, a new way of writing poetry.

Another instance of overstressing, by means of clauses, occurs in *Abschied*:

> Wie war ich ohne Wehr, dem zuzuschauen,
> das, da es mich, mich rufend, gehen liess,
> zurückblieb, so als wärens alle Frauen . . .   (III, 62)

The sequence *das, da es mich, mich rufend, gehen liess, zurückblieb,* with its four verbs coming home to roost on the same branch, and the two consecutive *mich*, give the middle stanza of the poem a

G

slight taint as of parody or caricature, recalling Gellert's notorious
lines

> Lebe, wie du, wenn du stirbst,
> wünschen wirst, gelebt zu haben.

At least, the constructions in the following passages are not dis-
similar:

> und wandelt uns, auch wenn wirs nicht erreichen,
> in jenes, das wir, kaum es ahnend, sind;   (III, 429)

and from *Sonnets to Orpheus*:

> Sollen wir unsere uralte Freundschaft, die grossen
> niemals werbenden Götter, weil sie der harte
> Stahl, den wir streng erzogen, nicht kennt, verstossen . . .
>   (III, 336)

It would be an error to assume that in *Neue Gedichte* the style of
long sentences weighted with clauses is not balanced by contrasting
elements. In many poems the end of every stanza is also the end of
a sentence, as in *David singt vor Saul, Östliches Taglied, Abisag, Das
Einhorn, Der Ölbaumgarten, Pietà, Der Tod des Dichters, Der Stifter*
and many more. Short sentences, if rare, are not wanting in the
collection; in some poems they predominate, e.g. in *Eranna an
Sappho, Sappho an Eranna, Der Dichter, Die Laute* and in a few others.
We find also very short, and occasionally even incomplete, sentences
in *Neue Gedichte*: *Wir gedenkens noch* (III, 14); *Sie lag* (III, 17); *Der
Sommer summt* (III, 222); *Er lag* (III, 30); *Ich bin die Laute* (III, 207),
etc.

The style based on repeated and involved clauses comes to an
end with *Neue Gedichte*. In the *Duino Elegies* a more immediate
feeling calls for a simpler syntax. There are a few recurrences of
the earlier style, as this passage from the Fourth Elegy:

> Du, der um mich so bitter
> das Leben schmeckte, meines kostend, Vater,
> den ersten trüben Aufguss meines Müssens,
> da ich heranwuchs, immer wieder kostend
> und, mit dem Nachgeschmack so fremder Zukunft
> beschäftigt, prüftest mein beschlagnes Aufschaun, —
> der du, mein Vater, seit du tot bist, oft
> in meiner Hoffnung innen in mir Angst hast,
> und Gleichmut, wie ihn Tote haben, Reiche
> von Gleichmut, aufgibst für mein bischen Schicksal,
> hab ich nicht recht?   (III, 275–6)

This intricate and difficult sentence is spread over eleven lines. Yet
on the whole, the contrast in these poems between calm or weighty

statements and outbursts of emotion has its precipitate in their syntax in an alternation between simple sentences and turbid passages of elated song; the latter are syntactically more irregular. The great number of short and even elliptical sentences is significant, sentences like *Denn Bleiben ist nirgends. Stimmen. Stimmen* (III, 261); *O Bäume Lebens, o wann winterlich?* (III, 274); *Hier. Ich bin davor* (III, 275); *Alles. Die Adern voll Dasein* (III, 289).

In the *Sonnets to Orpheus*, Rilke's syntax has undergone a significant change: the short sentence now predominates. In many of the sonnets, the end of each stanza coincides with the end of a sentence, which gives these pieces a firm, harmoniously rounded form (Sonnets 18, 21, 25, 26 in Part I, and 1, 3, 6, 10–14, 16, 18–24, 27 in Part II). Very few sonnets consist of, or contain, one long period: 23 in Part I, 1, 5, 7 and 15 in Part II. In the case of the Seventh Sonnet in Part I, we can hardly even call it a long period: it is an evocation lacking subject and predicate, consisting of a string of participles and clauses, similar in this respect to the sonnet *Römische Fontäne* in *Neue Gedichte*. It is a floating, boneless formation, not without a delicate charm which, however, seems to be somewhat illegitimately acquired by the sacrifice of grammatical structure.

Of the many significant short sentences so frequent in the *Sonnets*, we can give no more than a selection: *Da stieg ein Baum* (III, 313); *Sie schlief die Welt* (III, 314); *Ein Gott vermags* (III, 315); *Das genügt* (III, 323); *Zwar war es nicht* (III, 344); *Wolle die Wandlung* (III, 354); *Schwarz sind die Sträucher* (III, 370). Moreover, there is a great number of elliptic sentences: *Und schlief in mir* (III, 314); *Für den Gott ein Leichtes* (III, 315); *Du, mein Freund, bist einsam, weil* . . . (III, 328); *Ein Ohr der Erde* (III, 358); *Schreien den Zufall* (III, 371).

The finest effects, however, are achieved by a combination of Rilke's manner of interlacing lines and verses with his new preference for short sentences:

> Wir gehen um mit Blume, Weinblatt, Frucht.
> Sie sprechen nicht die Sprache nur des Jahres.
> Aus Dunkel steigt ein buntes Offenbares
> und hat vielleicht den Glanz der Eifersucht
> der Toten an sich, die die Erde stärken.　　　(III, 326)

In this passage the end of two sentences coincides with the end of the line, while the third is spread over three lines. Monotony is thus avoided, and a rhythm links the long lines to the shorter ones, enhancing by contrast the effect of both. This happy combination of short with longer sentences is encountered in many of the *Sonnets to Orpheus.*

Questions

A form of sentence that pervades Rilke's poetry from first to last is the question. Questions have always been popular with poets; their suggestiveness is obvious, and it is understood that the majority of such questions is purely rhetorical. In Rilke's poems, interrogations are not only more frequent than usual; the character, too, of many of his questions is peculiar to his way of feeling, and therefore to his style. As a rule, they are not the facile rhetorical questions we encounter so regularly in all lyrical poetry (*Was zieht mir das Herz so? — Wie heisst König Ringangs Töchterlein? — Hör ich das Pförtchen nicht gehen? — Frühling, was bist du gewillt? —*). Rilke's questions are different: more searching, weighted with meaning and often with anxiety, and unlike the rhetorical questions that do not require an answer, many are quite unanswerable. With few exceptions, they are addressed not to the reader's imagination, but to God, to Fate, to the Angel. The tragic tone of many of Rilke's poems is often centred in such questions. Sometimes, a whole poem consists of one question, or string of questions only, or a question at the end of a poem compresses its meaning, its anguish, its perturbed uneasiness. Such a poem is *Der Auszug des verlorenen Sohnes*, with its heavy last line, in which all the bitterness of the preceding ones is gathered up and concentrated:

> Ist das der Eingang eines neuen Lebens?　　　　　(III, 25)

Significant in a similar way are the last lines of *L'Ange du Méridien*:

> Was weisst du, Steinerner, von unserm Sein?
> und hältst du mit noch seligerm Gesichte
> vielleicht die Tafel in die Nacht hinein?　　　　(III, 32)

and the hopelessly sad question that concludes one of the poems in the *Stundenbuch*:

> Wer lebt es denn? Lebst du es, Gott, — das Leben?　(II, 242)

One of the earliest poems consisting of a string of questions is *Der Nachbar*, in *Buch der Bilder*:

> Fremde Geige, gehst du mir nach?
>
> ·　·　·　·　·　·　·
>
> Spielen dich hunderte? Spielt dich einer?
>
> ·　·　·　·　·　·　·
>
> Und warum trifft es immer mich?　　　　　　(II, 42)

Later poems of this kind are *Schlaflied* (*Einmal, wenn ich dich verlier,* |
wirst du schlafen können ... III, 238), *Liebeslied* (*Wie soll ich meine
Seele halten, dass* | *sie nicht an deine rührt?* ... *Auf welches Instrument
sind wir gespannt?* | *Und welcher Spieler hat uns in der Hand?* III, 9),
and *Der Apfelgarten*, with its long, intense interrogation. Sometimes
the poet's thought is so tenuous, so delicate that only questions
will commensurably express it, like those in *Rosa Hortensie*:

> Wer nahm das Rosa an? Wer wusste auch,
> dass es sich sammelte in diesen Dolden?
>
> . . . .
>
> Sind Engel da, es zärtlich zu empfangen,
> wenn es vergeht, grossmütig wie ein Duft? (III, 242)

Here the poem begins with a question. In many instances, this is
Rilke's manner of determining its style from the start. What
could be more suggestive than the first lines of *Kretische Artemis*:

> Wind der Vorgebirge: war nicht ihre
> Stirne wie ein lichter Gegenstand? (III, 118)

or the following beginnings:

> Wo ist zu diesem Innen
> ein Aussen? Auf welches Weh
> legt man solches Linnen? (III, 225)

> König, hörst du, wie mein Saitenspiel
> Fernen wirft, durch die wir uns bewegen? (III, 19)

> War in des Wagens Wendung dieser Schwung?
> War er im Blick ... (III, 233)

Four of the *Duino Elegies* begin with a question:

> Wer, wenn ich schriee, hörte mich denn aus der Engel
> Ordnungen? (III, 259)

> O Bäume Lebens, o wann winterlich? (III, 274)

> Wer aber sind sie, sag mir, die Fahrenden ... (III, 278)

> Warum, wenn es angeht, also die Frist des Daseins
> hinzubringen, ... (III, 297)

The Fourth Elegy has a string of questions just before its end (*Wer
zeigt ein Kind* ...), and the Fifth ends, as it began, with a question.
Moreover, questions have a significant part in the *Elegies* everywhere, as the repeated *Hab ich nicht recht?* in the Fourth, *War es
nicht Wunder?* in the Seventh, *Habt ihr Beweise? Liebende, seid ihrs
dann noch?* in the Second.

As in the *Elegies*, many of the questions in *Sonnets to Orpheus* are of a philosophical character, addressed to Orpheus or to Fate, and incapable of being answered:

> Wo ist ihr Tod? O, wirst du dies Motiv
> erfinden noch, eh sich dein Lied verzehrte?   (III, 314)
>
> Wann aber sind wir? Und wann wendet er
> an unser Sein die Erde und die Sterne?   (III, 315)
>
> Aber sind sie's? Oder meinen beide
> nicht den Weg, den sie zusammen tun?   (III, 323)
>
> Gibt es wirklich die Zeit, die zerstörende?   (III, 372)

Not all the questions in the *Sonnets* are so pregnant with meaning; some might be called rhetorical:

> Wer zeigt mit Fingern auf einen Geruch?   (III, 328)
>
> Hörst du das Neue, Herr,
> dröhnen und beben?   (III, 330)

One even receives an answer:

> Ist er ein Hiesiger? Nein, aus beiden
> Reichen erwuchs seine weite Natur.   (III, 318)

A highly suggestive question in the *Sonnets*, the one that appeals most to our imagination, and one that reveals better perhaps than any other the value of the question-form as an aesthetic device, is the long-drawn-out one that begins the Seventeenth Sonnet of Part II:

> Wo, in welchen immer selig bewässerten Gärten, an welchen
> Bäumen, aus welchen zärtlich entblätterten Blütenkelchen
> reifen die fremdartigen Früchte der Tröstung?   (III, 360)

The Subjunctive

The subjunctive is not quite so extinct in German as it is in English, but its use is generally restricted to a few conventional forms, such as *wäre*, *hätte*, *könnte*, etc. There are not in German, as in the Romance languages, conjunctions that govern the subjunctive, and it is mainly used to express a wish, a possibility, a state of unreality. Rilke makes a wider use of the subjunctive and employs it even in its rarer and more unusual forms, in which it is hardly ever heard in speech, forms like *schwände*, *hübe*, *trüge*; in doing this, he sometimes widens the gulf that exists between his poetic language and common speech. Only Stefan George approaches, and at times surpasses, Rilke in the use of uncommon subjunctives:

> Vergeblich wäre wenn sie dich umschlängen
> und töricht wenn du zwischen ihnen föchtest.
> (*Der Teppich des Lebens, Vorspiel,* XIV)

In the first place, the subjunctive serves Rilke to express the metaphorical unreality so necessary to his thought: *so als wäre* . . ., *als hätte* . . ., *als ob* . . . A great number of his metaphors take this form. But he uses the subjunctive also independently of any conjunction: *käme doch wieder ein Tier.* — *Wüsste einer denn zu sagen* . . . Since the subjunctive necessitates the umlaut in many German verbs, it is probable that this determined Rilke's choice in some instances, for he often needs words with umlaut to fit them into his schemes of vowelling. Moreover, the subjunctive can express delicate shades of meaning, and this may well be one of the principal reasons for Rilke's preference, for any device that would help him to a greater accuracy and subtlety of expression was welcome to him.

The subjunctive is not particularly frequent in Rilke's work prior to *Neue Gedichte*; like other elements in his style, it is on the increase up to his central period. In the *Stundenbuch*, the subjunctive is by no means conspicuous; we find forms like *schriebe, bliebe, trüge*, but they are few and scattered through the poems. In the Requiems, we have *begänne, nachtrügest, fändest, hübest*, together with less unusual forms: *wüssten, dürften, hättest*, etc. In *Neue Gedichte*, examples are more numerous and typical:

und schwäre nur und bräche nicht mehr an	(III, 43)
und schösse nur nicht ab . . .	(III, 45)
und wissend, wie sie seine Trauer trügen	(III, 68)
ohne Sorgfalt, was die Nächsten dächten	(III, 231)
damit es nie erführe vom Verblühn.	(III, 242)

These subjunctives do not always avoid a certain preciousness which may, or may not, be intentional. The lines

. . . als dir einer böte,	
wenn er von seiner Freundin sagt . . .	(III, 236)

sound affected, but it may be argued that they are in keeping with the general tone of this most delicate and intricate poem (*Die Flamingos*). The subjunctive *hübe* is more difficult to bear, especially as a rhyming word; it occurs in *Skizze zu einen Sankt Georg*, a somewhat artificial poem in *Späte Gedichte*. In the same collection we have the modified form *höbe*:

liess ich, auch wenn ich ihn näher höbe,	
jenen Abstand dauern von vorhin;	
und das Einzige, das mich selbst verschöbe,	
ist der Schritt der Tänzerin.	(S. G., 128)

Rilke does not abandon the extensive use of the subjunctive in his later poems. In the Seventh Elegy we have: *schrieest, würbest, begriffe, trüge, käme, ständen, gälte, ständ', stärke, steh', würbe*, and since this is one of the longer elegies, the proportion of subjunctives in the others is not much smaller. It cannot be said that they are very conspicuous in the elevated language of these poems. In *Sonnets to Orpheus* and the later poems, subjunctives are less frequent, though still in evidence; in a single sonnet (14 of Part II), we have *prange, schliefe, käme, bliebe, blühten*.

The Participle

The participle, in its present and past form, is an integral part of Rilke's poetry. There was a rich tradition for its use in German poetry. Whole poems are based on it, as Goethe's *In tausend Formen magst du dich verstecken*, where we encounter the most unusual combinations, as *allschöngewachsene, allbuntbesternte, allherzerweiternde*; that, of course, is in the nature of a playful exception. Lenau has *duftverloren, felsentstürzt, mondbeglänzt*; Heine *alte, aufgeklärte Fenster*; Liliencron *kraftgärend, jagdgierzitternd, trümmertragend*. Yet Rilke's way of handling the participle is very different from these models, and we may say he had no real predecessor in the intensive as well as extensive use he makes of it. The present participle, as employed by him, has an enlarging effect: it suspends time and thus broadens lines and verses, while the past participle adds a dimension of time to them. These forms pervade Rilke's work in a combination of uses: as participles proper, as nouns, adjectives and adverbs. Here is an illustration of their use in a combination of different forms of the present participle:

> Drum reichen sie sich schweigend
> mit einem Neigen, Zeigende zu zeigend
> Empfangenden, geweihtes Wasser ...   (III, 88–9)

This passage has two participles as adverbs (*schweigend, zeigend*) and two as nouns (*Zeigende, Empfangenden*). A special case is the well-known *Römische Fontäne* (III, 79), where the soft, floating movement of the fountain is expressed in a vague sequence of present participles, unsupported by any firmer grammatical structure: the poem trickles away in a subdued andante. This sonnet has been compared with C. F. Meyer's *Der römische Brunnen*, because both poems were inspired by the same fountain in the Borghese Gardens in Rome. It is indeed interesting to compare the structure

of the two pieces. Meyer puts all his nine verbs in the active form
of the present indicative: *steigt, giesst, strömt, ruht,* etc., interrupted
and modified by three present participles: *fallend, sich verschleiernd,
wallend*; one of these is very effectively placed within the only clause
in the poem: *die, sich verschleiernd, überfliesst.* In Rilke's poem,
the proportion is very nearly reversed: eight verbs are in the form
of the present participle, and two only—*stand, macht*—appear in
the indicative form, each placed in a relative clause.

he following passages show Rilke's use of the past participle:

> ... ganz
> hingehalten von dem grossen Willen.
> Weit entrückt wie Mütter, wenn sie stillen,
> und in sich gebunden wie ein Kranz. (III, 47)

> während sie, geschwächt und ausgeruht,
> unbeholfen, um sich hinzugeben,
> eine ungewohnte Geste tut. (III, 57)

A combination of the present and past participles is often used to
great advantage:

> wie mit Zuversicht die Fahrt bekränzend,
> leichtgebunden um den runden Bug,
>
> . . . .
>
> aufgerichtet, hingerissen, rauschend,
> und im Tauchen mit den Wellen tauschend ... (III, 121)

By an accumulation of participles, Rilke can achieve truly grandiose
effects:

> angewachsen — sieh: zu welcher Masse,
> aufgehäuft aus altem schwarzen Hasse,
> und das Haupt zu einer Faust geballt,
> nicht mehr spielend gegen irgendwen,
> nein: die blutigen Nackenhaken hissend
> hinter den gefällten Hörnern, wissend ... (III, 213)

It is interesting to observe how lines taken from different poems
have a similar, almost identical ring when they are based on participles, which give them their characteristic, sweeping intensity:

> flügelschlagend, manchmal fast zu fassen (III, 57)
> dienend, voll Geduld, versuchend, wie ... (III, 248)
> hingeworfen, weinend, nicht mehr wagend (III, 151)
> angeschuldigt, aufgerissen, offen. (III, 187)

The features revealed by Rilke's use of the participle as an
adjective confirm those noted when dealing with the participle
proper: extension in space and time. The present participle has,

of course, always been extensively used as an adjective, and there
would be nothing remarkable in Rilke's doing so if his manner
did not differ from conventional use. When Goethe says *ein
singender Vogel — die scheidende Sonne — die sinnende Schöne — ein
blinkender Stern* (*Sehnsucht*), these participles are more informative
than descriptive. Rilke uses such informative participles too, but
whenever he can, he makes them pointedly descriptive, vividly
painting:

die auswärtswollenden Konturen	(III, 48)
der stauende Verlauf	(III, 77)
kriechende und fliegende Gesichte	(III, 148)
sein schwindendes Gehust	(III, 157)
das benehmende Gepolster	(III, 181)
nicht zu verwandelnde Gedanken	(III, 192)
mein strömendes Antlitz.	(III, 302)

The poet's use of the past participle as an adjective is still more
interesting, since it throws light on the great subtlety of his
technique. Rilke is very sensitive to the accumulated, concentrated
energy with which the past participle is endowed, an energy much
surpassing that of the adjective. There are a few precedents for
this use of the past participle in German poetry, e.g. Mörike's
lovely *die vertiefte Bläue* in *Mein Fluss*. The condensed power possessed by the participle used as an adjective derives from the expression of the past contained in it. It is felt when Rilke, instead of the
correct *kühne Entwürfe*, says *erkühnte Entwürfe* (III, 369): while the
former combination gives, by means of the adjective, a closer
definition of 'projects' and adds a descriptive touch, the latter
expresses the more graphic meaning that the projects have been
conceived by bold minds; the descriptive force is considerably
increased by this conception as well as by the more unusual character
of the word. The same participle occurs again in *deinem erkühnten
Gefühl die erglühte Gefühlin* (III, 287). In the same way, *ihr erhelltes
Haar* conveys more than *ihr helles Haar* would. This participle is
used with the corresponding adjective in the same sentence: *ihr
erhelltes Haar | war wie ein heller Saal* (III, 207). *Erhellt*, in the context,
may imply several things, e.g. that cosmetics had their part in
bleaching Tullia's hair, or that reflections from the sun have just
given it added brightness, or that jewels light it up; the variety of
possible meanings makes the word richer, more poetical, and moreover the participle, vibrating with accumulated energy, is more

suggestive than the adjective. Similarly, *vereinsamter Schrei* is more effective, because more dramatic, than *einsamer Schrei* (III, 306). *Beseligte Golfe* has a rather unusual ring, and a doubt may arise whether the straightforward *selige Golfe* might not be more appropriate. Yet the fullness of *beseligt*, the faint implication, conveyed by the participle, that in a distant past some deity made those gulfs blissful, and lastly the slight quaintness of the word—qualities that make it more poetic in the true sense of the word—fully justify the poet's choice.

The following selection, from *Neue Gedichte*, of characteristic past participles used as adjectives will convey an idea of the amazing variety and shades of expression Rilke could master by this means:

sein verfrühtes Gesicht	(III, 74)
sein weitgeschleudertes Vertrauen	(III, 129)
umgestürzte Würden	(III, 132)
ein kaum begonnenes Profil	(III, 81)
auf den unverhofften, oftenstellten Garten im beruhigten Geviert	(III, 165)
die vollgestellte Stadt	(III, 189)
der mitgefühlte Frühlingsmorgen	(III, 212)
die überfüllten Früchte.	(III, 248)

It would lead too far to comment in detail on the wealth of images and meanings condensed in these participles; a hint may suffice on the graphic quality of *getürmtes Wohnen* (III, 182), which, with two words, gives a most vivid picture of the high tenement houses of Naples with their crowded mass of humanity, or on the intense, sharply outlined sketch contained in *der eingeneigte Schreiber* (III, 211), a happy neologism that makes us see, in a flash, the bent, deferential, scholarly clerk to whom the emperor is dictating. *Der ungeschaffne Gang des Schwanes* (III, 51) is a magnificent, most original image expressed by means of a participle. A lesser poet might have been content with the word at hand, *der unbeholfne Gang*; Rilke's *ungeschaffen* is fresh, powerful, graphic.

Such examples show how the frozen past contained in the participle makes for economy of diction, and enables the poet to compress meaning and double meaning into a perspective vista in which present and past become simultaneous. Occasionally, Rilke overstrains the form:

> gewährtes Weiss und leichtgerührtes Blau
> gebauschtes Grün. (III, 197)

Sometimes Rilke even presses the participle into un-German or grammatically unsound constructions:

> so waren sie hörend   (III, 262)
>
> und sie lässt mit hochgehobnem Kinn
> alle diese Worte wieder fallen,
> ohne bleibend . . .,   (III, 201)

but such audacities are in the end justified by their effect.

In the *Elegies*, Rilke's use of the participle continues, with the difference that they take on a new significance: while in *Neue Gedichte* he uses these combinations mainly to achieve a more precise and graphic expressiveness, in the *Elegies* the meanings he arrives at are often as original as they are profound. They express certain novel conceptions and sensations that could be conveyed by participles only. Taken from their context and out of the atmosphere of the poem, such applications may at times appear somewhat strange, but within the poems they do not stand out as unusual or artificial:

> das verzogene Treusein einer Gewohnheit   (III, 260)
>
> im erschrockenen Raum   (III, 263)
>
> in der verwitweten Haut   (III, 279)
>
> das trabende Herz   (III, 280)
>
> ins verspätete Innre   (III, 284)
>
> der gärtnernde Tod   (III, 285)
>
> jeder ihn meinende Herzschlag   (III, 286)
>
> ein kümmerndes Tier   (III, 287)
>
> ein gebetetes Ding, ein gedientes, geknietes   (III, 290)
>
> der gerufene Ruf   (III, 289)
>
> das strebende Stemmen, aus vergehender Stadt   (III, 291)
>
> das behübschte Glück.   (III, 303)

The participle is less frequent in the *Sonnets to Orpheus*, yet when it does occur in this collection, it is always illuminating, and often particularly felicitous:

> die gefühlte Wiese   (III, 314)
>
> sein fühlender Süden   (III, 319)
>
> der geweinte Quell   (III, 320)
>
> die reine, sich weigernde Schale   (III, 327)
>
> eingetauschter Weltraum   (III, 341)
>
> ermüdende Sünden   (III, 347)
>
> das erschwungene Jahr   (III, 362)
>
> durchwinterte Eichen.   (III, 370)

Used as nouns, participles again exercise their enlarging and deepening effect: they give extension in time, and by reflection also in space. The present participle particularly seems to create this spatial sensation, while the past participle provides a deep anchorage in time. Take, as an instance, Rilke's *Der verwöhnende der Fraun* (III, 14; spelt with a small initial letter in the poem, because dependent on *Der Flüchtling,* but nevertheless used as a substantive in this connection). Rilke's term, which stands for something like *der Frauenverwöhner,* acquires extension in time and, indirectly, also volume in space; moreover, other qualities like softness and tenderness are infused into it. By the novel use of the present participle, the donjuanesque lover's power of seduction is thrown into relief and made plastic: while *der Frauenverwöhner* would be little more than a statement, *der Verwöhnende* gives the presence and action of the seducer, his apt poetic image. Similarly, *das Erglühende der Früchte* (III, 186) is charged with a continuous, wavelike radiance which the simple term *das Glühen der Früchte* does not provide.

The concentrated power of the past infused into nouns when made up of participles can be studied in the passage

> auf Pferde, sieben ziehende, verteilt,
> verwandelt Niebewegtes sich in Schritte . . .   (III, 77)

Niebewegtes is a most effective concentration into a single word of the sentence 'a thing that was never before moved'. It is much more than a convenient or picturesque abbreviation, for through being thus condensed, the term, like compressed steam, acquires a singularly compelling force. Here are some more examples of participles used as nouns:

die grossen Städte sind
Verlorene und Aufgelöste   (II, 271)

ein Schönverbundenes   (III, 62)

von Gewesnem ausgeweitet   (III, 85)

das Erleichternde der Öle   (III, 159)

ein vielleicht Seiender   (III, 166)

das Drängende von . . . Gärten   (III, 191)

überstarke Überlieferte   (III, 195)

ihr ineinander Genügten,   (III, 266)

and, most felicitous in its lyrical concentration: *frühe Geglückte* (III, 264)—only Rilke could have coined these words.

The use of participles as adverbs discloses the same enriching qualities:

> . . . verlächelnd schob der Laborant
> den Kolben fort, der halberuhigt rauchte.   (III, 150)
> hingegeben hebt er seine Hand   (III, 174)
> bis er draussen atemlos beschwörend
> seine Leere zu den Himmeln hebt   (III, 189)
> der ein . . . Lächeln glänzend zu enthalten schien (III, 197)
> überstürzt gesiegelt.   (III, 239)

Not many poets before Rilke have used the participle, preceded by *wie*, for similes (Goethe's *wie reingewaschen* in 'Mai' is rather an isolated case). With Rilke, this form is fairly frequent:

> wie verloren   (III, 61)
> wie weggeworfen   (III, 129)
> wie ertrunken   (III, 199)
> wie verrufen, wie vergiftet   (III, 200)
> wie mitgehoben   (III, 211)
> wie herausgegriffen, wie geschliffen.   (III, 219)

Rilke has few, if any, precedents in poetry for his use of participles in the comparative. It occurs mostly in his later poetry, where, in order to give expression to new shades of meaning, he sometimes abandons the road of tradition and seeks new paths. The possibilities of language do not always serve his purpose now. They would offer, e.g.: *wo er inniger fühlt — er wird erstaunter stehn*, where Rilke writes: *wo er fühlender fühlt — er wird staunender stehn*. The force of expression gained by this novel use of the participle is obvious, while in most cases the poet's sincerity and moderation succeed in overcoming any strain that might be caused by the strangeness of the innovation. The first four of the following examples are taken from *Neue Gedichte*, the rest from the *Elegies*, the *Sonnets* and from *Letzte Gedichte*:

> immer schwindelnder und blinder   (III, 179)
> die er, ungeduldiger, bedrohter, / weiterlebte   (III, 209)
> sie kniete knieender   (III, 217)
> im überfüllteren Blick   (III, 298)
> dass ich euch knieender nicht . . . hinnahm, . . .
> mich gelöster ergab . . .   (III, 302)
> er . . . griffe strahlender um sich   (III, 349)
> singender steige, preisender steige   (III, 356)
> die geschautere Welt.   (III, 462)

and, most unusual of all, *geborener*.[1] Rilke's skill and tact even

---

[1] *Aus Taschen-Büchern und Merkblättern*, Inselverlag 1950, p. 25.

make the superlative of a participle possible:

das zitterndste Bild	(II, 219)
deine leidendste Erfahrung	(III, 374)
aus den bebendsten Steinen	(III, 351)
die Schwindendsten	(III, 297)
handelndster Geist	(S.G., 37)

Fritz Kaufmann[1] has drawn attention to the double meaning in Rilke's combination, *erfahrene Frucht* (III, 327)—the participle here can be understood in the transitive as well as in the intransitive sense, meaning that the fruit has experience or that it is being experienced by him who tastes it. In another of the *Sonnets*, 22 of Part II, Rilke says *die mit Licht übertriebene Nacht*: the participle *übertrieben* is not employed in its conventional sense here, but felt almost as a new word by the addition of *mit Licht*; the word is, as it were, restored to its pristine sense, recreated as the participle it originally was, before usage made it an adjective.

Parentheses

Another characteristic feature of Rilke's style, but not of poetry generally, is the use of parentheses. In the work of other poets it is so rare that it may be ignored, and it is not difficult to understand why parenthesis has no place in poetry, which tends to eliminate whatever checks and disturbs direct communication. To Rilke it is a means of adding depth to certain passages in his poems; it provides him with yet another dimension, creates a sphere of aloof intimacy in which he can give expression to subtle shades of meaning, or it gives him the possibility of differentiating certain parts in his poems from the rest. Since, as we have seen, his rhythm is slow and soft, the retarding effect of parenthesis does not disturb him.

As a rule, and in opposition to general usage, Rilke encloses his parentheses in curves; in exceptional cases only does he use dashes (two of these rare instances occur in II, 308, and in III, 73). The curves often seem but a manner, or mannerism, of punctuation: a colon, one feels, would do just as well, or the phrase might have been enclosed between commas. Here is an instance where the colon might have been employed:

> Was wirst du tun, Gott, wenn ich sterbe?
> Ich bin dein Krug (wenn ich zerscherbe?)
> Ich bin dein Trank (wenn ich verderbe?),   (II, 198)

[1] 'Sprache als Schöpfung. Zur absoluten Kunst im Hinblick auf Rilke,' *Zeitschr. für Aesthetik und allgemeine Kuntswissenschaft*, Bd. 28.

commas in this:

> und sie hängten schliesslich wie Gewichte
> (zu verhindern seine Himmelfahrt)
> an ihn ihrer grossen Kathedralen
> Last und Masse,   (III, 40)

or in this:

> aber als der herrliche Behälter
> (goldgetrieben, köstlich, vielkarätig)
> fertig vor ihm stand . . .   (III, 151)

In the passage just quoted, it would seem that the use of commas
instead of brackets would make no difference at all, or might perhaps
even be felt as more organic. Why then does Rilke prefer the
brackets? It is because they push the thought back a little, thus
giving an almost imperceptible distance to the clause, one of those
nuances so important and dear to him.

It may be argued that brackets, in any case, are but a visual device
and do not necessarily influence the real test of a poem, its being read
aloud. But they do give the reader's voice a direction, make him
change his tone and volume, and even an ever so slight decrease
would suffice to fulfil the poet's wish for differentiation. Thus, if a
pause be inserted and the voice slightly softened in these instances,
the author's intention would be realized. Besides, we must not
forget that the poems will be far oftener read than heard.

The least interesting use of parenthesis occurs when it serves to
express an aside:

> denn nur noch so entsteht (das wissen wir)
> . . . der Heiland   (III, 36)
> nur (so sagt man) in den letzten Nächten . . .   (III, 153)

In some other cases, brackets have a weightier task than warding
off a phrase or adding distance to a thought: they create a dimension
in depth, or isolate a conception:

> Sie aber kam und hob
> den Blick, um dieses alles anzuschauen.
> (Ein Kind, ein kleines Mädchen zwischen Frauen.)   (II, 299)
>
> Jetzt fragte sie lange nicht wer
> sie sei (: eine ferne Verwandte)   (III, 175)
> (Note the sophistication of placing even the colon inside the brackets)
>
>   . . . als kündigte alles
> eine Geliebte dir an? (Wo willst du sie bergen,
> da doch die grossen fremden Gedanken bei dir
> aus und ein gehn und öfters bleiben bei Nacht.)   (III, 260)

Sie merken es nicht in dem Wirbel
ihrer Rückkehr zu sich. (Wie sollten sies merken.) (III, 266)

In passages like these, the sentences enclosed in brackets effect a dimensional enlargement of the poem, but they are still contained within its sphere. In a few instances, however, Rilke seems to be leaving the plane of the poem in order to explore a sideline: he pushes a thought outward:

bis es die unbekannten Munde schluckten,
die niemals reden. (Wo besteht und denkt
ein Hirn, um ihrer einst sich zu bedienen?)   (III, 50)

die andern Toten, welche bis ans Ende
aushielten. (Was will Ende sagen?)   (II, 342)

. . . diese gewährenden, diese
unsere Räume. (Was müssen sie fürchterlich gross sein,
da sie Jahrtausende nicht unseres Fühlns überfülln.) (III, 291)

Such asides are not without their danger, and sometimes all the poet's tact and feeling for form are required to find the way back into the original flow of the poem.

Brackets are also employed by Rilke to give relief to a metaphor that would be flatter or less colourful without their space and distance giving effect:

statt der Fetzen werden die ererbten
Bettbezüge, welche wehen wollen,
von den immer höheren Balkonen
(wie in Fliessendem gespiegelt) hängen.   (III, 182)

. . . dass nicht die Macht sie überfällt
die sie in ihm (so wie man Löwen hält)
vorsichtig nährten.   (III, 206)

The subtlest use of this technique is found in the Ninth Elegy:

. . . Lorbeer, ein wenig dunkler als alles
andere Grün, mit kleinen Wellen an jedem
Blattrand (wie eines Windes Lächeln) . . .   (III, 297)

Eines Windes Lächeln, a graceful simile in itself, gains in originality as well as charm by being applied to the edge of the laurel leaf; the curves place it, as it were, in a recess, thereby giving it a slight relief that brings out its full flavour. Such instances illustrate Rilke's mastery over minor technical devices, his highly developed sense for detail.

H

The strangest use of parenthesis occurs in a poem in *Späte Gedichte*:

> Da schwang die Schaukel durch den Schmerz — ; doch siehe,
> der Schatten wars des Baums, an dem sie hängt.
> (später) :
> Ob ich nun vorwärts schwinge oder fliehe . . .   (S.G., 85)

The word *später* in its curves strikes us a naïve, and at the same time not very effective, way of indicating the passing of time. If it were omitted altogether, the poem might gain by it.

CONDENSATION

THE German lyric can be very concise, and German poetry abounds in short and very short pieces. Rilke follows this trend, and from his beginnings, with few exceptions, he prefers short forms. As his art, during his middle period, became more delicate and complex, he had to choose between lengthening the individual poem and compressing more into it, and generally decided in favour of the latter course. In his early poems we still encounter lines and words that could have been left out without a loss. Rilke would adorn his poems with such words for the sake of their vowel music or alliterative sounds, sometimes irrespectively of their meaning, as when he says:

durch schmale, schmachtende Spalten;   (II, 55)

schmachtende Spalten, the adjectival participle introduced to provide a sound parallel to *schmale*, is of course absurd. Such decorative use of language persists in varying degree through Rilke's early production and is not quite extinct in *Buch der Bilder* and *Stundenbuch*, until finally the compact intensity of *Neue Gedichte* renders it impossible. This intensity called for a new and severe condensation: a wealth of meaning, vision and experience had to be compressed into the narrow frame of the short poem, generally of twelve to fifteen lines. The first, negative step in this direction was to remove all padding by the omission of everything that could be spared without obscuring the meaning. Rilke goes very far in this direction; not only does he throw all unnecessary ornaments overboard, but he forcibly compresses his thought, leaving a great deal to the reader's constructive imagination. He could now outline a situation with a minimum of words, clear-cut, rapid, dramatic:

> Sie folgten furchtbar; ihren bunten Tod
> von ferne nach ihm werfend, während er
> verloren floh, nichts weiter als: bedroht.   (III, 74)

> Da plötzlich war der Bote unter ihnen,
> hineingeworfen in das Überkochen
> des Hochzeitsmahles wie ein neuer Zusatz.   (III, 103)

Since the first lines of most poems in *Neue Gedichte* lead the reader in *medias res* with a minimum of exposition, or even

without that, the title now becomes indispensable for their understanding:

> ### Der Turm
> Erd-Inneres, Als wäre dort, wohin
> du blindlings steigst, erst Erdenoberfläche . . .   (III, 83)
>
> ### Die Versuchung
> Nein, es half nicht, dass er sich die scharfen
> Stacheln einhieb in das geile Fleisch . . .   (III, 148)
>
> ### In einem fremden Park
> Zwei Wege sinds. Sie führen keinen hin.
> Doch manchmal, in Gedanken, lässt der eine
> dich weitergehn.   (III, 61)
>
> ### Eine Sibylle
> Einst, vor Zeiten, nannte man sie alt.
> Doch sie blieb und kam dieselbe Strasse
> täglich.   (III, 137)

This conciseness is often more than the mere omission of redundant words or phrases, it is a genuine condensation: the thought
appears, as it were, foreshortened in perspective:

> Kaiser sein heisst unverwandelt vieles
> überstehen bei geheimer Tat . . .   (III, 211)
>
> ### Das Gold
> Denk, es wäre nicht: es hätte müssen
> endlich in den Bergen sich gebären
> und sich niederschlagen in den Flüssen
> aus dem Wollen, aus dem Gären . . .   (III, 153)

Kretische Artemis begins with these lines:

> Wind der Vorgebirge: war nicht ihre
> Stirne wie ein lichter Gegenstand?   (III, 118)

What condensation in these three words, *Wind der Vorgebirge:* how
simply and effectively they conjure up the Greek landscape with
its sharp contours and pale colours under the light of early dawn!
The last lines of *Der Doge* are typical for Rilke's art of firm
contraction:

> Was die Signorie
> in seinem Innern zu bezwingen glaubte,
> bezwang er selbst. In seinem greisen Haupte
> war es besiegt. Sein Antlitz zeigte wie.   (III, 206)

The minute and lengthy descriptions in pieces like *Hetärengräber*
and *Die Rosenschale* are rather exceptional in *Neue Gedichte*, the
bulk of which give the impression of thought and sensation tightly
packed into a narrow space. Nothing of importance is omitted,

and there are hardly any elliptic sentences; the conciseness is accomplished by precision of thought and expression. In many cases, we do not even feel it as conciseness: the poem *Der Dichter*, in eight short lines, sums up Rilke's poetic destiny, more than that, the tragic destiny of every poet when inspiration leaves him, yet we do not feel the poem as unduly terse in relation to its great theme. Each of Rilke's poems at this period seems to exhaust its theme, boldly delineated with few strokes of the utmost precision, while the omissions silently complete the picture.

Condensation goes even further in the *Elegies*. They are long poems, yet they seem too short for what the poet has to say, and they are made heavy, slow and at times even obscure by the wealth of thought and experience that have been compressed into them. In many a passage we feel, behind the words, a background of experience (*Erlebnis*) that is only partly expressed in them:

> Und ihr, hab ich nicht recht,
> die ihr mich liebtet für den kleinen Anfang
> Liebe zu euch, von dem ich immer abkam,
> weil mir der Raum in eurem Angesicht,
> da ich ihn liebte, überging in Weltraum,
> in dem ihr nicht mehr wart . . .   (III, 276)

These six lines contain, *in nuce*, an account of Rilke's emotional attitude to people, yet admirable as the condensation is, it will be fully comprehensible only to those who have studied his life story. Here is another condensation, in four lines, that can hardly be improved upon:

> Und wir, Zuschauer, immer, überall,
> dem allen zugewandt und nie hinaus!
> Uns überfüllts. Wir ordnens. Es zerfällt.
> Wir ordnens wieder und zerfallen selbst.   (III, 295)

Within such general abbreviations Rilke has, moreover, personal short cuts where his thought seems to leap from stone to stone, as in a brook:

> Uns, die Schwindendsten. Einmal
> jedes, nur einmal. Einmal und nicht mehr. Und wir auch
> einmal. Nie wieder.   (III, 297)

> Sie sagt:
> Weit. Wir wohnen dort draussen . . . Wo? Und der Jüngling
> folgt. Ihn rührt ihre Haltung. Die Schulter, der Hals-, vielleicht
> ist sie von herrlicher Herkunft.   (III, 304-5)

> Und höher, die Sterne. Neue. Die Sterne des Leidlands. (III, 307)

While the *Elegies*, owing to their form as long poems, still allow Rilke to compress or enlarge his material at will, no such liberty is granted him by the sonnet-form of *Sonnets to Orpheus*. Here, all is severe compression, even more so than in *Neue Gedichte*, because the subject matter of these short poems is akin to that of the *Elegies*, which in comparison appear almost diffuse. Rilke himself writes in this connection:[1]

> But there is something in the very nature of these poems, in their condensation and abbreviation (frequently stating lyrical totals, instead of setting out the stages necessary to the result), that makes them more likely to be grasped by the inspiration of one similarly focused than generally 'understood'.

We have to distinguish, however, between the condensation of Rilke's poetic material itself and the expression this condensation found in his style, for the two are not the same. In the *Sonnets*, Rilke is frequently compelled to have recourse to elliptical sentences, he speaks in a kind of poetic telegraph style of the utmost conciseness:

> Und schlief in ihr. Und alles war ihr Schlaf.   (III, 314)
>   Das verrinnt.
> In Wahrheit singen, ist ein andrer Hauch.
> Ein Hauch um nichts. Ein Wehn im Gott. Ein Wind. (III, 315)
> Aber die Lüfte . . . Aber die Räume . . .   (III, 316)
> Reine Spannung. O Musik der Kräfte!   (III, 324)

A longer quotation will shed more light on this technique: in Sonnet 11 of Part I, Rilke gives expression to the thought that horse and rider come to a cross-roads, that the rider knows how to make his horse turn in the direction he wishes to take, that the two gallop along, seemingly one, while in reality worlds separate them— could this sequence be expressed with fewer words than these:

> Weg und Wendung. Doch ein Druck verständigt.
> Neue Weite. Und die zwei sind eins.
> Aber sind sie's? Oder meinen beide
> nicht den Weg, den sie zusammen tun?
> Namenlos schon trennt sie Tisch und Weide.   (III, 323)

In some passages, Rilke makes use of poetic allusion, and there remains a great deal for the reader to complete:

> Was wissen wir von ihrem Teil an dem?   (III, 326)
> Erkennst du mich, Luft, du, voll noch einst meiniger Orte?
> Du, einmal glatte Rinde,
> Rundung und Blatt meiner Worte.   (III, 341)

[1] Quoted from the Introduction to J. B. Leishman's *Translation of the Sonnets to Orpheus*, 1936, p. 10 (Briefe aus Muzot, 220).

Unlike the poems in *Neue Gedichte*, we feel many of the sonnets as condensations, extreme formulas of abbreviation beyond which it would not be possible to go without becoming very obscure. To have reached just this stage of balance is the success, the triumph, of these poems—a triumph comparable to that of Goethe's *Selige Sehnsucht*, where the profoundest experience has found expression in a crystalline cipher. In the *Sonnets* obscurity, when encountered, is more apparent than real, i.e. we can overcome it by filling in and connecting what the poet's condensation has left out or compressed, as shown in the example of horse and rider. Sonnets 18, 19, 22, 23 of Part I, and 23 of Part II, are instances of such extreme condensation.

Letzte Gedichte provide several examples of successful condensation, though nothing that surpasses the *Sonnets* in this respect. One of the most effective occurs in *Klage*:

> Früher. Klagtest? Was wars? Eine gefallene
> Beere des Jubels, unreife!
> Jetzt aber bricht mir mein Jubelbaum,
> bricht mir im Sturme mein langsamer
> Jubelbaum.   (III, 412)

The whole poem is very compact, but these five lines in it are an extraordinary feat of emotional condensation: in them, a great accumulation of suffering has found its pathetic expression in a minimum of words. Similar in this respect, i.e. built almost entirely on poetic allusion, is this passage from another poem:

> Ausgesetzt auf den Bergen des Herzens. Steingrund
> unter den Händen. Hier blüht wohl
> einiges auf; aus stummem Absturz
> blüht ein unwissendes Kraut singend hervor.
> Aber der Wissende? Ach, der zu wissen begann,
> und schweigt nun, ausgesetzt auf den Bergen des Herzens.
>   (III, 420)

Again, as in the preceding poem, this is almost more in the nature of a repression than an expression, as if pain and despair, welling up, were being pushed back with force. An infinity of thought and feeling has been compressed into these six lines, and in what we have to read between them.

Finally, *Der Magier* may be mentioned as a supreme instance of the ease and elegance with which Rilke could express a line of thought

with the utmost graphic brevity, creating an apt dramatic beauty
of its own:

> Er ruft es an. Es schrickt zusamm und steht.
> Was steht? Das andre; alles, was nicht er ist,
> wird Wesen.   (III, 431)

And the last stanza:

> Entscheidung fällt. Die Bindung stellt sich her.
> Er weiss, der Anruf überwog das Weigern.
> Doch sein Gesicht, wie mit gedeckten Zeigern,
> hat Mitternacht. Gebunden ist auch er.   (III, 431)

REPETITION

REPETITION is a familiar artistic device in the epic, where identical or similar actions are covered by recurring formulas, or persons and things given the same epithets whenever they appear on the scene. In lyric poetry repetition is not so widely used nor so generally expected or accepted, except perhaps for refrain-like repetitions in ballads and similar poems. From his earliest to his latest productions, Rilke makes an extensive use of repetition as an artistic expedient. His honesty here bluntly contravenes the rule of elegant variation, he even seems to proclaim a counter-rule: repeat whenever it enhances the effect. There is something almost uninhibited in his repetitions, when he drives home a point in a manner we might call naïve were it not, after all, deliberate and intentional. We think of a poem like *Herbst* (II, 54), with its seven *fallen* (or *fällt*), in nine lines; of *Bangnis* (II, 48), where *welken Walde* occurs three times in the first five lines, and *Vogelruf* twice. There is a contrast between the high complexity of some of Rilke's stylistic devices and the simplicity implied in repetition. Rilke's repetition is usually massive and heavy, without gradations, very forthright; it is rarely rhythmical or refrain-like as in older German lyrics (*Schlafe! Was willst du mehr?* — Goethe; *Wenn ich ihn nur habe* — Novalis; *Schweig stille, mein Herze* — Mörike, etc.). We encounter this kind of repetition in a few poems in *Neue Gedichte* only, e.g. in *Das Karussell* (*und dann und wann ein weisser Elephant*, III, 80), and in *Lied vom Meer* (*Uraltes Wehn vom Meer*, III, 190). More characteristic for Rilke is a passage like this:

Ich leg meine Hand auf den Arm der Frau,
meine graue Hand auf ihr graues Grau,   (II, 123)

where we have three repetitions in one line. (Compare C. F. Meyer's: *den Felsen umschleichest du grau auf dem Grau* — 'Noch Einmal'.) Again:

Raum-brauchen, ohne Raum von jenem Raum
zu nehmen . . .   (III, 110)

überhäuft mit Himmeln, überstarke
Überlieferte, die überstehn . . .   (III, 195)

In the last passage we have a massing of words with the prefix *über,* a deliberate overcrowding in order to give the lines exceptional fullness. The *Sonnets to Orpheus* contain many instances of repetition:

> ... die Schwere,
> gebt sie zurück an der Erde Gewicht;
> schwer sind die Berge, schwer sind die Meere.
> Selbst die als Kinder ihr pflanztet, die Bäume,
> wurden zu schwer längst ...   (III, 316)

(Compare, in *Neue Gedichte*: *von seiner Schwere schwer*, III, 77).

> ... wie der Winter, der eben geht.
> Denn unter Wintern ist einer so endlos Winter,
> dass, überwinternd, dein Herz überhaupt übersteht.
>   (III, 356)

> Unabgeschmackt
> scheint dir das Kommende. Jenes so oft
> dir schon Gekommene scheint dir zu kommen ... (III, 370)

> Wie ergreift uns der Vogelschrei ...
> Irgendein einmal erschaffenes Schreien.
> Aber die Kinder schon, spielend im Freien,
> schreien an wirklichen Schreien vorbei.
> Schreien den Zufall.   (III, 371)

The following heavy repetition, five times in four lines, occurs in *Letzte Gedichte*:

> Schutzlos
> ist sie wie wir, wie Tiere im Winter, schutzlos.
> Schutzloser: denn sie erkennt die Verstecke nicht. Schutzlos,
> so als wäre sie selber das Drohende. Schutzlos
> wie ein Brand ...,   (III, 466)

and, from the same collection, the finest example perhaps of what Rilke could achieve by repetition:

> Da beugte der alte
> Gott zu dem Alten langsam sein altes
> Antlitz. Nahm ihn im Kusse aus ihm
> in sein Alter, das ältere.   (III, 404-5)

These examples show how deliberately Rilke avoided 'elegant variation' which for a poet with his large resources of vocabulary could not have been difficult. He repeats with a technique similar to a musician's, who reiterates the notes of his theme until it is fully established in the hearer's consciousness. But this technique is by no means fixed, it shows interesting variations:

> Sie spricht zum Gotte, und der Gott vernimmt sie,
> und alle hörens gleichsam erst im Gotte:
> Ersatz kann keiner für ihn sein. Ich bins.
> Ich bin Ersatz. Denn keiner ist zu Ende,
> wie ich es bin.   (III, 105)

We might call this modulating repetition: first three times *Gott*, then twice *Ersatz*, followed by two *keiner*, and again three *bin*; a pattern of recurring repetition with different words. In the next example the repetition is rhythmical:

> Er ging hinauf unter dem grauen Laub
> ganz grau und aufgelöst im Ölgelände
> und legte seine Stirne voller Staub
> tief in das Staubigsein der heissen Hände. (III, 26)

Grau is repeated in the first two lines, *staubig* in the next. Later in the poem, this rhythmical repetition continues very effectively with the sentences: *Ich finde dich nicht mehr. — Ich bin allein. — Warum ein Engel? — Ach, es kam die Nacht*, the first repeated three times, the others twice.

There is yet another, less unfamiliar kind of repetition, which we might call emotional repetition. Unlike the kind just treated, emotional repetition is found extensively in lyrical poetry, as Goethe's *Komm, ach komm in meine Brust!* Mörike's *O Fluss, mein Fluss im Morgenstrahl! Empfange nun, empfange . . .*, George's *und Rosen Rosen waren um sein Kinn*. We would not expect to find a great deal of emotional repetition in *Neue Gedichte*, where it occurs occasionally only, and is subdued in character:

> deine Nächte, König, deine Nächte —,
> und wie waren, die dein Schaffen schwächte,
> o wie waren alle Leiber schön. (III, 19)

> O Jesus, Jesus, wann war unsre Stunde? (III, 28)

> Du aber sei, du Mund, dass wir es hören,
> du aber, du Uns-Sagender, du sei. (III, 29)

In the last example, *du* is repeated five times in two lines.

In the *Duino Elegies*, on the other hand, there is a great deal of emotional repetition, of which a few characteristic examples only:

> Sondern die Nächte! Sondern die hohen, des Sommers,
> Nächte, sondern die Sterne, die Sterne der Erde.
> O einst tot sein und sie wissen unendlich,
> alle die Sterne: denn wie, wie, wie sie vergessen! (III, 288)

> Aber ein Turm war gross, nicht wahr? O Engel, er war es, —
> gross, auch noch neben dir? Chartres war gross . . . (III, 292)

> Erde, ist es nicht dies, was du willst: unsichtbar
> in uns erstehn! — Ist es dein Traum nicht,
> einmal unsichtbar zu sein? — Erde! unsichtbar! (III, 300–1)

The poet's liberated faculty for the expression of joy similarly asserts itself in the *Sonnets*:

> sie kanns, sie kanns!
>
> . . . . . .
>
> sie singts, sie singts!   (III, 333)
> singender steige, preisender steige   (III, 356)
> Aber er trug auch, er trug, dein Baum der Ekstase. (III, 362)

The most dramatic instances of emotional repetition undoubtedly occur in *Letzte Gedichte* and *Späte Gedichte*, where the poet proceeds from double to triple repetition:

> Hier bin ich, hier bin ich, Entrungene,
> taumelnd.
> Wag ichs denn? Werf ich mich?
>
> . . . . . .
>
> Wag ichs denn? Werf ich mich?   (III, 402)
> Das Ding zu machen, Herr Herr Herr, das Ding . . . (III, 446)
>
> Wann wird, wann wird, wann wird es genügen . . .
> Sind nicht, sind nicht, sind nicht vom Buche
> die Menschen geschlagen.   (S.G., 99)

WORD ORDER

PERHAPS the only part of poetic technique in which Rilke (the young Rilke at least) displays a certain gaucheness is the order of words. He is, in this respect, somewhat below the standards of his contemporaries, taking over usages that belong to an earlier period, when it was not unusual for poets, and especially minor poets, to transpose subject and verb and other parts of speech, which were thus shifted in order to comply with the rhythm, or to bring the rhyming word to the end of the line:

> Wenn nach heisser Sehnsucht langen Leiden
> Sie ans Herz sich endlich dürften pressen
>
> > (Lenau)
>
> Ins Museum bin zu später
> Stunde heut ich noch gegangen.
>
> > (C. F. Meyer)

Rilke's earliest poems contain many instances of such old-fashioned transposition; a passage like the following, with its clumsy inversion in both lines, is typical of this unlovely style:

> Zur seiten ihr der Gatte kann
> sie trösten mehr in keiner Weise;   (I, 24)

similarly, the position of the words *noch sich* at the beginning of a line, and followed by *auf den*, is very awkward in

> Lose Lichter haschen spät
> noch sich auf den Dächerkanten,   (I, 30)

and analogous lapses occur in

> Bald hättest, alte Rathausuhr,
> du nimmer dürfen Stunden weisen   (I, 94)
> dort findet Mutter Nacht er lehnen.   (I, 47)

In the period immediately preceding the *Stundenbuch*, when he was under the spell of Jacobsen, Rilke was very fond of the Saxon genitive, and passages like these abound:

> des Himmels violette Tinten   (I, 18)
> des Winters weisse Sohlenspur.   (I, 120)

Although the Saxon genitive is not at all unusual in German poetry and even prose, the extensive use Rilke makes of it borders on affectation. Another mannerism of this period is still more marked, and often becomes irritating: the transposition of the adjective behind its noun and at the end of the line, so as to catch the rhyme:

> Nischen rings, die eingebauten (I, 19)
>
> und die Nacht war schwarz, die schwüle (I, 83)
>
> Ein heisser Eid, ein gramerpresster. (I, 95)

(Compare Lenau's

> doch diese Wehmut, die herbe...
> Auf dem Teich, dem regungslosen.)

Such mannerisms, however, disappear fast with the poet's advance in taste, and in the *Stundenbuch* there is hardly a trace of them left. In Rilke's central period we find few deviations from the normal word order: he is now free from certain mannerisms and no longer in need of contortions. In *Neue Gedichte*, the word sequences fit so smoothly into the schemes of metre and rhyme that no strain is noticeable; Rilke has not only caught up with his early deficiency in this respect, but has become a master in arranging the sequence of words in his poems to the best advantage. It is only occasionally now that he adopts a more unusual word order to emphasize a point, as when, by postponement, he gives relief to the straining of the horses in the line

> auf Pferde, sieben ziehende, verteilt ... (III, 77)

Equally effective, in the same poem, is the position of the words *langsam zuletzt*, at the end of a long period:

> so kommt es durch den stauenden Verlauf
> des Tages, kommt in seinem ganzen Staate,
> als ob ein grosser Triumphator nahte,
> langsam zuletzt ... (III, 77)

In *Samuels Erscheinung vor Saul*, instead of the correct version: *noch ehe die Starrende beschrieb*, Rilke very effectively turns the words round:

> Und da die Starrende beschrieb, noch ehe,
> da war ihm schon, er hätte selbst gesehn ... (III, 133)

The first line of *Der Balkon* is similarly incorrect:

> Von der Enge, oben, des Balkones
> angeordnet ... (III, 184)

Since *Balkones* is the only end word in the poem without a rhyme, its placing at the end of the line is a deliberate device to give emphasis to the inserted *oben*.

These instances from *Neue Gedichte* are isolated, but later, in *Letzte Gedichte*, the *Duino Elegies* and *Sonnets to Orpheus*, Rilke begins to cultivate strange and novel inversions and transpositions, invented or adapted from other languages, to stress a passage, give relief to a particular word, or give a new turn to the whole sequence. With their Latinisms and Gallicisms these transpositions somehow violate the spirit of the language; they are definitely, perhaps intentionally, un-German. The most unusual effect is often obtained by a genitive and verb preceding, instead of following, the noun to which they belong:

> Manche, des Todes, entstand ruhig geordnete Regel. (III, 352)

This is really more than a new word order: it is a violation of the rules of German syntax—and yet Rilke's sentence is impressive with its quiet and monumental dignity due to the word order which, though obviously forced, somehow establishes itself as natural, at least within the poem. It is a tribute to Rilke's power that he can bring off such feats, create a poetical atmosphere that tolerates not only the unusual, but even the manifestly incorrect. Rilke adds an explanatory note to the sonnet from which this first line is taken, and in this connection it is interesting to note how odd, how un-German, even the prose of this note reads, almost as if it had been translated from the French:

> Bezugnehmend auf die Art, wie man, nach altem Jagdgebrauch, in gewissen Gegenden des Karsts, die eigentümlich bleichen Grotten-Tauben, durch vorsichtig in ihre Höhlen eingehängte Tücher, indem man diese plötzlich auf eine besondere Weise schwenkt, aus ihren unterirdischen Aufenthalten scheucht, um sie, bei ihrem erschreckten Ausflug, zu erlegen.

Neither word order, nor rhythm, nor punctuation of this piece can be called German.

It is not easy to explain this development in Rilke's style: was it unconscious, brought about by reading French and translating from it, or by living in a French environment, or was it a conscious new orientation? These foreign-sounding sequences need not necessarily be French, some recall a Latin word order, others that of Hölderlin's later poems:

> Ihr holden Schwäne,
> Und trunken von Küssen
> Tunkt ihr das Haupt . . .
>
> (*Hälfte des Lebens*)

The *Elegies* are rich in such novel word sequences:

> Den sie von weitem erkennt, ihren Jüngling, was weiss er ...
>   (III, 269)
>
> Wo, ach, hin sind die Jahre ...   (III, 270)
>
> ... und in die Falten des Vorhangs
> passte, die leicht sich verschob, seine unruhige Zukunft
>   (III, 271)
>
> ... doch an deinem Körper verliert sich,
> der es flächig verbraucht, das ... Gesicht.   (III, 280)
>
> Diese, des Herzens, Verschwendung.   (III, 290)

If such transpositions are arbitrary, it is certain that somehow Rilke succeeds in making them acceptable to us; strange as they may be, they fit into the style of the *Elegies*. The strong impression they produce is hard to define: the immediate effect is not only one of novelty, but of heightened poetic language:

> Nicht dass du Gottes ertrügest
> die Stimme, bei weitem.   (III, 262)
>
> Sondern die hohen, des Sommers,
> Nächte ...   (III, 288)

The boldness of such sequences also communicates an impression of grandeur, often of a sombre and tragic colouring:

> Aber,
> das uns finster verschweigt, das ... Schicksal   (III, 285)
>
> O Bäume Lebens, o wann winterlich?   (III, 274)
>
> Durch den sich Vögel werfen, ist nicht der
> vertraute Raum ...   (III, 441)

These transpositions often have an enlarging effect, like the participle, as may be seen in the last example quoted that makes us feel space and the flight of birds through it; if we establish the correct word order, this effect is diminished: *der vertraute Raum, durch den sich Vögel werfen*. ... The sombre greatness of Rilke's new word order sometimes makes us think of Rembrandt and El Greco, perhaps because such passages illuminate the poem with unexpected flashes of a mysterious brightness. A tormenting residue often remains, as from a passage like

> wo die Modistin, Madame Lamort,
> die ruhlosen Wege der Erde, endlose Bänder,
> schlingt und windet und neue aus ihnen
> Schleifen erfindet ...   (III, 282)

Similar instances from *Späte Gedichte* and the *Sonnets* confirm these impressions:

> Nun, wie das Grüne, das Blaue heisse,
> dürfen wir fragen ...   (III, 333)
>
> Ach, der Erde, wer kennt die Verluste?   (III, 342)
>
> Wenige ihr, der einstigen Kindheit Gespielen   (III, 348)
>
> treiben sie ihre, des Kreischens, Keile   (III, 371)
>
> schreit, den er donnernd bewohnt, sein rötlicher Himmel
>   (III, 390)
>
> Welches, unter dein Bild, heft ich ...   (III, 423)

LANGUAGE

Texture

Was man mit 21 Jahren schreibt ist ein Schrei — denkt man bei einem Schrei daran, ob er hätte anders geschrieen werden müssen? Die Sprache ist noch so dünn um einen in diesen Jahren, der Schrei dringt durch und nimmt eben nur mit, was an ihm hängen bleibt. Die Entwicklung wird immer die sein, dass man sich die Sprache voller, dichter, fester macht (schwerer), und das hat dann freilich nur Sinn für einen, der sicher ist dass auch der Schrei in ihm unablässig, unaufhaltsam zunimmt, sodass er später, unter dem Druck unzähliger Atmosphären, aus allen Poren des fast undurchdringlichen Mediums gleichmässig austritt.[1]

This passage is interesting and revealing: Rilke speaks of the necessity of making his language 'fuller, denser, firmer (heavier)'. There are indeed two styles of poetic language that might be aptly described by the words light and heavy; borrowing a term from science, we might speak of the specific gravity of language. For a typical example for the light style, let us turn to Heine:

> Ich hab' im Traum geweinet,
> Mir träumte, du lägest im Grab.
> Ich wachte auf, und die Träne,
> Floss noch von der Wange herab.
>
> (*Lyrisches Intermezzo*)

What makes this style light? It progresses rapidly, the words being but the bare means for conveying a thought or sensation which, however, is not poetically condensed in them; i.e. they convey the meaning without themselves indirectly expressing, or even becoming, the meaning. In the heavy style, on the other hand, words and poetical means become so intimately connected by various devices, such as interdependence of meaning and sound, alliteration, vowelling, assonance, associations, a significant use of syntax and grammar, that in the end they become inextricably interwoven. While in a poem like the one just quoted, the language is an open-work structure, something like a scaffolding, the heavy language resembles a very closely woven carpet. In the light style, each of the words used may be necessary, and their sequence and arrangement equally so, yet they will be hardly remembered as words: they float by, carrying the poetic meaning as a river carries flowers, swiftly, lightly, on its surface. In the heavy style attempted by Rilke and other poets, there is an aura radiating from each word,

---

[1] Letter to N.N., Dec. 26, 1911.

connecting it in a sense other than that of logic or causality, to those that precede and follow: 'Les mots s'allument de reflets réciproques, comme une virtuelle trainée de feux sur des pierreries'.[1] Maupassant expresses a similar thought: 'Les mots ont une âme: la plupart des lecteurs, et même des écrivains, ne leur demandent qu'un sens. Il faut trouver cette âme qui apparaît au contact d'autres mots. . . .' When looking for a counterpart to Heine's lines by a contemporary of his, we might quote the first stanza of Droste-Hülshoff's *Im Grase*:

> Süsse Ruh, süsser Taumel im Gras,
> Von des Krautes Arom umhaucht,
> Tiefe Flut, tief, tieftrunkne Flut,
> Wenn die Wolke am Azure verraucht,
> Wenn aufs müde, schwimmende Haupt
> Süsses Lachen gaukelt herab,
> Liebe Stimme säuselt und träuft,
> Wie die Lindenblüt auf ein Grab.

The reader will immediately notice how much more static these lines are; not limited to conveying a meaning, they interlace, 'light each other up with reciprocal reflections', so that their progress is considerably slowed down; they almost seem to stand still, like trees in a forest, intertwining their branches and stretching their roots downwards. Various attractions connect them: repetition (two *süss* in the first line, a third in the sixth; two *Flut* and three *tief* in the third line); a particularly sonorous vowel music and assonance (*Ruh, Flut, Azur; Taumel, Kraut, Haupt; Gras, Lachen, Grab; süss, müde, Lindenblüt; säuselt, träuft; tiefe, Liebe, Stimme*). Moreover, the more uncommon words, like *Arom, Azur,* are full of associations, as also *Lindenblüt, Grab.* The statement of fact contained in the nine lines is scanty and vague compared to that contained in Heine's four, yet the sensations conveyed are more graphic and therefore leave a deeper, more lasting, impression. Heine's stanza contains four simple main sentences and one clause, while the grammatical structure of Droste's lines is much looser: they consist of a somewhat indeterminate invocation (*Süsse Ruh* . . .), qualified by an adjective clause and three parallel conditional clauses, the last of which is elliptic, lacking the initial *wenn.* Heine's stanza, moreover, does not contain a single adjective, against nine in the second example, one of them a present participle (*schwimmend*), another a composite past participle (*tieftrunken*).

The texture created by the heavy style implies a system of words,

[1] Mallarmé, *Divagations.*

comparable to the system of colours in a painting. The meaning of 'valeurs' in painting is the interaction and dependence of colours upon each other; each colour determines its neighbour and counterpart in a gradation of intensity, lightness, firmness, texture, transparency in a most delicate, easily disturbed balance. The same is true of words in a poem; in a broad sense, it applies to all poetry, but more particularly to that composed in what we called the heavy style. In the light style, the words move along rapidly, and thus have little time to react upon one another, and as they float in a thin atmosphere, they do not touch closely. Their interaction, therefore, will be slight, and they need not be so delicately attuned as the intimately interwoven words of the heavy style. In the second stanza of the poem quoted (*Im Grase*), a disturbance occurs that illustrates this point:

> Wenn im Busen die Toten dann,
> Jede Leiche sich streckt und regt,
> Leise, leise den Odem zieht . . .

While a general term like *die Toten* does not give offence, *Leichen* (corpses) as stretching and heaving within the bosom, are felt as too corporeal, destroying the poetic illusion: a wrong 'value', not attuned to the atmosphere created by the poem.

Rilke, in his central period, had acquired a very delicate sense of word values, and his *Neue Gedichte* are masterpieces of a dense, uniformly though not monotonously woven word texture. Various means and devices are now at the poet's disposal to reveal 'cette âme qui apparaît au contact d'autres mots': first, on the negative side, we note the absence of a rapidly progressing movement, supported by a wealth of active verbs in the indicative mood; on the positive side, his words are bound together by accumulations of related vowel sounds and by assonances, while alliteration takes care of the consonants. The frequency of adjectives and participles contributes to density and heaviness, and repetition, rhyme, the poet's peculiar syntax with its clauses and subjunctives, as well as a slow tempo, do the rest. Yet such methods are not infallible in themselves; a fine feeling for values is needed to keep words constantly attuned not only to each other, but also to the structure and flow of the poem that exist prior to these devices, and are partly independent of them.

Since the dense texture of heavy language relies on such a delicate balance of values, represented mainly by words, the principal danger for the poet handling it must consist in lapses from the standard he has himself established. In view of this ever-present danger, it is the more remarkable how firmly Rilke has in hand the numerous devices he commands. If we compare his words to musical notes, in his over-sensitive style a word that was only a quarter-note wrong would immediately cause a disturbance, while in the fast flowing, unconnected style even a wrong half-note might pass unnoticed. We can read the whole of *Neue Gedichte* without ever being aware of a misplaced or discordant word. C. M. Bowra points out the incongruity of one of Rilke's similes:

> The image of hair pulled from the armpit is disgusting in itself and quite inadequate to the sense of loss which pervades the rest of the poem . . . it is hard not to ascribe this failure in taste to his very sensibility.[1]

It is evident that the simile in question, speaking not of hair from the armpit only, but of pubic hair as well, leads deliberately towards the sexual sphere; the poet obviously wishes to bring out that part of David's lament where he says: 'Thy love to me was wonderful, passing the love of woman'. The question in this connection, however, is not whether we approve of this particular image or not, but whether the texture of the poem is disturbed by the admittedly daring and unusual simile:

> Irgendein Fremder sollte dich zerstören,
> und der dir innig war, ist nichts dabei
> und muss sich halten und die Botschaft hören;
> wie wunde Tiere auf den Lagern löhren,
> möcht ich mich legen mit Geschrei:
>
> denn da und da, an meinen scheusten Orten,
> bist du mir ausgerissen wie das Haar,
> das in den Achselhöhlen wächst und dorten,
> wo ich ein Spiel für Frauen war,
> bevor du meine dort verfitzten Sinne
> aufsträhntest, wie man einen Knaul entflicht;
> da sah ich auf und wurde deiner inne:—
> jetzt aber gehst du mir aus dem Gesicht.   (III, 127–8)

We may not wish to follow Rilke all the way, we may disapprove with Dr. Bowra; but within the verbal system of the poem, the transition is perfect, and there is no discord.

This word harmony within the heavy style is the more remarkable as Rilke's vocabulary is vast, containing a surprising number of unusual, rare and foreign words, also words of his own making, paraphrases in similes like the one just dealt with, etc. The mastery

---

[1] *The Heritage of Symbolism*, p. 70.

acquired with *Neue Gedichte* is never lost, it persists through all of Rilke's later work, with occasional slight lapses only in those poems he did not publish during his lifetime.

Diction

> Die armen Worte, die im Alltag darben,
> die unscheinbaren Worte, lieb ich so.[1]
> Aus meinen Fenstern schenk ich ihnen Farben,
> da lächeln sie und werden langsam froh.   (I, 260)

Rilke published these lines in 1899. Yet turning over the leaves of the volume in which they are printed, we encounter on every page words like *Silberschwingen, Liedintervalle, Monstranz, Rosenerben, Aureolenglanz, Purpurzelte, Madonnenschein, hellgesellt, herbstverhangen* and many more of this kind. If Rilke's alleged love of simple words was more 'wishful thinking' than fact then, it was not to become reality at a later stage either. His language lacks the popular simplicity, that direct, natural utterance of speech that springs from a close union of the poet with the people or with a popular tradition. This trait he shares with the poets not only of his own, but also of a previous generation; Mörike was perhaps the last great lyrical poet in Germany to enjoy the immense advantage of such a tradition. When Rilke started writing, poetry had, for a considerable time, been dependent on a language which, if it cannot be called wholly artificial, was nevertheless cut off from the life-giving forces that well up from the deep springs of a homely tradition. It had been living on a great past, and thoughtlessly squandering a good part of that noble legacy, until Liliencron swept away the false accents with the power of his unfettered naturalness, while Stefan George, with intention and effort, and Hofmannsthal, with seemingly effortless ease, led German poetic language back to the purity of its fountain heads. These poets were able to purify the language to a certain extent, but it was beyond their powers to restore to it all the youthful vitality it had lost during the nineteenth century.

Goethe's range extended from the simple language of the *Volkslied* to the sublimity of his philosophical poetry in the second part of *Faust*; Mörike could write *Schön-Rothraut* and *Das verlassene Mägdlein* as well as *Peregrina* and *Um Mitternacht*. Storm retains some of the popular accents, while in Hebbel's, Droste-Hülshoff's, C. F. Meyer's lyrics they are on the wane; Liliencron has them again, if

---

[1] In the first version: die zagen, blassen Worte.

on a narrower and different scale, but his manner was so personal that no tradition could be founded on it, although he influenced many of his contemporaries. Hofmannsthal has popular undertones, due partly to his Austrian milieu, where the connection between poetry and popular tradition had never been wholly severed, partly to his close affinity with Goethe's lyric poetry. George lacks these undertones and was dependent on a somewhat stilted poetic language of his own creation.

That was the general situation in Germany and Austria when Rilke begun writing his first verse, and like all serious-minded poets of his generation, he had to carve out his own path which was beset with dangers and pitfalls. If he did not succeed in avoiding all of them, it is nevertheless remarkable how soon he began moving consciously in a given direction, and with what single-minded tenacity he followed it. Among several tasks he set himself in 1904 (hardly any of which he accomplished), was that of reading in Grimm's famous dictionary of the German language:

... das Lesen in dem grossen deutschen Wörterbuche der Gebrüder Grimm, daraus einem Schreibenden, wie mir schien, viel Zufluss und Belehrung kommen kann. Denn eigentlich müsste man doch alles, was in die Sprache einmal einge-treten ist und da ist, kennen und zu brauchen wissen, statt mit dem Zufallsvorrat, der gering genug ist und ohne Auswahl, auskommen zu wollen.[1]

Here we have the rare and remarkable case of a poet endeavouring to study his own language historically in order not to be dependent on the 'accidental store' of words otherwise at his disposal: another proof of the young Rilke's lack of assurance and spontaneity, his repressed and self-conscious attitude at that period. For the 'accidental-store' of words served most poets very well, as it probably served Rilke too, in spite of his misgivings. We do not know which words in his vocabulary he owes to his reading of Grimm's dic-tionary, but it is a safe guess that they were not many, and mostly those with an archaic ring he uses in poems with medieval settings only.

His earliest language, far from being markedly original, is as varied as it is unselective, and contains a surprisingly large number of words belonging to the insincere style commonly called *Gold-schnittlyrik*, words like *traun, just, wahrlich, traut; Bronnen, Stübchen, Lenz, Wonne, Dirne, Mädel; Blondköpfchen, Bräutchen, Frauchen, Mütterchen, Grossmütterchen; Stimmung, Zauber, Erotik, Brunnen-poesie, Dörfchen, Häuschen, Strassenkapellchen; plauschen, liebeln,*

[1] *Briefe aus den Jahren 1902 bis 1906*, 1930. Brief 62, p. 157.

blinken, gucken, erlauschen, verdämmern, umzittern. Composite words are popular and conspicuous at this period: *Goldgeglast, Lichtgeglänze, Silberhobelspäne, Madonnenhände, Blätterleichenschau, Rhythmenzittern, Quellenquirlen, Sterbestundenstille, Dämmerdustgeschwel* and the monster *Götterbildermarmorweisse.* Combinations of words are in the same poetic vein: *ein blondes Glück, silberne Kiele, des Schmerzes Eisenreif, atlasblasse Abendmeere, das schwüle Stadtgebrause, die moderne Bauschablone, in prunkenden Gebreiten, purpurbunte Einsamkeiten.* This lengthy list of words, all culled from the first volume of the Collected Works, and showing the very young poet's superficial imagery and inebriation with words, is given as a contribution of some interest for the study of Rilke's development: it testifies to his delight in creating and combining words rich in associations in what was then considered to be 'poetic language', though in most cases they were ready-made clichés only, or at best clichés made to order in imitation of existing ones. Rilke soon abandoned this youthful style, already in *Frühe Gedichte* words like those quoted above are much rarer than in the preceding collections, and in *Buch der Bilder* and the poems that follow very little is left of them.

Buch der Bilder is characterized by the simultaneous display of the rich and the austere style, the former prevailing in the cycle *Die Zaren*, the latter in that called *Die Stimmen*. It is obvious that Rilke had some difficulty in getting rid of a tendency towards ornateness; we cannot help feeling that the ornate style with its crushing wealth of epithets, metaphors, painting nouns and composite adjectives came more naturally to him than the austere, at times slightly forced, simplicity of *Die Stimmen*. Two examples from the collection will show the difference:

> das grosse gibt dem Mutterantlitz Raum,
> und rechts und links hebt eine mandelschmale
> Jungfrauenhand sich aus dem Silbersaum. (II, 104)

Four long composite words, in addition to enjambment, long period, forced word order, are typical for these lines from *Die Zaren*. Set against this *Das Lied des Trinkers*, from *Die Stimmen*:

> Es war nicht in mir. Es ging aus und ein.
> Da wollt ich es halten. Da hielt es der Wein.
> (Ich weiss nicht mehr, was es war.) (II, 124)

Here we have main sentences only of the simplest construction, no adjectives, all words, except *halten*, of one syllable only.

A mannerism Rilke shares with other poets of the period is a preference for uncommon plurals like *Herzensfinsternisse, Sehn-süchte, Fürstenmunde, Vergangenheiten, Resonanzen, Brünste, Parke* and others. In the *Stundenbuch* we encounter *Traurigkeiten, Alltage, Ängste, kleine Glücke*, and even in the later poem such plurals are not totally abandoned.

In the *Stundenbuch*, Rilke's diction has become much simpler. Remnants of his ornate style are found in words like *Harfendämmerungen, Samtsandale, der Schönumscharte, tönende Vertröster*, but they are relatively few and do not determine the vocabulary, which now avoids decorative and ostentatious display. On the other hand, the *Stundenbuch* is not economical with words. Periphrasis and circumlocution are features of its style: Rilke does not seek the precise word, but endeavours to express a wealth of meaning by using a great number of related words, which appear one behind the other like hills in a range of mountains:

> Nach jedem Sonnenuntergange
> bin ich verwundet und verwaist,
> ein blasser allem Abgelöster
> und ein Verschmähter jeder Schar,
> und alle Dinge stehn wie Klöster,
> in denen ich gefangen war.
> Dann brauch ich dich, du Eingeweihter,
> du sanfter Nachbar jeder Not,
> du meines Leidens leiser Zweiter,
> du Gott, dann brauch ich dich wie Brot. (II, 233)

Sometimes each word in such a sequence is heavy with its own meaning:

> Weinberg, Weide, alter Apfelgarten,
> Acker, der kein Frühjahr überschlägt,
> Feigenbaum . . . (II, 217)

This is not, as the reader might assume, a cumulative succession of words as in the previous example; each of these nouns had a special meaning for Rilke: the vineyard was connected with an experience in Italy, the pasture with Russia, the apple orchard with Sweden, the field with Germany, the fig tree with Capri. Unless he has made a study of the poet's life and letters, the reader will hardly be able to understand these underlying associations, yet he may sense the weightiness of such a sequence of words, their impregnation with emotional experience.

The vocabulary of *Neue Gedichte* is varied and rich; it embraces simple and elaborate, even sophisticated, words, and welds these elements together into a homogeneous style. In his central period, nouns and verbs are the main features of Rilke's diction. If the appropriate noun is not found in the language, Rilke creates it from a verb or an adjective. Infinitives used as nouns, already found in previous collections, are now very numerous:

dieses Nichtmehrfassen	
sein ängstliches Sich-Niederlassen	(III, 51)
das Dunkelsein der Kathedralen	(III, 38)
mit jenem Äussersten von Sein und Neigen,	
Hinhalten, Niemals-Gebenkönnen, Dastehn ...	
Raum-brauchen ... fast nicht Umrissen-sein	(III, 110)
ihr frühes Hingegebensein	(III, 156)
das Lichterniedertreiben,	(III, 220)

and these from adjectives:

das Plötzliche der Köpfe	(III, 39)
das Ungemässe	(III, 16)
ihr namenloses Rosa	(III, 112)
Grün wirklicher Grüne.	(III, 63)

The last quotation is a good instance of Rilke's power to imbue and transform words: in isolation, *Grün wirklicher Grüne* is not just uncommon, it sounds precious, but in their context the words lose every trace of affectation and become perfectly natural:

> Doch als du gingst, da brach in diese Bühne
> ein Streifen Wirklichkeit durch jenen Spalt,
> durch den du hingingst: Grün wirklicher Grüne,
> wirklicher Sonnenschein, wirklicher Wald.   (III, 63)

As we enter the world of the *Elegies*, we sense a different atmosphere with entirely new constellations of words. Rilke's vocabulary has undergone a profound change: the main characteristic now is that we find a number of words constantly recurring. And words so different from those hitherto preferred by Rilke! Many are homely words, the old, old words of poetry, like *Herz*, *Mutter*, *Hand*, *Gesicht*, *Nacht*, *Stern*. Statistical methods cannot, as a rule, do justice to poetry, but it may be interesting to make deductions from the frequency of some words constantly recurring in the *Elegies*. Here is a selection of such words (the number indicates their frequency in the *Elegies*): *Herz* (23), *Engel* (18), *Liebende* (17), *Tod*, *Tote* (16), *rein* (13), *Gesicht*, *Angesicht*, *Antlitz* (12), *Raum*, *lieben* (12 each), *Hand*, *Sterne*, *Mutter*, *Nacht* (11 each), *Ding* (10), *Schicksal*, *Erde*, *Tier* (9 each), *Glück*, *Jüngling*, *Mädchen* (8 each),

Geliebte, Dasein (7 each), *Kind, Vogel, Gefühl* (6 each), *Baum, Lächeln, Vater, Blut, Tag, Frühling, Gott (Götter), Held* (5 each). With the exception of *rein* (which will be dealt with in detail with the adjective) and *lieben*, all these words are nouns; they are plain words of the type that stand for much, embodying a wealth of common human experience and therefore of poetic associations. Yet if we look more closely at some of these words, we find that in Rilke's mouth they are less simple than they appear: they have become imbued with special meanings peculiar to the poet, and to him alone; his emotions and experiences have, to some extent, been superimposed on them. The most obvious of those words is, of course, *Engel*, used by Rilke in a very personal meaning, not always easy to understand; another is *Raum*, very different in these poems from its conventional use in German poetry (*wenn über mir im blauen Raum verloren* — Faust); in the *Elegies*:

> Wirf aus den Armen die Leere
> zu den Räumen hinzu, die wir atmen . . .   (III, 260)

> weil mir der Raum in eurem Angesicht,
> da ich ihn liebte, überging in Weltraum . . .   (III, 276)

Moreover, words like *Mädchen, Ding, Erde, Tier, Kind*, are iridescent with added meanings. Other words have successfully resisted such changes: *Mutter, Sterne, Nacht, Baum, Haus, Hand* retain their age-old meanings without associative values.

In spite of their frequent recurrence, the plain words are not dominant in the diction of the *Elegies*, being offset by words and phrases of a subtler, more involved nature. But they permeate, with their recurrent motives, the texture of these poems, adding to it strength, simplicity, greatness.

The old, plain words have a similar part in the *Sonnets*. *Engel*, being peculiar to the *Elegies*, occurs only once in the *Sonnets*, and then in its more conventional sense; for the other words, the frequency is: *Tod, Tote* (14), *Herz, Gott, rein* (13 each), *Erde, Baum, Ohr* (8 each), *Mädchen* (7), *Raum* (5), *Schicksal* (4). A greater harmony reigns in the *Sonnets* between these homely words and the rest of their vocabulary. A few foreign words—*Metarmophose, Apparate, Antennen, polyphon, transparent* and others—act as foils, and a number of compound words, purely descriptive, are not felt as contrasting, or if so, rather in a stimulating sense— *Bruderzorn, Rosseblut, Himmelsstillen, Knabenstolz, Doppelbereich, Frühlings-schleier*, etc. In the great economy of these poems, all words become weightier, fraught with meaning and associations, and this is true of every category of word.

Letzte Gedichte contain many new words and phrases. Their diction is in part experimental: Rilke attempted to express new thoughts and experiences, and this led him to invention and novel word combinations. While the neologisms will be dealt with in a special chapter, we will quote here a few of the novel idioms and combinations created by Rilke:

> an gestern begonnenem Fenster   (III, 406)
>
> Es rauscht
> Wind ihres Aufgangs im Laub seines Leibes.   (III, 411)
>
> jenes grüne Gefülltsein der schönen Bäume   (S.G., 146)
>
> stand ohne Geländer, Eigentümer der Schmerzen...
>   (S.G., 20)
>
> blinder Bissen wölbt sich ohne Gröbe.   (S.G., 128)

Foreign Words

For centuries the use of foreign words had been a spiny problem in German language and literature. It was felt as a patriotic duty by many German poets and writers to avoid these foreign elements like the plague. Even Goethe, not a chauvinist, under the influence of Herder, in 1773 and again in 1787, purged his *Götz* (1771) of foreign—mostly French—words, replacing even *Papa* by *Vater*; later, he invents *Einhelfer* for *Souffleur*, uses *geviert* for *quadratisch*. Schiller, in his *Braut von Messina*, translates *Piedestal* with *Fussgestell des Ruhmes* (I, 7, 801). Gottfried Keller, in his revision of *Der grüne Heinrich*, rejects a great number of foreign words, and in this connection replaces *Bonbons* with *Zuckerzeug*, *gratis* with *Dreingabe*; Liliencron invents monstrosities like *Flachgespräch* for *causerie* (how much better is Rilke's translation, *Geplauder*! S.G., 124), *Sicherhafen* for *Asyl*.[1] Rilke not only does not share his compatriots' prejudice in this matter, he even introduces foreign words where their German equivalents had long been established. Perhaps his Austrian milieu and upbringing had something to do with this insouciance; to this day, Austrian aristocrats express nuances by using otherwise slightly out-of-date French or Latin words like *desparat* or *ridikül*.

Of his contemporaries, only Stefan George resembles Rilke in this unconcern about the foreign word, although the number em-

---

[1] Quoted from O. Weise, *Ästhetik der deutschen Sprache*, 5 Aufl., 1923.

ployed by him is much smaller, and he rarely equals Rilke's skill in handling them. In his early period, when the associative and musical qualities of words attracted him, Rilke indulges in a lavish and often uncritical use of foreign words of all kinds. In a single short poem in *Larenopfer* he has (perhaps influenced by the monologue in *Faust?*), *Skolar, Pandekten, Theologie, Medizin, Alma Mater, Prachtregister, Magister* (I, 52). *Im Kreuzgang von Loretto*, in the same collection, contains *Säulenarabesken, Fresken, Heilmirakel, Tabernakel,* as well as the names *Loretto* and *Tintoretto* (I, 32). In other early poems we encounter the words *Diphtherie, Gouvernante, Tramway, Mietskaserne, parzellieren.* Words of a more decorative character are *Katafalk, Monstranz, Serale, Syringen.* In *Buch der Bilder* we find, among others, *Resonanzen, Devisen, Draperien, Violinen, Diät, sakrosankt;* in the *Stundenbuch, Levite, Blasphemie, Drama, Fabrik, Scharlatan, Theologe, Gamme, Monogramm, Kultur, Fieberkrise, Embryo*—most of these words, startling as some of them may appear in isolation, are very naturally embedded in the flow of the language, and carried away on it without causing a whirl or a break. For it is not the use of the foreign word in itself that is important, but the way it is introduced into the fabric of the poet's language without producing a disturbing friction. In this respect, Rilke reveals himself as an accomplished master in *Neue Gedichte*, where the great number of foreign words, many never before used by a German poet, have the mission of supplying the precise term, a specific colour, or the needed nuance. Without showing a marked preference for the foreign term, Rilke never hesitates to use it when accuracy of expression or the necessity for a subtle shade seem to call for it. If this necessity arises more frequently for him than for most of his contemporaries, it is because his poetry is more precise, more delicately coloured, and lastly because Rilke is no linguistic purist, and intolerant of any restriction coming from an outside agency. What interests the student of his style is whether these un-German words stand out as foreign elements, or whether the poet succeeds in amalgamating them in his poetic language. In the great majority of cases, we accept Rilke's foreign words as natural and legitimate, it may even happen that we hardly notice he is using a word that hitherto had not been at home in the language. Thus, *Dekor des Sommertags* is felt as happily appropriate in *Béguinage* (III, 88), as likewise *deines Herzens Initial* in *Klage um Jonathan* (III, 127); *Trireme* is both natural and necessary in *Delphine* (III, 121), and even as daring a neologism as *Fermen*, from the French *ferme,* does not give offence in *Römische Kampagna* (III, 189). *Das Chrys-elephantine*, certainly a far-fetched and very ornamental word, has a legitimate place in *Die Marienprozession*: the term forcibly expresses the exotic and precious loveliness of the image borne in the procession:

> Die Böschung Schauender unschliesst die Schiene,
> in der das alles stockt und rauscht und rollt:
> das Kommende, das Chryselephantine,
> aus dem sich zu Balkonen Baldachine
> aufbäumen, schwankend im Behang von Gold.   (III, 91–2)

Rilke uses French words without restraint and makes us feel that they are almost as familiar to him as German ones, so that their avoidance or translation might have seemed more artificial than their use. We note, among others: *estaminets, monseigneur, tapis-vert, avenue, venerie, train, clavecin, contreforts, bibelots, jabot, fragile.*

Accuracy of expression, it was said, sometimes calls for the foreign word. Thus the phrase *ihre Hände liegen im Konkreten* (III, 165), said of the quiet moments enjoyed by the insane, admir-ably gives the precise suggestion, just as the combination *willig, primitiv,* in the preceding poem (III, 163), is as natural and unobtru-sive as it is expressive: the German and the foreign adjective are bound together by sense as well as by sound (the only vowel they contain is '*i*'). A similar combination is *offen und konkav,* which we feel as indispensable to Rilke's description of the poppy (III, 235). In other instances, the foreign word contributes the exact shade just because it has a foreign ring, and therefore no German word could possibly approach it in suggestiveness. *Fatal* is such a word, which, preceded by *Marionetten, Waldskelette, General, Galeeren, Arsenal,* in the magnificent combination *strahlend und fatal,* brings the poem *Spätherbst in Venedig* (III, 204) to its apt climax. In a similar way, *Triumphator* is the keyword in *Der Marmorkarren* (III, 77), *die Pendüle* a necessary accessory in *Der Junggeselle* (III, 244), *in privater Wehmut* delicately and accurately expressive in *Das Bett* (III, 230).

The cases where such words remain foreign in an irritating sense, where we feel they are not fully incorporated in the language of the poem, are the exceptions that confirm Rilke's habitual felicity in the handling of this difficult material. Many readers will think that *elegante Pseudonyme* (III, 198), although very apt, would perhaps be more appropriate in a prose essay than in a lyric, and likewise that *in dem Kostüme eines Schmerzes*, and *hingerissen von enormen Stürmen* (III, 159), if intentionally painted in glaring theatrical hues, are neither wholly convincing nor strike us as being in good taste. And *vertönende Theorbe*, to rhyme with *Räucherkorbe* (S.G., 18) reminds us unfavourably of Rilke's early efforts.

The vogue of foreign words, which reached a climax in *Neue Gedichte*, subsides in the *Elegies*, where they are much rarer; we may mention *attische Stelen* (III, 267), *Kontur des Fühlens, Scenerie* (III, 274), *Modistin* (III, 282), *Pylone* (III, 291). In *Sonnets to Orpheus*, the most significant are *wachsende Apparate* (III, 335) and *Antennen* (*Die Antennen fühlen die Antennen*, III, 324). From the context—*die leere Ferne trug*—it is clear that Rilke speaks of wireless antennae, and the passage is another instance of the pure, unforced naturalness with which the poet makes use of a modern technical term (in 1922, a wireless antenna was not as familiar as it is to-day), if it suits his purpose. (A similar case occurs in *Späte Gedichte*, 97: *Glaubt nicht, dass die längsten Transmissionen | schon des Künftigen Räder drehn*). There is no display in it, nothing of the pose of being up-to-date and progressive that sometimes disturbs us in the work of other poets; Rilke uses *Antennen* naïvely, as he would use any other fitting metaphor, and this accounts for the conviction the passage carries. The sonnets also contain examples of Rilke's happy faculty of assimilating particularly sonorous foreign words without making them sound pompous or affected:

> Errichtet keinen Denkstein. Lasst die Rose
> nur jedes Jahr zu seinen Gunsten blühn.
> Denn Orpheus ists. Seine Metarmophose
> in dem und dem.   (III, 317)

> Blumenmuskel, der der Anemone
> Wiesenmorgen nach und nach erschliesst,
> bis in ihren Schooss das polyphone
> Licht der lauten Himmel sich ergiesst . . .   (III, 345)

The poet's skill in handling these difficult words does not only achieve that they blend perfectly with the German ones, so different in sound and character, but that the two kinds react upon each other, enhancing their respective effectiveness by contrast. The full associative and musical content of the Greek words in the lines quoted is brought out, and yet they do not give the impression of being isolated, they seem to come from a source not so very far removed from the German words. In the daring and exquisite passage *das polyphone Licht der lauten Himmel*, no other word perhaps could give the note of fullness and colour. Rilke is not afraid of placing these foreign words in exposed positions by using them for rhymes: in making *Metarmophose* rhyme with *Rose*, which, although not of German origin, has become a homely German word, he approaches the two words to each other, creates a bridge between them. The repeated use of the Greek name Orpheus in the sonnet is another device for making *Metarmophose* appear less isolated. In addition, Rilke creates phonetic analogies by using full-sounding German words like *Rosenschale, Blumenmuskel, Schooss, Ruhewink, Blätterränder*.

Späte Gedichte contain a great number of foreign words. It cannot be gainsaid that generally they blend well with the tone of these poems, but since their style is sometimes cramped and not free of a certain artificial coloration, the final effect is not invariably as happy and convincing as in *Neue Gedichte*. While words like *Voluten, Kabel, Transmissionen* cause no break, others are sometimes a trifle far-fetched and heavily scented, like

als gingen sie durch Lüfte, durch Porphyr	(S.G., 41)
der aride verbrannte Mund	(S.G., 79)
die Amöbe	(S.G., 128)

Names

From foreign words it is but a step to names. R. L. Stevenson says: 'None can care for literature itself who do not take a special pleasure in the sound of names'.[1] Rilke uses them freely, with the same insouciance he shows when introducing foreign words, and with the same purpose: to illuminate the poem with a particular light, to provide a shade only a name, only this name, could supply. A significant example is found in the first line of *Die Flamingos*:

In Spiegelbildern wie von Fragonard . . .,   (III, 236)

where the French painter's name provides colour as well as sound: it evokes certain delicate and voluptuous colour schemes, and moreover its long *a–o–a* is a soft and rich vowel sequence hardly to be found in another word, let alone a German one. (The whole vowel sequence of the line is of the most melodious: i–i–e–i–e–i–o–a–o–a). Later in the same poem, another name occurs, that of *Phryne*, and again it is the seductive association of the classical name as well as the long *ü*-sound that prompted the poet's choice.

---

[1] Quoted by Carlos Baker. Hemingway, the writer as artist, 1952, p. 50.

Both names are used in similes, both are uncommon enough to strike
the reader as unexpected, yet before there is time for more than a
faint surprise, they have already been accepted as part of the very
specific language of the poem. In other instances, names, always
coupled with their sound values, contribute local colour, as the
musical *San Giorgio Maggiore* in *Venezianischer Morgen* (III, 203), or
the string of Russian names (*Orloff, Newa-Quai, Ljetnij Ssad*) in
Nächtliche Fahrt (III, 191), while *Ispahan oder Schiras* (III, 366) is
evocative of the splendours of exotic gardens. Sometimes the name,
without being resounding, serves as a qualifying term, almost like
an adjective, as in the passage *unter Bäume wie von Dürer* (III, 248),
or *kleine Tage wie bei Patenier* (III, 84). Like many a poet before
him, Rilke also makes use of the suggestiveness of classical names
such as *Tullia* (*Es war Tullias Dunkelheit*, III, 207), *Meroë* (*warfen
sie aus ihren Herzen / immer wieder Meroë*, III, 153), *Daphne* (*die
verwandelte Daphne*, III, 355), *Eurydike* (*sei immer tot in Eurydike*,
III, 356), *Heloise* (*dass sie wachsend Heloisen / überstehn und überschrein*,
III, 216). The name of Orpheus is a case apart: it pervades the
Sonnets to Orpheus as an ever recurring magical invocation, symboliz-
ing the perpetual presence of the God of song: 'For in the utterance
of a name is power, creative, possessive power'.[1]

In the poem *Auferstehung* Christian names contribute to period
colour, with the date added as on a tombstone:

> und warten nur noch auf Erich
> und Ulriken Dorotheen
> die sieben- und dreizehnjährig
> (sechzehnhundertzehn)
> verstorben sind in Flandern . . .   (III, 72)

Names in the *Elegies* are of a more intimate character, the
majority being closely related to the poet's deepest experiences.
It may be felt that at least some of these names are perhaps too
personal, lacking in universal appeal and fully intelligible only to
those who have made a close study of the author's life. *Gaspara
Stampa* is such a name, occurring in the First Elegy, as likewise
die Tafel in Santa Maria Formosa, and the ancient mythical hero
Linos. In other elegies, we encounter *Tage Tobiae*, with its obsolete
biblical genitive, *August der Starke, Chartres, Bilder von Karnak,
Seele der Etrusker* and, most startling of all, in the Tenth Elegy,
hinter dem Pschent-Rand hervor.

[1] G. H. W. Rylands, *Words and Poetry*, 1928, p. 79.

K

The names of flowers in Rilke's poems deserve special mention. His love of precision is admirably documented by the use of these names which are rarely vague (and then with some reason), but generally very specific. He never names his flowers at random, relying on their inherent poetical associations, as other poets not infrequently do (e.g. Stefan George, who mentions together, as if they flowered at the same time, *Rosen* and *Mimosen*, or *Rosen* and *Violen*). In Rilke's poems, each flower named is organic: it is the flower of the period, of the season, of the place and lastly of the poem itself, in which its name must have the right colour and sound. But he does not invariably feel the need to be specific, and sometimes deems the general term more appropriate:

> Hinter ihr . . .
> erhoben sich . . . die Blumen und die Halme . . .   (III, 109)
>
> der Blüten leichte Schenkung   (III, 436)
>
> zwischen die Blumen, gegenüber dem Himmel.   (III, 422)

In most cases, however, the correct and suggestive name of the flower or plant is given, often a rare or unusual one: *der Zauber von Erdrauch und Raute* (III, 318) is suggestive of the dead; the flower the poet finds in a Roman sarcophagus—and which could be more homely and remote at the same time, which more poetical?—is *Bienensaug* (III, 322); of the poor, the poet says

> sie duften wie Melissen,
> und ihre Blätter sind gezackt und zart: (II, 284)

Melissen occur again in *Schlaflied*:

> . . . mit einer Masse
> von Melissen und Sternanis;   (III, 238)

a meadow in an early poem is covered with *Klee, Löwenzahn, Schierling* (I, 148); *Astern, Berberitzen* occur in an autumn poem in the *Stundenbuch* (II, 263). A simile in *Die weisse Fürstin* is rather startling:

> Ihre Hälse waren
> wie Stengel von Rhabarber, stimmenstrotzend.   (I, 383)

The tree from which Absalom is found hanging is specified as *die Terebinthe* (III, 139); the flowers in *Die Sonnenuhr* are *Majoran und Koriander* (III, 234). A smile is likened to a tuberose (III, 201); *Jasmingeruch* is introduced in *Übung am Klavier* (III, 222), *abgestandener Jasmin* in *Die Parke* (III, 200). The flower the boy is crushing in his fingers is *eine Blüte des Konvulvulus* (S.G., 114). At the end of the Tenth Elegy, we read

> . . . sie zeigten vielleicht auf die Kätzchen der leeren
> Hasel, die hängenden . . . (III, 308)

The word for *Hasel* had first been *Weide*, but when Rilke found out that willow catkins do not hang, he changed his manuscript accordingly. Here is what he writes to a correspondent in this connection:[1]

> Es gibt also keine 'hängenden' Weidenkätzchen . . . Die Gedichtstelle, die ich auf die sachliche Richtigkeit hin kontrollieren wollte, steht und fällt damit, dass der Leser, mit dem *ersten* Gefühl, gerade dieses *Fallende* der Kätzchen ergreife und auffasse, sonst verliert das dort gebrauchte Bild allen Sinn. Es muss also die durchaus typische Erscheinung dieses Blütenstandes aufgerufen werden . . . Ich weiss also, was ich wissen musste, und vertausche im Text 'Weide' gegen 'Hasel'.

Of course, these investigations were not made for the sake of botanical, but of poetical accuracy; as Rilke points out in his letter, he wishes the reader to have the right image. It is typical for Rilke that, in another simile, he does not speak of a bird that has flown off a tree, but specifies, although the image of just a bird flying off a tree might have been sufficient in this instance:

> . . . vielleicht ein Pflaumenbaum,
> von dem ein Kuckuck hastig abgeflogen. (III, 62)

By naming both tree and bird, Rilke infuses colour into the image.

In addition, we have the poems dealing wholly with flowers, as *Blaue Hortensie*, *Rosa Hortensie*, *Der Schlafmohn*, *Persisches Heliotrop*, the anemone (*Sonnets*, II, 5), and the poet's favourite flower, the rose, sung in *Sonnets*, II, 6, in *Die Rosenschale*, *Das Roseninnere*, the French cycle *Les roses*, as well as in a great number of similes and allusions.

Neologisms

It is the poet's prerogative to coin new words; from times immemorial poets have not been content with the existing vocabulary, even in new meanings and arrangements, but have boldly created new words where the old ones would not serve their purpose. And dwelling near the source of language, the poet is entitled to such creation, which has often permanently enriched the language. In this word-creation he will naturally meet with many limitations, imposed by his desire to be understood, by good taste,

---

[1] Letter to E. Aman-Volkart, June, 1922.

a consideration for what the language will tolerate. The successful test of the new word is that it is accepted, at least within the poem where it occurs. It may well be felt as new, but such novelty must be integrated into the language at large as well as into the specific language of the poem. This postulation is often disregarded, especially by poets who create their new words on intellectual considerations, and with a conscious challenge: such words will not be confined to a particular poem, but occur again and again. An instance is Stefan George's *Ewe*, coined from the adjective *ewig*, and used in the meaning of an epoch, a word he employs in poetry as well as prose; another is *Denkbild*, loaned from the Dutch, a translation of *Idee*, of Greek origin. New words of this kind, we feel, lack spontaneity: they are the outcome of thought or contain a programme; something intentional clings to them and often makes them unpoetic. A word like *Sterbling* (mortal), also created by George, if free of such intellectual origin, will not be readily accepted because it evokes the association of something contemptible by the analogy with words like *Wüstling*, *Feigling*, *Rohling*. New words are dangerous ground, and their creation is a severe test not only for a poet's creative power, but for his taste and tact as well.

A poet will hardly ever be able to invent a new word outright, for it would be unintelligible; he must make use of analogy and of existing words in new combinations, making a verb out of a noun, a noun from an adjective, a compound word from two words or a word and a prefix or ending. Goethe was great in creating such composite words, which seemed to form most naturally on his lips, many to enrich the language permanently (*Blütentraum*, *Morgenglanz*, *Lebensglut*, *Liebeswonne*), others to serve as examples for similar formations (*Bruderquelle*, *Gipfelgang*, *Frühlingstritt*, *wälder-wärts*, *feuchtverklärt*, *wärmefühlend*, *wellenatmend*, *jünglingsfrisch*). We noted that such composite words were a mannerism of the young Rilke, and as if consciously on his guard against these tempting and facile forms in his later work, he uses them very sparingly after *Buch der Bilder*. Those he produces are more descriptive than ornamental, like *schwergesässig* (III, 144), *Marktfrucht* (III, 281), *küsselos* (III, 18) or contractions on a logical basis: *Herzraum*, *Herzwerk* (III, 462), while a few are poetical in the traditional way, yet moderate in effect, like *abendklar* (III, 86), *blick-verschwenderisch* (III, 183), *mädchenhändig* (III, 320), *winterwährig* (III, 302). Such composite words are almost exceptional in Rilke's later production, when most of his neologisms start from a different basis. One of his ways is making adjectives out of nouns by adding an appropriate ending, mostly *ig*: *gemütig* (III, 460), *traumig* (III, 119), *blumig, schwungig* (III, 281), *torig* (III, 349), *knabig* (S.G., 100). We feel these words as new, but in a refreshing way, and accept them without difficulty in their context: *Rühms mit blumiger, schwungiger Aufschrift* (III, 281)—this gives an immediate picture of the script on old apothecary's jars, we might say the two adjectives imitate that script in their expressive quaintness. Other new adjectives are formed with the ending *lich*:

seliglich	(II, 317)
rühmlich	(III, 319)
krönlich	(III, 306, 419)
frühlinglich	(II, 116)
säglich	(III, 364)
beschämlich.	(III, 386)

Others, less unusual, take the ending *bar*:

rufbar	(III, 346)
mitfühlbar	(III, 406)
verbindbar.	(III, 467)

A few adjectives are formed by adding *e, en* or *isch*:

aprilen	(III, 466)
(this occurs also with Werfel):	
lorbeern	(III, 335)
sternisch	(III, 323)
antikisch.	(III, 322)

There are some endings in the language that may be added to almost any word; such an organic ending is *in*, used to transform a masculine noun into its feminine counterpart. Some words thus formed, however, have a very unusual ring, as Hölderlin's *Fremdlingin* in *Die Nacht*; Rilke, in analogy, forms *Übertrefferin* (S.G., 139), *Werferin* (III, 10), *Jünglingin* (III, 119) and, strangest of all, because coined from a neuter, *Gefühlin* (III, 287). Other unusual nouns obtained by endings are

Fühlung	(III, 325)
Rühmung	(III, 319, 320)
Hütung	(III, 394)
Angewöhner	(II, 240)
Vermöger	(III, 337)
Beschwerer	(III, 357)

The last word quoted, *Beschwerer*, existed in the language in the combination *Briefbeschwerer* (paper weight); it is not difficult to see the poet's need for the word: it is a poetical contraction for beings that impose their weight on everything:

> Da gehn wir umher wie Beschwerer,
> legen auf alles uns selbst, vom Gewichte entzückt. (III, 357)

Prefixes were used to form these neologisms:

Gequäl	(III, 39)
Getast	(II, 298; III, 143)
Genist	(III, 313)
Gerinn.	(III, 379)

A new word created in analogy to *Sintflut* is *Sintfeuer* (S.G., 80), another, shortened from *Inständigkeit*, *Instand* (III, 460) (compare Hopkins' 'inscape').

The separation of prefix from verb is often irksome to Rilke, and in such cases he contravenes the rules of grammar by leaving the two together, an innovation very peculiar to him, as it is but rarely found with other poets. Werfel has *hinström ich*, and similar forms are found in poems of the expressionistic school. The effect created by such irregular forms is one of compressed intensity, the verb appears much more compact, and this heightened energy, together with the startling novelty of the contraction, increases the impact:

ansing ich euch	(III, 264)
hinstürmte der Held	(III, 286)
und nun aufstand er	(III, 392)
überfloss sein Herz	(III, 402)
aufschau!	(III, 419)
wer vordenkts	(III, 394)
er anschaute knieend.	(III, 460)

Some new verbs are formed from nouns or adjectives:

sie klugte	(II, 297)
hinter ihr hurtigt das Blut	(III, 119)
er vermochte niemals . . . ihr abzuneinen	(III, 159)
der wellende Besatz	(III, 197)
die Landschaft finsterte hin	(III, 406)
das Grün verernstigt sich	(III, 455)
früht das Gefühl.	(III, 320)

Some of these new verbs are rendered acceptable by their context

only. A word like *verkeuschen*, e.g., positively ugly in isolation, is
not felt thus in the poem:

> Wie viele Griffe in das Leere
> hat reines Wasser wunderbar verkeuscht . . . (S.G., 112)

> bis sie ihres Auges Bleiche
> hinhalsend bergen in der eignen Weiche.   (III, 236)

The last quotation is a fine example of Rilke's art in creating a
new word where the poem requires it. *Hinhalsen*, of course, does
not exist in the language, and in the infinitive it sounds absurd,
although, in natural analogy to a word like *um-armen*, it is formed
by a prefix added to a noun. But used in the present participle
and in the context of the poem, the new word is so expressive and
blends so perfectly with the poem's word texture that its novelty
is overlooked: most readers will not even notice it as a new creation,
so naturally and effortlessly does it express the long, wavy movement of the flamingoes' necks.

A similar instance of the importance of a neologism is

> . . . und bald
> mondets empor . . .   (III, 306)

Here the new word, *mondet*, is above all an abbreviated metaphor:
in a single word, if expresses a sequence like 'looms up on the
horizon like the moon'. We cannot say, in this instance, that the
word is not felt as new: its very quaintness adds, is meant to add,
to the strange lunar landscape described. It is a perfect creation of
consummate art, reflected also in the sound: followed by *empor*,
it provides an accurate and lovely inverted symmetry of long
'*o*' and short '*e*', just as *hinhalsend*, with its two '*h*', added alliteration to its expressiveness of meaning. Rilke's new words of his
best period are embedded in the language as well as in the meaning
and sound texture of the poem; they are legitimate creations. In
one instance, Rilke uses a non-existing past tense, because he needs
the full u-sound:

> und es rufte im Abgrund;   (III, 385)

the obsolete weak tense here is not only justified, it becomes, for
its sound as well as for its quaintness, a poetic necessity, and the lines
acquire a strange expressiveness by it.

Archaisms

There is hardly a poet who does not make use of archaisms
now and then. Such lost or disused words almost invariably contain

something worth preserving which lives on in poetry, if nowhere else; moreover, they add colour, and a dimension stretching into the past. These very qualities make them also difficult to handle, for the colourfulness of archaic words, if overstressed, can cheapen a poem by dressing it up, as it were, in historical costume. Of Rilke's contemporaries, Stefan George is very fond of archaisms, which he uses in a slightly defiant manner, as if to challenge modern speech with their truer ring: he says *Fahr* for *Gefahr, Drusch, Kür, Kürung, Sende, Hornungschein, Mär, Zähre,* and such words, because of their planned and studied use, clearly stand out as archaic even in George's somewhat scented style. Rilke seeks to avoid this; his archaisms are neither frequent nor regularly recurring, and generally met with in poems with medieval themes only. Thus we encounter *Schauben und Hauben* in *Totentanz* (III, 146), *Helm und Haubert* in *Sankt Georg* (III, 217), *den erhobenen Henzen* in *Skizze zu einem Sankt Georg* (III, 379), *der dürren Haare Schelfe* in *Die ägyptische Maria* (III, 156), *tumb* and *Magenkraft* in *Legende von den heiligen drei Königen* (II, 75). If to this short list we add *gorer Abfall* (III, 398), *der er pflag* (III, 18), *Frauenzimmer* (III, 160), *im geelen Amber* (III, 181), *die duffen Tauben* (III, 193), we have practically exhausted the number of rare or archaic words used by Rilke; they provide the right touch of colour in the right place and are, in every instance, attuned to the poem as only Rilke's mature art and almost infallible ear could attune them.

The Adjective

Rilke's adjectives justify the attention often bestowed on the epithet as a particularly important element in poetic language. We can trace their evolution and changes as his language grows and develops. To a great extent, his earliest poems rely for their effect on a lavish use of adjectives which, with nouns and other words, share a somewhat superficial ornateness. The composite adjective is the poet's favourite at this period, as can be seen in creations like *goldsonnig, glückverschneit, märchenallein, sehnsuchtsblass, frühfrostfahl, hellgesellt, muttermatt, kinderkühl, frühlingfrierend*—most of these, if talented, artificial and lacking in taste. There are a few exceptions in the early poems, where the adjective is really qualifying:

kapellenloser Glaube	(I, 129)
mäuschenstille Plätze	(I, 131)
rotrote Blüten.	(I, 295)

We have seen that *Buch der Bilder* is the turning point for this early style. From now on the adjective becomes less frequent and is no longer employed to permeate a whole poem with colouring matter, but rather to supply specific dashes of colour wherever they are needed. The adjective has now become organic, it is an element in a structure, to be used sparingly and with discretion; this implies that it must lose its former heavy ornateness and become a qualifying term of graphic, expressive simplicity. It must, without altogether renouncing colourfulness, combine a maximum of precision and brevity. In *Buch der Bilder*, we still find a certain number of decorative, and even of compound adjectives: *die seidene Stille, das samtene Dunkel, die mandelschmale Hand, die hochbelohnten Ziele*; but these are much rarer now, and set off by more simply descriptive, if often emotionally charged, epithets:

mein armes, warmes Leben	(II, 19)
das durstlose Mädchen	(II, 28)
die mutige Erinnerung	(II, 115)
verkohlte westliche Wälder.	(II, 134)

The adjective is at approximately the same stage in the *Stundenbuch* where, besides rarer forms of the earlier period like *lichtzitternd, mailich*, we have very simple and expressive epithets:

wurzelhaftes Haar.	(II, 211)

and the very felicitous and beautiful

flugbereite Güte.	(II, 245)

The tendency towards a strictly testifying, clear and simple adjective is accentuated in *Neue Gedichte*, where forms like these are frequent:

seine leichten Hände	(III, 49)
ihr runder Tanz	(III, 82)
der ruhige Rubin	(III, 152)
ein leerer Morgen	(III, 170)
die glatten Traber.	(III, 191)

Another group of adjectives in the same collection is significant for the novel way in which they are combined with nouns to which they had never before been applied. Taken by themselves, these adjectives have nothing unusual, but when Rilke says

deine frühe Flanke	(III, 14)
warm wie dein Gedanke,	(III, 14)

the new and stimulating combination reflects happily and significantly on both adjective and noun. Other instances are:

ihr bunter Tod	(III, 74)
erlauchter Ausgang	(III, 75)
waches Violett	(III, 237)
windiges Licht	(III, 83)
der liebe Geruch	(III, 175)
deine nordische Erinnerung	(III, 179)
ohnmächtige Konturen	(III, 191)
der lautere und lichterlohe Engel	(III, 249)
die schuldlosen Bäume.	(III, 468)

Sometimes Rilke couples his adjectives for emphasis:

O du wilde weite Werferin	(III, 10)
ein unverwandtes warmes Land	(III, 24)
die schlanke adelige Uniform	(III, 69)
in dem schmalen langen harten Kinn	(III, 71)
alt, veraltet, ratlos	(III, 104)
ein dunkles unverwundnes grausames Etwas	(III, 62)
goldgetrieben, köstlich, vielkarätig.	(III, 151)

In *Das Karussell*, such coupling is employed to emphasize the rhythm:

ein kleines blaues Mädchen	
ein böser roter Löwe	
mit der kleinen heissen Hand	
dieses atemlose blinde Spiel.	(III, 80-1)

Another case is that of an adjective in turn qualified by an adverb:

ruhiggelb	(III, 78)
der fertig-volle Garten Eden	(III, 161)
schlicht entschlossen	(III, 161)
schuldlos-schuldig	(III, 162)
ein sanftgesinnter langmütig lange Wartender.	(III, 90)

Composite adjectives, formed by an adjective and a noun, or by two adjectives, are now often very felicitous:

atemwarm	(III, 112)
das abendklare Wasser	(III, 86)
ein firnisklares Lächeln	(III, 197)
der flüssigklare Spiegel	(III, 228)
das immersüsse Land	(III, 126)
tieftiefinneres Geläut.	(III, 211)

In the *Elegies*, Rilke's adjectives have gained in imaginative and poetic expressiveness. In the elevated language of these poems, their chief use is no longer, as it was in *Neue Gedichte*, to serve as strictly qualifying terms: they are again emotionally charged, but on a different plane: they now often express certain half-tones, unusual associations difficult to define, but which may be adumbrated by means of the adjective; a residue of mystery often remains:

die riesige Ruf	(III, 261)
neue, warme, entgehende Welle des Herzens	(III, 265)
unvordenklicher Saft	(III, 273)
auf unsäglichem Teppich	(III, 282)
die ruhlosen Wege	(III, 282)
im versprechlichen Spiel	(III, 288)
dieser voreilige Vorteil	(III, 297)
die grimmige Einsicht	(III, 302)
aus dem tonlosen Los	(III, 308)
das wachsam warme Tier	(III, 294)

    (Compare: die warmen Tiere, II, 242; in den starken wachsamen Tieren, III 384)

das kleinblütige Heilkraut.	(III, 281)

The use of adjectives to convey a specific, at times stylized, colour is still more noticeable in the *Sonnets*:

die schmale Leier	(III, 315)
lichte Profile	(III, 335)
allmähliches Meer	(III, 341)
der unendliche Empfang	(III, 345)
im unbrauchbaren Raum	(III, 351)
aus dem wagrechten gelben Tag	(III, 367)
die unerhörte Mitte	(III, 373)
das mürrische Schicksal.	(III, 369)

The *Sonnets* also contain characteristic accumulations similar to those noted in *Neue Gedichte*:

doppeldeutig, sonnig, erdig, hiesig	(III, 325)
hell, elend, unendlich zerstörbar	(III, 363)
ins reine, ins hohe, ins torig offene Herz,	(III, 349)

and significant instances of adjectives used as nouns:

das alte Schlimme	(III, 320)
ein buntes Offenbares	(III, 326)
Warmes der Mädchen	(III, 347)
das Irdische.	(III, 374)

Such forms tend to monumentalize the adjective, make it stand out as strong, simple and more general than in *Neue Gedichte*, where greater precision was the poet's aim, and adjective-nouns like *ein Starkes* (III, 374) would have been avoided as too vague. In the large, intense, yet at the same time miraculously light and transparent style of the *Sonnets* such forms enhance the volume and contribute to the grandeur of outline.

In Rilke's early poems, an ever-recurring adjective is *leise*; it is so frequent, occurring in every third or fourth poem, that a list of contexts would be monotonous. After the *Stundenbuch*, this adjective becomes much rarer. Peculiar to Rilke, since we do not encounter it elsewhere with his meanings, is *heil*. It occurs frequently, as the following selected quotations show, and is an instance of a predilection that has led to happy results, for almost invariably this adjective has the freshness of a new, though not too new, word; the old meaning of *heil*—sane, healthy, unharmed—has only been adapted in new or unusual combinations:

als würde etwas heil	(III, 163)
welche heil ist und geschont	(III, 188)
die heile Helle des Ausblicks	(III, 205)
o ihr Seligen, o ihr Heilen	(III, 316)
zwar ist kein Hören heil	(III, 330)
der heile Vogelschrei	(III, 371)
die heile Leier	(III, 392)
zu der heilen Feier	(III, 373)
heilen Bewusstseins	(III, 420)
in heiler Genüge	(S.G., 103)
schweigsam, einfach und heil	(S.G., 105)
im Scheine der heilen Flamme.	(S.G., 164)

Another such adjective typical for Rilke is *rein*. Its literal meaning, 'pure', is modified by overtones peculiar to Rilke, and in his later poems it often acquires the meaning of 'absolute'; there exist, moreover, shades between these meanings that defy translation. In *Neue Gedichte* this adjective is still rare, and generally occurs in its original meaning:

er wurde nur ganz rein	(III, 41)
ein wenig reine Einsamkeit.	(III, 89)

In the *Elegies* and *Sonnets*, *rein* increases very considerably in frequency, and its meaning changes in the manner alluded to above; the following is a selection only of the most significant passages:

ihrer Geister reine Bewegung	(III, 262)
das reine Dauern	(III, 267)
ein reines, verhaltenes schmales, Menschliches	(III, 268)

Hat er die innige Einsicht
in ihr reines Gesicht nicht aus dem reinen Gestirn?

(III, 269–70)

für einen reinen Vorgang	(III, 277)
dein reines Geheimnis	(III, 284)
schrieest du rein wie der Vogel	(III, 287)
ein reiner, bejahender Tag	(III, 288)
das Reine, Unüberwachte	(III, 293)
das reine Zuwenig	(III, 282)
ein erworbenes Wort, reines	(III, 298)
rein wie im Innern einer gesegneten Hand.	(III, 307)

This selection from the *Elegies* can be supplemented with an equally significant one from the *Sonnets*:

reine Spannung	(III, 324)
ein reines Wohin	(III, 335)
rein eingetauschter Weltraum	(III, 341)
ein reines Tier	(III, 344)
ein Spielen von reinen Kräften	(III, 350)
in den reinen Bezug	(III, 356)
der unerschöpflich Eines, Reines, spricht.	(III, 358)

In *Letzte Gedichte* and *Späte Gedichte* the word is hardly rarer, but we will give a few quotations only:

der Gipfel reine Verweigerung	(III, 420)
des allerreinsten Gastes	(III, 436)
mit dem reinen Untergang	(S.G., 106)
Weils keiner meistert, bleibt das Leben rein.	(S.G., 148)

The examples given show the great versatility the word assumes in Rilke's poetry: it has a different ring in almost every passage, and this diversity is brought about by the nouns to which it is attached, or by the context and general trend of thought. In *ein reines Tier* (III, 344), the meaning is the simple, original one; in other combinations, it moves away to more abstract and involved meanings: *das reine Dauern, das reine Zuwenig, reine Spannung, das reine Wohin, die reine Richtung, im reinen Hirtenamt*, etc. We need not be concerned here with an explanation of these different meanings;

the importance of the word for Rilke's style lies in its faculty of abbreviation, in the way an ancient, very simple word is put to many new uses without visible effort. In each of these cases the word assumes a very positive quality: it is undoubtedly one of the most serious, expressive superlatives the poet can bestow upon a thing, a relationship, a direction, a state, if he calls them *rein*. It is no mean achievement to have adapted this simple word to such varied possibilities of meaning, a genuine enrichment of the language brought about by the poet's earnest and imaginative intensity alone, without recourse to any manipulation or device. The permeation with the poet's spirit creates an almost new word: 'It is the common words that have the finest triumphs in poetry, because they necessarily have the greatest suggestive power behind them'.[1]

An interesting peculiarity of Rilke's style is the way in which he uses adjectives in the comparative or superlative. In many instances, the comparative is not genuine inasmuch as it does not indicate a real comparison; it is a general increase of the adjective only in order to give it a heightened significance, or a greater nervous tension. (Cf. Hölderlin:

> Und der geheimeren,
> Tiefern Schmerzen des Lebens
> Hast du manche gelernt von mir.
> [*An Diotima*].)

südlichere Tage	(II, 51)
zum fruchtbarern Ausdruck	(III, 270)
aus geölter, glatterer Luft	(III, 278)
die wärmere Landschaft	(III, 327)
im steileren Abstieg	(III, 379)
mit innigerm Flug	(III, 260)
das schönere Zögern	(III, 350)
der stillere Instinkt.	(III, 359)

Rilke even puts words in the comparative that denote absolute values and are thus incapable of an increase, as *gelb*, *ewig*:

stummer, ruhiggelber als ein goldnes	(III, 78)
ewiger glänzt euer Lächeln.	(III, 316)

Rilke's superlatives, if much rarer, are equally unusual, though hardly conspicuous in his style; more genuine than his comparatives,

---

[1] Lascelles Abercrombie, *The Theory of Poetry*, 1928, p. 138.

they may be felt as a legitimate means of concentrating emphasis
upon one point:

der goldenste Ring	(II, 188)
dein stärkstes Schauen	(III, 181)
die reizendsten Freuden	(III, 281)
seine süsseste Leistung	(III, 284)
die reifeste Rundung	(III, 307)
die unvereinlichsten Kontraste.	(S.G., 22)

Again, adjectives like *golden* or *unvereinlich* are not capable of comparison; Rilke lets his need for expression overrule grammatical
rules or linguistic usage.

Colloquialisms

A survey of Rilke's vocabulary would not be complete without
a consideration of those 'unpoetic' everyday words he uses in some
of his poems in order to introduce a particularly strong note of
colour. Such colloquialisms are unevenly distributed in contemporary German poetry. Liliencron is very fond of them; while
Hofmannsthal seems to ignore them, Stefan George abhors and
avoids them. Later, with Franz Werfel and expressionistic poetry,
these words invade the German lyric for a while, but they are used
in a spirit very different from that in which Rilke occasionally
employs them. He does not brag with them nor does he throw
them about in unselective profusion; they are strong accents in his
language, used sparingly and with an artist's economy. While
they are totally absent from most poems, we find them clustered in
others, e.g. in the cycle *Die Stimmen* in *Buch der Bilder*, from which
the following selection is taken:

dieses Vieh, der Tod	
schmutzige Karte	
grauer Grind, Kot	(II, 124)
übergeben, Diät	(II, 125)
kauft für alt, Ausverkauf	(II, 127)
abgetragen, Mist	(II, 130)
brennen mit kleiner Flamme.	(II, 134)

These 'ugly' words sound very un-Rilkean, and they are really not
typical for his diction, since the cycle in question was evidently
written in an experimental vein. There are hardly any such words

in the *Stundenbuch*, but a few 'strong' words are found in *Neue Gedichte*:

entgegenstank	(III, 143)
trieb ihm Eis in den Schweiss	(III, 143)
Beischlaf	(III, 144)
beissender Schweiss verleidet ihnen Stirne und Steiss	(III, 145–6)
bettheiss	(III, 156)
ihren Mund voll Mist	(III, 169)
er kann es sich leisten	(III, 169)
ich bin entzwei	(III, 129)

Rilke's later poems also contain a restricted number of common or unpoetic words, some with a certain commercial ring, others not far removed from slang:

und ob!	(III, 332)
Erde, die frei hat	(III, 333)
fertig gekauft	(III, 303)
Hunde haben Natur	(III, 304)
billige Winterhüte	(III, 282)
die farbenechten Himmel	(S.G., 18)

Interjections

Interjections are remnants from the beginnings of language, when sound and meaning were one.

Ein kundgebender Ausruf des Schmerzes, des Jubels, der Klage, stellt demnach das Urphänomen des (sprachlich) Lyrischen dar; in der Interjektion Ach! wurzelt sozusagen alle Lyrik.[1]

It is but natural, therefore, that interjections should always have had a large place in poetry, the rememberer and keeper of the youth of language. In his early and middle work, Rilke distinguishes himself from the almost universal usage of poetry by being very economical with interjections: they would not fit his introverted, soft and subdued style. His occasional *o* and *ach* acquire a greater weight by their scarcity. Thus, in *Buch der Bilder*, the poem *Kindheit* is distinguished by the regular recurrence of a plaintive *o* in the last line of each stanza:

O Einsamkeit, o wunderliche Zeit, O Trauer ohne Sinn,
o Traum, etc.   (II, 29)

---

[1] Wolfgang Kayser. *Das sprachliche Kunstwerk*, 2. Aufl. 1951, p. 336.

Since Rilke is so sparing with his interjections, they contribute to the poems where they occur a note of grave and intense sincerity:

<blockquote>

O wie sind die Tiere so viel treuer ... (II, 45)

</blockquote>

In *Neue Gedichte*, interjections are hardly more frequent, and mostly soft or *sotto voce*:

<blockquote>

Ach es kam die Nacht (III, 27)

o namenlose Scham (III, 26)

o wenn er steigt ... (III, 83)

Ach, sie hätte gern in jenem Land
noch ein wenig weilen mögen ... (III, 162)

Oh dass ihr stille bliebt (III, 166)

ach, sie haben nicht denselben Gang. (III, 221)

</blockquote>

Still subdued, interjections now also help to express a heightened feeling, even a delicate, quietly glowing joy:

<blockquote>

o süsses Lied (III, 9)

O du wilde weite Werferin (III, 10)

O wie blüht mein Leib aus jeder Ader (III, 15)

O wie fühlt dich ein
treibender Feigenbaum. (III, 190)

</blockquote>

With the *Elegies* and *Sonnets*, interjections acquire a new importance, and finally come into their own. Not only are they much more frequent now, but they leave the semi-obscurity in which they lingered before and come into the open with a note of deep sorrow or of pure, ringing joy, with a fullness they never had before (we are including in the appellation 'interjections' such words as *wehe, weh mir, ja, siehe,* etc.):

<blockquote>

Und dennoch, weh mir,
ansing ich euch ... (III, 264)

O Lächeln, wohin? O Aufschaun: ...
weh mir: wir *sinds* doch. (III, 265)

O des Blutes Neptun, o sein furchtbarer Dreizack.
O der dunkele Wind ... (III, 269)

Wo, ach, hin sind die Jahre ... (III, 270)

Wo, o wo ist der Ort ... (III, 281)

O staune, Engel, dann wir sinds,
wir, o du Grosser, erzähls ... (III, 291)

Ach, in den andern Bezug,
wehe, was nimmt man hinüber? (III, 298)

in — o unendlich — in uns! (III, 300)

</blockquote>

L

O reine Übersteigung!

O Orpheus singt! O hoher Baum im Ohr!   (III, 313)

O Musik der Kräfte!   (III, 324)

O Erfahrung, Fühlung, Freude-, riesig!   (III, 325)

O du verlorener Gott!   (III, 338)

Ach, der Erde, wer kennt die Verluste?   (III, 342)

O diese Lust, immer neu, aus gelockertem Lehm!   (III, 369)

Personal Words

Some words used by Rilke are his very own, i.e. he uses them in combination and for meanings in which they are not commonly used.

Il y a des mots dont la fréquence chez un auteur, nous révèle qu'ils sont en lui tout autrement doués de résonance, et par conséquent, de puissance positivement créatrice, qu'ils ne le sont en général. C'est là un example de ces évaluations personnelles, de ces grandes valeurs-pour-un-seul, qui jouent certainement un très beau rôle dans une production de l'esprit où la singularité est un élément de première importance.[1]

A typical group of such words are those beginning with the prefix *über*: *übersteigen, überleben, überschreiten* and, most characteristic of all, *überstehen*. All these words express a transcendency: the passing of a crisis, overcoming of anguish and despair, the overstepping of a goal, a survival. *Überstehen*, as employed by Rilke, is more poignantly specific than in common use, it is charged with certain overtones that make us think of tension and anguish in the poet's life. Its object may be the wind (*so muss er sehn wie er / dich übersteht*, III, 190), or a symbolic person (*dass sie wachsend Heloisen / überstehn und überschrein*, III, 218), or the skies (*sind die Himmel stark, wie voller Leuen, / die wir unbegreiflich überstehn*, S.G., 141). It is also used without an object:

. . . überstarke

Überlieferte, die überstehn.   (III, 195)

(Note the three *über* in close succession)

wo noch eins übersteht,

ein einst gebetetes Ding . . .   (III, 290)

Steht. Übersteht.   (III, 393)

da er in des Knaben Unterliegen

gründete das Überstehn des Manns   (S.G., 118)

trinkt es Zukunft, atmet, übersteht.   (S.G., 87)

[1] Paul Valéry, *Introduction à la poétique*, 1938, p. 54.

The meanings of *überschreiten* are similarly surcharged in Rilke's poems:

Denn dass einer jene überschreite ...	(III, 216)
(from a poem that ends with the words *überstehn und überschrein*)	
und er gehorcht, indem er überschreitet	(III, 317)
wo ist ein Herz, das er nicht überschritte.	(S.G., 39)

Übertreiben occurs in many new meanings and combinations:

das ihre Einsamkeit noch übertreibt	(III, 93)
Schauspieler, aufgetürmte Übertreiber	(III, 110)
wo das Alleinsein alles übertrieb	(III, 168)
bis an Städte, die man übertreibt	(III, 231)
in die blendend mit Licht übertriebene Nacht	(III, 367)
das erregte übertriebene Licht.	(III, 409)

Two words peculiar to Rilke, i.e. hardly ever used by other poets, and certainly not in the particular sense he gave them, are *verwöhnt* (or *verwöhnen*), and *geschont* (*schonen*). In a way, Rilke was himself 'pampered', cushioned from the impact of a hostile world, and he knew it. Here are some of the contexts in which he uses the word:

Und es war der schlanke	
Flüchtling, der verwöhnende der Fraun.	(III, 14)
Ich verwöhnte ihn zwar.	(III, 125)
Fürstlich verwöhnte Fenster sehen immer,	
was manches Mal uns zu bemühn geruht	(III, 203)
empfand sie plötzlich den verwöhnten Park.	(III, 222)
und das verzogene Treusein einer Gewohnheit	(III, 260)
... die grüne metallene Seide	
fühlt sich unendlich verwöhnt und entbehrt nichts.	(III, 281)

The meaning of *schonen, geschont* is somewhat akin to *verwöhnt*:

Derselbe Baum,	
dessen Kränze toten Pharaonen	
für das Ewige die Stirnen schonen,	
neigte sich.	(II, 309)
... Worte ...,	
nicht die seinen (denn was wären seine,	
und wie schonend wären sie vertan)	(III, 135)
Und dann gleitet oben eine Weite	
weiter, welche heil ist und geschont	(III, 188)
... oder durch geschonte	
Parke graue Edelsitze zeigten	(III, 231)
Hoher Vorwurf, dicht vor dem Herzen erhoben,	
das nicht so wogend empfand, das sich schonte.	(S.G., 77)

Another word specific to Rilke, the most important perhaps, is *Beziehung, Bezug*. Its meaning is relation, correlation, relationship in a philosophical, even a metaphysical, sense, and it is therefore a difficult word to acclimatize in the language of poetry. Words so charged with intellectual or transcendental meaning are as a rule shunned by poets as not direct, not vivid enough. *Bezug* is Rilke's poetic version for the more prosaic *Beziehung*, yet even the shorter word is so heavily charged with sometimes vague and not always identical meanings that it may lead a chain of thought away from the poem. *Beziehung* occurs once in *Buch der Bilder, Bezug* in the later poems only, not in the *Stundenbuch* or in *Neue Gedichte*.

> ... bringe
> doch mich auch in Beziehung zu dem Vielen   (II, 56)
>   Seltsam
> alles, was sich bezog, so lose im Raume
> flattern zu sehen ...   (III, 262)
>   Ach, in den andern Bezug,
> wehe, was nimmt man hinüber?   (III, 298)
> und der Zauber von Erdrauch und Raute
> sei ihm so wahr wie der klarste Bezug   (III, 318)
> steige zurück in den reinen Bezug   (III, 356)
> was jene ... durchstürzte mit unendlichem Bezug (III, 386)
> überall Lust zu Bezug und nirgends Begehren   (III, 417)
> Und nur die Stirne baut sich etwas dauernd
> hinüber aus verflüchtigten Bezügen   (III, 463)
> um aus dem unbeschreiblichen Bezug
> herauszufallen wie ein Stein?   (S.G., 113)
> handeln wir aus wirklichem Bezug.   (III, 324)

We cannot here be concerned with the elucidation of the difficult word, only with its place in Rilke's poetic language. To many readers, it will appear as slightly disturbing, not fully integrated. The appropriateness and felicity of the term may be said to vary a good deal: in some places it is fitting, in others it will be felt as a heavy, almost foreign, element. In the first quotation, from *Buch der Bilder*, the clumsiness of the passage, so unusual for Rilke, is almost pathetic: *Bringe doch mich auch in Beziehung zu dem Vielen* is prosy and pedestrian, a thought not purified in the flame of poetry. In the combinations *aus dem unbeschreiblichen Bezug* and *aus verflüchtigten Bezügen*, the adjectives, and in the second instance also the plural, introduce a note of exaggeration, almost of affectation, not quite in keeping with the abstract character of the word. On the other hand, adjectives like *klar, rein, wirklich* seem to benefit the vague and iridescent term, providing a kind of anchorage for the plurality of its possible meanings. A relation can really exist only between two or more things: it is disconcerting that Rilke uses the word in an absolute sense, for relationship as such, apart from anything related. When he says: *alles, was sich bezog,* the contrast makes the meaning clear: on the one hand a system of established relationships, on the other looseness, chaos, disintegration. In the passage: *Ach, in den andern Bezug, wehe, was nimmt man hinüber?* the word stands for 'the other system of related values', meaning death or an existence after death—a very daring and at the same time effective abbreviation or compression of thought, acceptable at least to those familiar with Rilke's way of feeling and his mode of expression. In other instances, the meaning is not so unambiguous, but we must not forget that a certain vagueness, profundity, even ambiguity and obscurity, so objectionable in many other fields, have their legitimate place in poetry: it is the poet's prerogative to create new words for new meanings, which may not always be immediately understood. *Bezug* is not a word used by other poets, but it is obvious, from the examples quoted, that Rilke felt a need for it and attempted to give it a place in his poems, with what seems to us varying success. It is conceivable that future generations will see no difficulty where we struggle for understanding as well as appreciation. At present, Rilke's poetry is the only place where *Bezug* exists with the particular meanings he implied. In those cases where it is not felt as organic within the poem, it must be judged as a disturbing factor in his poetic style.

THERE is some confusion in the use of the words metaphor and simile: the former is the substitution of one thing or conception for another, the latter a genuine comparison between two things, generally of a different nature or belonging to different categories, like abstract and concrete. The metaphor has been called an applied comparison, or we might describe it as a short cut to one:

> Grau, teurer Freund, ist alle Theorie,
> Und grün des Lebens goldner Baum —

this is a poetical condensation of: Life is like a golden tree in full foliage, *golden*, in turn, being used in its symbolical connotation of 'ever fresh', or 'immortal'. The word 'imagery' may express the use of both metaphor and simile, and would perhaps have been more appropriate in the following quotation:

> I think we should always be prepared to judge a poet, to the exclusion of all other qualities, by the force and originality of his metaphors.[1]

Even if we do not follow Read as far as his 'to the exclusion of all other qualities', a poet's command of imagery must be considered a central factor of his poetic powers, and in this respect, Rilke's position in German poetry is exceptional.

German lyrical poetry is very rich in metaphors, much less so in similes. With Rilke it is the reverse, at least in his central period: his wealth of similes is so extraordinary that they leave little room for metaphors; in his early poetry, on the other hand, metaphorical language predominates. The German language itself inclines towards metaphor, as is seen in the easy transformation of nouns or adjectives into verbs: *Ein Tännlein grünet wo — es blaut die Nacht — tauten die Tränen*, and in the facility for forming compound nouns or adjectives: *Lebenstiefe, Lebensflut, Tatensturm, Donnerwort, Zeitenstrudel, Mottenwelt, Ebenbild, segenduftend, neuglühend* (the last group culled from the first pages of *Faust*). We would expect the young Rilke to yield extravagantly to the temptation offered by the language, and indeed his early collections are full of metaphorical periphrases in more or less dubious taste:

> das Regenwasser röchelt in den Rinnen (I, 55)

---

[1] Herbert Read, 'The Nature of Poetry,' in *Collected Essays in Literary Criticism*, 1938, p. 98.

dass mit des Liedes Silberzwirne
er seiner Liebsten Herz umspinnt (I, 62)
Matt . . . wankt Abend auf goldenen Schuhen (I, 134)
Am Tag trug ich den engen Ring
der feigen Pflicht (I, 171)
Schon blinzt aus argzerfetztem Laken
der Götternacken der Natur (I, 120)

In his endeavour to keep aloof from the cliché, Rilke can be very hard on our imagination, and his early metaphors are often more cerebral than visual:

singen wie mit ihren Haaren (I, 344)
[Die Rosen] schreiten zwei zu zwein,
und sie halten sich um die Hüften (I, 285)
. . . sucht müd, gestützt auf Strahlenkrücken
die Sonne . . . ihr Valladolid. (I, 97)
(Compare Meyer's *Meine Strahlen sind geknickte Speere* — in *Zwiegespräch*)

Girls that sing with their hair, roses walking in twos holding each other by the hips—these things, even if one could imagine them, are extremely unpoetical. This kind of metaphor is found in many early poems; in *Buch der Bilder* the spate subsides somewhat, and metaphors do not only become rarer now, but are more carefully elaborated and integrated when they occur. The decorative metaphor becomes the exception:

[die Mädchen] lächeln nur, lichter als Perlenschnüre,
die man an Schalen von Silber hält. (II, 14)

There is a tendency towards greater clarity and simplicity:

Gefügig räumt sich alles in den Schrei.
Das ganze Land scheint lautlos drin zu liegen,
der grosse Wind scheint sich hineinzuschmiegen . . . (II, 48)
Der Abend wechselt langsam die Gewänder (II, 62)
[Meine Seele] hat keinen Garten, sie hat kein Bett,
sie hängt an meinem scharfen Skelett
mit entsetztem Flügelschlagen. (II, 130)

The *Stundenbuch* is permeated with metaphors and metaphorical language. They are part of the thought-content of these poems rather than means towards its expression; we might call them approaches to Rilke's theme, God, and hesitate considering them as elements of the poet's style:

Du bist die Zukunft, grosses Morgenrot,
über den Ebenen der Ewigkeit.
Du bist der Hahnschrei nach der Nacht der Zeit,
der Tau, die Morgenmette und die Maid,
der fremde Mann, die Mutter und der Tod. (II, 252)

Instead of being decoratively descriptive and painting, Rilke's
metaphorical language is now more direct and gripping:

> Da neigt sich die Stunde und rührt mich an
> mit klarem, metallenem Schlag . . .
> und ich fasse den plastischen Tag.   (II, 175)
>
> Ich lebe mein Leben in wachsenden Ringen . . .   (II, 175)
>
> die dunklen Höhenzüge der Kamele
> umgaben es mit der Gebirge Pracht.   (II, 280)

This firmness is still on the increase in *Neue Gedichte*. It is no
longer as if the poet were coaxed by the language into facile metaphors; regardless of their ornamental beauty, he shapes his word-
pictures to intense, clarifying sharpness:

> Wenn, auf meiner Brüste Hügeln
> stehend, mein Gefühl nach Flügeln
> oder einem Ende schreit.   (III, 8)
>
> mein festes Lied ist nicht gerissen   (III, 20)
>
> [die Kathedrale steht] in dem alten
> Faltenmantel ihrer Contreforts   (III, 33)
>
> Willkürlich von Gewesnem ausgeweitet . . .
> ladet der Platz zum Einzug seiner Weite
> die fernen Fenster unaufhörlich ein.   (III, 85)
>
> die Gassen haben einen sachten Gang   (III, 86)
>
> Die Stille kostet langsam . . .
> Beere um Beere aus der süssen Traube
> des Glockenspiels . . .   (III, 87)
>
> Die kleine Insel hat die Augen zu   (III, 93)
>
> Ohne zu kauen frass sein Schritt den Weg   (III, 99)
>
> alle seine trächtigen Sinne warfen . . .
> Frühgeburten . . . Und schon hatten seine Sinne Enkel
>   (III, 148)
>
> Völker schlugen über ihm zusammen   (III, 154)
>
>   Sie verkaufen
> das Hohle aus ihrer Hand.   (III, 169)

A metaphor like *und schon hatten seine Sinne Enkel* is dangerously on
the borderline of the cerebral, but within the poem it becomes
readily acceptable.

In the *Elegies* Rilke's metaphors undergo another transformation,
this time towards a greater sprituality. They now contain more
abstract elements, condensations of thought, suppressed symbols:

> das verzogene Treusein einer Gewohnheit   (III, 260)
>
> das, was man war in unendlich ängstlichen Händen,
> nicht mehr zu sein . . .   (III, 262)

```
        . . . von Holzglut zu Holzglut
geben wir schwächern Geruch                        (III, 265)
diesen Urwald in ihm, auf dessen stummem Gestürztsein
lichtgrün sein Herz stand.                         (III, 272)
Wer sass nicht bang vor seines Herzens Vorhang?    (III, 274)
        . . . in der eine Antwort
langsam erwacht und über dem Hören sich anwärmt    (III, 287)
             Denn mein
Anruf ist immer voll Hinweg                        (III, 292)
        Die Schmerzen aber sind ja
unser winterwähriges Laub, unser dunkeles Sinngrün (III, 302)
ein Stück geschliffenes Urleid                     (III, 305)
             . . . und manchmal
schreckt ein Vogel und zieht, flach ihnen fliegend
                      durchs Aufschaun,
weithin das schriftliche Bild seines vereinsamten Schreis
                                                   (III, 306)
```

Once, in the evocation of the angels in the Second Elegy, a series of metaphors sustains an outburst of lyrical ecstasy:

```
Frühe Geglückte, ihr Verwöhnten der Schöpfung,
Höhenzüge, morgenrötliche Grate
aller Erschaffung, — Pollen der blühenden Gottheit,
Gelenke des Lichtes, Gänge, Treppen, Throne,
Räume aus Wesen, Schilde aus Wonne, Tumulte
stürmisch entzückten Gefühls . . .                 (III, 264-5)
```

The spirituality is bolder still in the *Sonnets*. Here again, as in Rilke's early work, metaphors outstrip visual possibilities—but with a difference. They now move in a world of their own, where our imagination cannot follow them unless we previously translate them into symbols. Thus, in a passage like *o hoher Baum im Ohr* (III, 313), we must see *hoher Baum* as well as *Ohr* symbolically to avoid the jarring note if we tried to visualize them otherwise, and a similar translation will prove necessary, in varying degree, in the following instances:

```
ein Mädchen machte sich ein Bett in meinem Ohr   (III, 314)
soll ein Mann ihm folgen durch die schmale Leier? (III, 315)
Nie versagt ihm die Stimme am Staube              (III, 319)
Immer wieder von uns aufgerissen,
ist der Gott die Stelle, welche heilt.            (III, 359)
und leicht befremdet, wenn ein Baum sich lang
besann, mit dir nach dem Gehör zu gehn.           (III, 373)
```

There is not much difference in the character of Rilke's metaphors in *Letzte Gedichte*. We will mention only *Man muss sterben, weil man sie kennt* (III, 411), a poem wholly written in metaphorical language, and the highly significant, graphic metaphor in *Klage*:

Früher. Klagtest? Was wars? Eine gefallene
Beere des Jubels, unreife!
Jetzt aber bricht mir mein Jubelbaum,
bricht mir im Sturme mein langsamer
Jubelbaum.   (III, 412)

Such a passage is a highlight of Rilke's metaphorical thought, as compelling and beautiful as his *Pollen der blühenden Gottheit* in the Second Elegy.

Similes, as we have noted, are not particularly frequent in German poetry, and those that occur are mainly of a vague and general nature: *des Menschen Seele gleicht dem Wasser — ich singe wie der Vogel singt — freudehell wie ein Sternenblick* (Goethe); *der Tod, das ist die kühle Nacht — du bist wie eine Blume — mein Herz gleicht ganz dem Meere* (Heine)—all these are poetical similes, i.e. they are employed for their inherent beauty as much as for the associations they call forth. Of the many uses of Rilke's similes, such poetical embellishment is only a minor one. 'Imagery is an essential to poetry for the reason that its finish, exactitude, reality are indispensable to thought which reaches out beyond the bounds of commonplace observation and speculation.'[1] Note the words 'exactitude and reality': they might be called, together with 'beyond the bounds of commonplace observation', the key for the understanding of Rilke's imagery, for his similes are fundamentally different from those in the German tradition. The associations they evoke do not aim at lifting a passage into a beautiful world of poetry, nor do they simply compare one thing to another. 'In the dream of a poet things come together, not because they are being identified, but because they are thought and felt together in an emotional unity.'[2] This is only partly true of Rilke's imagery, in which things are identified as well as felt together in an emotional unity. French poets, Baudelaire, Verlaine and the Symbolists, contributed to his art a spirit of exactitude very far removed from the romantic vagueness so often encountered in the German lyric. It is a searching, painstaking, at times even ruthless accuracy, comparable to the portrait painter's striving for his sitter's likeness. And Rilke likes his comparisons to illuminate the scene with a flash of short duration;

[1] P. Gurrey, *The Appreciation of Poetry*, 1938, p. 63.
[2] Karl Vossler, *The Spirit of Language and Civilization*, 1933.

in his poem *An Hölderlin*, he finds words of rebuke for those poets who exploit their similes:

> Wie sie doch alle
> wohnen im warmen Gedicht, häuslich, und lang
> bleiben im schmalen Vergleich. Teilnehmende.   (S.G., 37)

But this applies to the poet's central period only; Rilke's art in the handling of similes undergoes the same purification noted in other instances: they progress from the superficial, the flashy, even the vulgar to the genuine, the fitting, the profound. The first and the last stage, vastly different as they are, have in common an indisputable originality: if at times far-fetched, Rilke's similes are, with few exceptions, invariably new, but the early ones share with his metaphors a cerebral artificiality:

> den Blumen fliesst der Duft herab wie Tränen.   (I, 298)

The moon is likened to a tamtam (I, 41), to a yellow melon (I, 69), to a white boat about to land in a lime tree (I, 122), to a silver coin (I, 239). On the other hand, Rilke can be trite in his early similes:

> und leise rieseln seine Töne
> wie Blütenregen in das Land.   (I, 62)

> und gross wie eine Nachtviole
> geht dir die dunkle Seele auf . . .   (I, 131)

Other early similes, if still somewhat affected, are on a higher plane:

> Nur ein matter Falter schwirrt
> rastlos durch das Land, das kranke . . .
> Einsam, wie ein Gottgedanke
> durch die Brust des Leugners irrt.   (I, 127)

This simile is particularly interesting because it reverses the process of comparison: instead of explaining or illustrating a thought by a more familiar object or action, a thing seen is here being compared to a thought, the fluttering butterfly to an isolated thought of God in the atheist's mind—a comparison that would never have occurred to a naïve poet. There is an analogy to this in Klopstock's

> Also spricht sie und eilt. So fliegt ein grosser Gedanke
> Feurig zum Himmel empor zu dem, von dem er gedacht war.

Here is another of these interesting, laboured early comparisons:

> und sie hält sich wie das Hohle
> einer Muschel Gott ans Ohr.   (I, 344)

(compare a later version in *Neue Gedichte*):

> Das Ohrgehäng erklingt an ihrem Ohre;
> sie aber hebt San Giorgio Maggiore
> und lächelt lässig in das schöne Ding.   (III, 203)

Buch der Bilder presents the same medley in this as in other aspects of the poet's style: original similes, somewhat difficult to visualize,

> sind bleich die Perlen, die in sieben Reihn
> wie weisse Kinder knien um seinen Nacken . . .　　(II, 102)

> als trügen seinen gründenden Granit
> blinde Schildkröten, die sich rühren,　　(II, 145)

are found side by side with others that reveal an artist's vision:

> Und während hier, wie Westwind warm,
> der Ochs ihr Ohr umschnaubt . . .　　(II, 76)

> Ah, was ist das für ein schöner Ball;
> rot und rund wie ein Überall . . .　　(II, 128)

It is hard to say what is poetically gained by imagining pearls as white children kneeling around a neck, while the absurd likening of the ball to an 'Überall', whatever that may be, is accepted as apt and fitting: logic plays a small part in the aesthetics of similes.

The majority of similes in the *Stundenbuch* must be considered, like the metaphors, as part of poetical thought rather than as elements of style. Those, on the other hand, that are employed by the poet with a view to creating a vivid image by means of a comparison, are generally attuned to the mystical character of the poems by a certain biblical greatness or simplicity, and their originality consists mainly in the novel way in which things are brought together that have never been compared before. Or has money ever been likened to the east wind?

> das Geld wächst an, hat alle ihre Kräfte
> und ist wie Ostwind gross . . .　　(II, 290)

Other examples from the *Stundenbuch*:

> Noch gestern war die Stirne wie ein Stein
> im Bach, geründet von den Tagen,
> die nichts bedeuten als ein Wellenschlagen　　(II, 190)
> die Städte: wie hohles Holz zerbrechen sie die Tiere,　　(II, 289)

and lastly one that shows how skilfully Rilke could embed his similes in the flow of the poem, creating a flawless harmony:

> mit jenem Leben, das wie Andacht leise
> und warm wie Atem aus den Feldern bricht.　　(II, 276)

With *Neue Gedichte* Rilke's poetry blossoms into full flower, and while every element shares in the maturing of the poet's style, similes seen even more affected than other devices. They are not only improved in taste and used to better advantage, but also more

precise and at the same time more profound. It may have been
Rodin's influence towards closer observation that helped to bring
about this transformation. In these poems the variety of similes,
ranging from the simple to the complex, from the subtle to the
monumental, is as amazing as their gradation, colour, versatility
and above all their precision. A simile cannot, of course, be precise
in itself; it may be used by the poet with a view to giving colour,
or adding beauty, or providing associations, or, as in Rilke's case in
Neue Gedichte, with the aim of making a thing or a situation more
vivid by providing the reader with the means of seeing and feeling
them as he saw and felt them. Although a number of Rilke's
similes always retains a certain cerebral quality, the majority are
now sharply seen and revealing in the sense that they illuminate
the thought in a flash. Rilke's striking originality in this respect is
partly due to the extreme sensibility that made him experience
sensations no one had felt before, or if so, not with his sense of
emotion or suffering. To see heat rise from a hot hish is a very
common experience, so common indeed that it causes no sensation
at all. In Rilke's sensibility this observation is coupled with a sense
of loss, and thus he is able to use it in a simple, yet most revealing,
comparison:

> Wie Tau von dem Frühgras
> hebt sich das Unsre von uns, wie Hitze von einem
> heissen Gericht. (III, 265)

If the poet, in his early work, sacrificed beauty to originality, now
he does not hesitate to give up a conventional conception of beauty
for accuracy, but his similes, though often poetically unlovely in
the conventional sense and at times even offending, acquire a convincing firmness based on their inherent truth. He rarely uses them
as touches of colour, to light up a poem; they are indispensable to
him for revealing the nature of a thing, a mood, an action:

> der Bote . . .
> hineingeworfen in das Überkochen
> des Hochzeitsmahles wie ein neuer Zusatz.
> . . . des Gottes
> heimlichen Eintritt, welcher seine Gottheit
> so an sich hielt wie einen nassen Mantel . . .
> Und gleich darauf, als klärte sich die Mischung,
> war Stille; nur mit einem Satz am Boden
> von trübem Lärm und einem Niederschlag
> fallenden Lallens, schon verdorben riechend
> nach dumpfen umgestandenen Gelächter. (III, 103)

None of these similes (all taken from the first lines of *Alkestis*), is beautiful in the traditional sense of poetic beauty: the poet is indifferent to the unpleasant sensations such similes may cause if they only have the revealing, sharply delineating intensity he demands of them.

It will give an idea of the great variety of similes now at Rilke's disposal if we group them together according to a predominant quality; such a division, if artificial like most groupings, is useful to draw attention to their different scope and uses. We continue the series of arresting images, begun with those from *Alkestis*:

> der Blinde . . . geht und unterbricht die Stadt,
> die nicht ist auf seiner dunkeln Stelle,
> wie ein dunkler Sprung durch eine helle
> Tasse geht.   (III, 174)

> (Compare, in the Eighth Elegy:
>   Wie vor sich selbst
> erschreckt, durchzuckts die Luft, wie wenn ein Sprung
> durch eine Tasse geht.)   (III, 295)

> und kleine Tage wie bei Patenier, . . .
> durch die die Brücken springen wie die Hunde,
> dem hellen Wege immer auf der Spur . . .   (III, 84)

> ein Lächeln, wie aus lauter Flicken   (III, 173)

> und drin die Gärten sind auf gleiche Weise
> gekleidet und wie Waisen gleich gekämmt   (III, 94)

> holt sie aus springenden Lidern zwei wache
> Blicke und zeigt diese harte Sache,
> wie man aus einem geheimen Fache
> schöne ererbte Steine nimmt.   (III, 229)

The following group is related to the foregoing, but the accent is more on the originality created by the poet's bold imagination that strikes out in regions where he is a pioneer:

> Und seine Sinne waren wie entzweit:
> indes der Blick ihm wie ein Hund vorauslief, . . .
> blieb sein Gehör wie ein Geruch zurück.   (III, 100)

>   In den Munden
> die glatten Zähne wie ein Reiseschachspiel
> aus Elfenbein in Reihen aufgestellt.   (III, 96)

> und seine Maske, die nun bang verstirbt,
> ist zart und offen wie die Innenseite
> von einer Frucht, die an der Luft verdirbt.   (III, 30)

> und die Gelenke lebten wie die Kehlen
> von Trinkenden   (III, 107)

Wie in der Hand ein Schwefelzündholz, weiss,
eh es zur Flamme kommt, nach allen Seiten
zuckende Zungen streckt —: beginnt im Kreis
naher Beschauer hastig, hell und heiss
ihr runder Tanz sich zuckend auszubreiten.   (III, 82)

Wie in einem Schlaftrunk Spezerein,
löst sie leise in dem flüssigklaren
Spiegel ihr ermüdetes Gebaren;
und sie tut ihr Lächeln ganz hinein.   (III, 228)

Note the poet's precision when he speaks, not of a fruit, but of the inside of a fruit that is decaying; how he sustains the image of the liquid, quoted above, from *Dame vor dem Spiegel*, when he continues

Und sie wartet, dass die Flüssigkeit
davon steigt; dann giesst sie ihre Haare
in den Spiegel und, die wunderbare
Schulter hebend aus dem Abendkleid,
trinkt sie still aus ihrem Bild . . .   (III, 228)

Remarkable, too, is the inevitability of the simile in *Bildnis* (of Eleonora Duse), where the actress must lift her fate, because it is 'a vessel without a foot' which she cannot put down; or the (perhaps too extreme) audacity in the simile of the adventurer's look (III, 209)

welcher war: als hätte er von Rosen
Kinder, die man irgendwo erzog.

This startling image convinces before it is intellectually grasped, before we understand that women for him were no more than roses he had lifted to his face, even if he had children by them.

Not a few of the similes in *Neue Gedichte* are indirect, i.e. the comparison is, as it were, oblique, an action being likened to a thing, or a thing to an action:

mit einem Blick, als ob er löge   (III, 177)

Leicht, wie nach ihrem Tode,
trägt sie die Handschuh, das Tuch   (III, 175)

sie stand wie mühsam in der Fensternische.   (III, 68)

The following is among the most involved of these oblique comparisons:

Denk, dass einer heiss und glühend flüchte,
und die Sieger wären hinterher,
und auf einmal machte der
Flüchtende kurz, unerwartet, kehr
gegen Hunderte — : so sehr
warf sich das Erglühende der Früchte
immer wieder an das blaue Meer . . .   (III, 186)

We are shown a fugitive who suddenly turns round to face his pursuers: thus, the poet says, the glowing colour of the oranges throws itself continuously against the blue sea. A more dramatic way of suggesting a violent contrast of colour can hardly be imagined.

Where the poet needs a chiaroscuro effect, this indirectness can tail off into a certain vagueness, a deliberate obscurity or half-light of similes; in these instances, he uses words like 'a bright object', or 'water', or 'the grave':

> . . . war nicht ihre
> Stirne wie ein lichter Gegenstand?   (III, 118) ✓
>
> Alles was durch meine Kinderjahre
> namenlos noch und wie Wasser glänzt   (III, 15)
>
> ihm Himmel hinter Grün und Dunkel zeigend
> wie einen unbekannten Gegenstand   (III, 79)
>
> wie noch unbestimmbar, wie noch nicht   (III, 185)
>
> und dich weitergeben wie das Grab   (III, 11)
>
> wie Ruhm in der Luft.   (III, 346)

The next group shows the cerebral quality of Rilke's similes; cerebral because the things adduced for the comparison are experiences only an intellectual or exceptionally sensitive person could have. Again, the normal process of the more familiar, or actually observed thing explaining an unfamiliar, or abstract thing, is reversed, as in *Der Marmorkarren*, where the actually observed advance of the cart through the traffic of the great city is likened to the interruption by the hero of the commotion in a drama:

> wie der Held das Drängen in den Dramen
> erst sichtbar macht und plötzlich unterbricht:
> so kommt es durch den stauenden Verlauf
> des Tages . . .   (III, 77)

The most notable instance of this reversion, however, is *Der Schwan* (III, 51), where the toil of life is likened to the 'uncreated' walk of the swan, and his launching into the water to dying; but the poem is called The Swan and is really about the swan, which, first on the ground and then in the water, is felt as a symbol of life and death: so this poem is rather a symbolist one than one containing a simile. The two: observed swan and emotionally felt transition from life to death, are inextricably interwoven in this poem, until they attain a mysterious unity.

Here are a few more examples of oblique similes:

> Ein Gespenst ist noch wie eine Stelle
> dran dein Blick mit einen Klange stösst   (III, 181)
> wie sich aus eines Traumes Ausgeburten . . .
> der nächste Tag erhebt, — so gehn die Gurten
> der Wölbung aus dem wirren Kapitäl   (III, 39)
> Im Sturm, der um die starke Kathedrale
> wie ein Verneiner stürzt, der denkt und denkt.   (III, 32)

Finally, here is a selection to show that Rilke did not always forgo the opportunity of poetic heightening offered by similes; he could light up a passage and add beauty to it by a striking, if simple, comparison, or by the associations that accompany it:

> Ich zittere wie eine Bitte   (III, 10)
> Sein wirres Leben lag
> verlassen wie verrufne Meeresküste
> unter dem Sternbild ihrer stillen Brüste.   (III, 18)
> bisweilen durch ein Lächeln unterschieden,
> für das ein Antlitz seiner Stunden Frieden
> bewahrt hat als ein stilles Zifferblatt   (III, 35)
> So seh ich, Jesus, deine Füsse wieder . . .
> wie standen sie verwirrt in meinen Haaren
> und wie ein weisses Wild im Dornenbusch   (III, 28)
> . . . von der leichten Leier,
> die in die Linke eingewachsen war
> wie Rosenranken in den Ast des Ölbaums   (III, 100)
> . . . um sich durchzustreiten
> durch die Erde, wie ein junges Jahr   (III, 162)
> wirst du schlafen können, ohne
> dass ich wie eine Lindenkrone
> mich verflüstre über dir?   (III, 238)

Some poems in *Neue Gedichte* are built entirely upon an intricate interplay of images, as *Die Gazelle*:

> Verzauberte: wie kann der Einklang zweier
> erwählter Worte je den Reim erreichen,
> der in dir kommt und geht, wie auf ein Zeichen.
> Aus deiner Stirne steigen Laub und Leier,
>
> und alles Deine geht schon im Vergleich
> durch Liebeslieder, deren Worte, weich
> wie Rosenblätter, dem, der nicht mehr liest,
> sich auf die Augen legen, die er schliesst,
>
> um dich zu sehen: hingetragen, als
> wäre mit Sprüngen jeder Lauf geladen
> und schösse nur nicht ab, solang der Hals

M

das Haupt ins Horchen hält: wie wenn beim Baden
im Wald die Badende sich unterbricht,
den Waldsee im gewendeten Gesicht.   (III, 45)

We had to quote the whole poem to show how the poet approaches
his subject with a series of ethereal images and comparisons that take
their starting point from the gazelle, then lead farther and farther
away from it until, like water to a fountain, they fall back to it
in a beautiful arch, only to leave it once more in the last image
of the bathing woman, so startling and at the same time so
convincing—the whole giving an eerie sensation, brought about
by an extraordinary feat of artistry. The technical skill of such
a poem is enough to take our breath away, yet it is skill to a
purpose, not displayed for its own sake: a magician, the poet
succeeds in conjuring up before our eyes the gazelle as seen and felt
by him, the creature moving with inimitable swiftness and grace.
It is the real gazelle and the gazelle of dreams, of Oriental tales and
fables, the gazelle of this moment and the gazelle of all times. The
technique serves only to fix these moving, superimposed and hence-
forth inseparable images, blend them into a whole as delicate and
firm as blown glass. A similar feat is achieved in *Persisches Heliotrop*,
when the poet, starting off with the rose, introduces the heliotrope
by way of contrast, leads away from it over the Bulbul to the distant
and strange image of the vowels (a true poet's simile, very Rilkean),
and back again to the flower, adding, as a last touch, its fragrance
in the closing lines.

Greatness, often with a sombre note, is the characteristic of the
poetic similes in the *Elegies*:

                  . . . die ihr unter den Händen
euch reichlicher werdet wie Traubenjahre   (III, 267)
wie aus geölter, glatterer Luft   (III, 278)
sondern die Väter, die wie Trümmer Gebirgs
uns im Grunde beruhn   (III, 273)
                  Wie ein gestreckter
Arm ist mein Rufen.   (III, 292)

Some of the similes in the *Elegies* are quite peculiar to Rilke,
being as striking as they are unexpected:

                  Sind wir in ihre
Züge soviel nur gemischt wie das Vage in die Gesichter
schwangerer Frauen?   (III, 266)
                  dem eigenen Lächeln
sind sie voran wie das Rossegespann in den milden
muldigen Bildern von Karnak dem siegenden König (III, 285)

[die Kirche] reinlich und zu und enttäuscht wie ein
                    Postamt am Sonntag   (III, 303)

              die halbe Sicherheit des Vogels,
der beinah beides weiss aus seinem Ursprung,
als wär er eine Seele der Etrusker   (III, 295)

              und selbst den eigenen Namen
wegzulassen wie ein zerbrochenes Spielzeug.   (III, 262)

The similes of the *Sonnets* are perhaps still more spiritual, often of an ethereal delicacy:

              Ein zum Rühmen Bestellter
ging er hervor wie das Erz aus des Steins
Schweigen.   (III, 319)

              Die Erde
ist wie ein Kind, das Gedichte weiss   (III, 333)

Wir aber nehmen an Kraft ab, wie Schwimmer   (III, 336)

oder jene so offenen, wie das Aug
eines frohen erwachenden Hirten   (III, 322)
       (said of sarcophagi)

dein Duft... plötzlich liegt er wie Ruhm in der Luft (III, 346)

und Warmes der Mädchen, wie Beichten,
von euch gebend, wie trübe ermüdende Sünden   (III, 347)
       (said of flowers)

flehend nah wie das Gesicht von Hunden.   (III, 368)

Finally, a number of similes found in *Letzte Gedichte* and *Späte Gedichte*, that will on the whole confirm the characteristics of those in the *Elegies*, only that some of them are harder, more ruthless, in their unconventional newness:

          Abschiede biegen sich wie grüne Ruten.   (S.G., 40)

          Liebende kamen abendlich zusammen
          und starrten sich bei Nacht wie Schmieden an   (S.G., 79)

          Dennoch es heult bei Nacht wie die Sirenen der Schiffe
          in mir das Fragende, heult nach dem Weg   (III, 393)

          Man muss ihnen die harte Gegenwart
          ausnehmen, wie ein künstliches Gebiss   (III, 413)

          wie ein volles Theater, bild ich ein grosses Gesicht,
          dass deines hohen mittleren Auftritts
          nichts mir entginge.   (III, 470)

Perhaps the most transcendental of Rilke's similes, in the sense of pure poetry, is this:

     Wie der Abendwind durch geschulterte Sensen der Schnitter
     geht der Engel lind durch die schuldlose Schneide der Leiden.
                                                       (III, 469)

DEVELOPMENT AND GROWTH OF
RILKE'S STYLE

Frühe Gedichte and *Buch der Bilder, first edition*

RAINER MARIA RILKE was a careful and exacting stylist, yet unlike some other poets, he was not fascinated by form as such. To him, form was a means to an end only, and the end was the poem, his poem. In Rilke's letters we find many passages dealing with poetry: there are the series of letters addressed to his Polish translator and those to a young poet, dealing almost exclusively with his art; yet, except for a notable passage in a letter to his publisher, and a few very general remarks about style in other letters, we cannot quote a single sentence relating to style, diction or other questions of poetic technique. Unlike Rückert, Platen, Liliencron, the mature Rilke would never write a poem to try his hand at some interesting verse form, or to explore the possibilities of a certain rhyming scheme. To him, poetry meant pure expression, and therefore he could not, except in his earliest work, approach it from the outside, from the realm of form. He had, moreover, little of the innovator and nothing of the rebel in his nature; mere novelty did not attract him. If his later style becomes markedly individual, very distinct and personal, this was achieved by a permeation of all the elements of contemporary language and form as he found them, with his maturing craftsmanship and personality. These elements were gradually transformed and assimilated until Rilke's poetic thought and the instrument for its expression were in complete harmony.

Rilke's poetry provides the rare opportunity of studying a poet's steady development and progress. In his letters and prose works, the poet himself frequently gives expression to his conviction that a poet must mature, and in the characteristic, often quoted passage from *Malte Laurids Brigge* (V, 27), he asserts that the stuff poets write when very young counts for nothing; only after years of silent meditation, of sustained and painful experience, can a poet hope to find 'the first word of a poem'. Speaking *pro domo*, he does not realize how much his conviction is at variance with the fact that so many great lyrical poets have given their best when very young and quite without experience; we might even say, in contrast to Rilke's theory, that poetry is an outburst that more often resembles the blossom than the fruit. Most poets are born, not made, and as in spring the flowers burst forth overnight, so youth is the moment when the mighty forces of life combine with the poet's natural gift to create a flame-like exuberance of production. Few indeed are the lyrical poets whose art is seen to improve with their maturing years, and notable, on the other hand, is the number of those who later abandon poetry, either to become silent altogether, or to turn their creative powers to the epic, the drama, the writing of prose. Rilke's often repeated assertion does not even quite fit his own case, for he could still be called a young man when he wrote *Buch der Bilder* and the *Stundenbuch*. But on the whole it is true to say that maturity brought out his best gifts and suppressed his worst defects; his poetry, more perhaps than that of any other poet, marks the stages of a 'gradus as Parnassum'.

This process was slow and progressive. Rilke was by birth Austrian, more precisely Bohemian. An admixture of Slav blood as well as his early surroundings account for his personal melody, which is soft, slow, musical:

> Mich rührt so sehr
> böhmischen Volkes Weise,
> schleicht sie ins Herz sich leise,
> macht sie es schwer.   (I, 61)

These often quoted lines show the Slav character with its melancholy softness. The young Rilke was by no means strikingly original; in his early works we encounter much of the general style of the Austrian school: a mild impressionism, very open to moods (*Stimmungen*), rather fastidious in the choice of words, aesthetic, slightly sensuous, softly expressive. His earliest poems, although not important for their own sake, must be of interest to us as the starting point of his poetical career.

A certain virtuosity was a feature of Rilke's style from the very beginning, and in his juvenilia we already encounter many of the characteristics of his later manner. His art of rhyming is perhaps the most conspicuous, but alliteration, vowelling and enjambment are present as well, which shows how instinctive these devices were with him, how much they belong to his original equipment. As a young poet, he has not yet learnt to use them with discretion; a youthful tendency to show off such arts to what he considers their best advantage is unmistakable, and this trait is especially marked in his treatment of rhyme. The young Rilke of the Prague and Munich periods shows an almost childish delight in making long, difficult or unusual words rhyme in a novel manner. While his other technical resources are somewhat subdued, all are marked by an adolescent lack of taste and assurance, which, by their naïvety, to some degree counteracts the virtuosity, making it more apparent than real.

The main source for this relative technical achievement was Rilke's natural talent for form: he was a born poet in the sense that Mozart was a born musician, endowed with a specific, irrepressible gift. Such talent is by no means as universal as is sometimes believed; minor artists may possess it, while great masters have to acquire laboriously the technical foundation of their art. What then prevented the springtime of Rilke's poetry from being as radiant as that of most young poets? Why are his first productions so bad that they have hardly any attraction for us, and are of no account in his collected works? The cause may partly lie with his unhappy childhood and youth which, together with a hereditary disposition, resulted in a repressed character incapable of natural, spontaneous expression. Rilke somehow could not sing out, the song was stifled in his throat, and his marvellous technical facility, coupled with this unhappy character, might have turned out to be more of a handicap than an asset, had he not striven so hard to find a balance in later years. It was because the faculty of writing musical, mellifluous, varied verse came so easily to him as a youth that he re-iterated those insistent warnings, directed to himself perhaps as much as to the young poets he addresses, to beware of the production of this age and the cheap satisfaction they might bring.

Rilke's poetry of his first period (*Larenopfer*, 1896, *Traumgekrönt*, 1897), was the production of a very gifted, but severely repressed, youth, lonely in spite of many contacts, deprived of the stimulating intercourse with congenial or admired friends, not widely read, inexperienced and as yet untravelled. Nor was he in love. The influences he had felt were of a rather casual nature, probably mostly those of poets he had read at school as a boy. He was not living at the centre of a movement, and therefore lacked the opportunity of feeling the stimulus of the best contemporary minds, heard few critical voices and thus had no standards for improving his taste and judgment. All this is true of other young poets; but it must be admitted that the young Rilke was particularly clumsy, '*weltfremd*', in these as in other respects. He was not even good at choosing his own books: had friends, e.g. Jakob Wassermann, not suggested to him some of the authors that later were to influence him so greatly, he might not have discovered them for himself.

The models we discover for his first poems were mainly Heine, Lenau, Mörike, C. F. Meyer and Liliencron. The fact that Rilke only mentions Liliencron when, in a letter to Hermann Pongs,[1] he gives an account of the poets who influenced him at this early period, shows that the other influences must have been either unconscious, or appeared too negligible to be mentioned. Indeed they were such as a young poet who had attended a German school could hardly escape at one time or another. Heine thus dominated several generations with an influence as vague and general as it is constant, relating more to genre and tone than to specific forms and devices. One example may stand for many:

> Die Sonne schmolz, die hehre,
> ins weisse Meer so heiss. —
> Zwei Mönche sassen am Meere,
> ein blonder und ein Greis.   (I, 77)

While such a poem is almost pure Heine, even to the point of caricature, there are others where the influence is diluted, and the model discerned more or less vaguely through the general outline.

Mörike's influence, so different from Heine's, is more difficult to trace. It is surprising that Rilke never mentions Mörike's name anywhere. The Swabian poet's natural perfection is so inconspicuous that it is hard to define his style by naming characteristic elements in it; it does not rest on any particular combination of devices, but on the poet's genius for hitting upon the right word, the right rhythm, the right intonation in a most natural, quietly convincing and seemingly effortless manner. Rilke seems to have been most influenced by his melody: we noted that his favourite rhyming scheme, abaaab (with variations), has probably been taken over from Mörike, with whom it occurs several times.

Conrad Ferdinand Meyer, on the other hand, is much more colourful and sharply outlined. In contrast to Heine as well as to Mörike, he is not the nonchalantly singing poet, but the conscious artist who carefully moulds and shapes his poems. His combination of intelligence, culture and sensuous colour achieved rounded little masterpieces, a species rare in German poetry, where, as a rule, the first fine careless rapture predominates over the artist's conscious effort. Meyer's influence produced, in Rilke's cycle *Aus dem*

---

[1] Published in *Dichtung und Volkstum*, Bd. 37, 1936.

dreissigjährigen Kriege (I, 80 ff.), a few close imitations, especially in rhythm, but the influence of the Swiss poet's technique of alliteration and vowel music will be fully felt at a later stage only.

It is Liliencron's chief merit to have revitalized the language of poetry, grown stale in endless imitation of the German classics, especially Schiller. With his bracing everyday words and his sometimes nonchalant, but always musical, metre Liliencron invades, long before Stefan George, the withering flower beds of German poetry like a refreshing breeze. His use of language and metre is direct and unaffected, his rhymes are remarkable for their purity. But in spite of his admiration, the values Rilke could take over from Liliencron were superficial ones only, such as pure rhymes and certain 'modern' words, hitherto banned from poetry; the elder poet's best qualities—his naturalness, honesty and freshness—were denied to Rilke, whose personality was wholly antithetical to the masculine Liliencron. We mentioned *Der Engel* (I, 36), as a close imitation of Liliencron's manner; similar reminiscences may be found in *Im Sommer* (I, 73), *Wintermorgen* (I, 42), *Es kommt in prunkenden Gebreiten* (I, 190), as well as in other early poems.

Rilke mentions Stefan George as another admired model, but it is difficult to find traces of his influence in the early work. George's harsh diction was the very opposite of Rilke's soft melody. Perhaps some of the younger poet's many decorative words were shaped after similar ones he may have encountered in George's poems, such as *silbriges Dunkel, blasser Karmin, das trümmergrosse Rom, die Purpurgolfe* (from various George poems).

All these influences were unco-ordinated in Rilke's early style; at that period, he could write more or less 'in the manner of' each of the models that influenced him, without amalgamating such reminiscences into a whole. His style is an inorganic mixture, and though marked by unmistakable talent and soon also by a certain originality, there is something provincial about it in the sense that it lacked a wide background, a rich and uniform tradition, and above all a sure taste. The uncertainty of Rilke's early style is accentuated by the word order, often reversed for no better reason than to fit the metre, by affectations like the frequent placing of the adjective after the noun (*Glühwürmchen hängt, das regungslose*), by the indiscriminate mixing of pointedly common words with stilted and solemn ones, by the preponderance of ornate epithets, quaint rhymes and a somewhat laboured alliteration. Among the dreary sentimentalities and false heartiness in *Larenopfer*, we sometimes encounter a flash of the later Rilke, as in the poem *Mittelböhmische Landschaft*:

> . . .
>
> Im hellsten Licht
> keimt die Kartoffel; dann
> ein wenig weiter Gerste, bis der Tann
> das Bild begrenzt.
> Hoch überm Jungwald glänzt
> so goldig-rot ein Kirchturmkreuz herüber,
> aus Fichten ragt der Hegerhütte Bau; . . . (I, 101)

The sureness of touch with which the 'unpoetic' potato is introduced, followed by *Gerste* and the beautifully sober name *Hegerhütte* render the poem graphic and firm in outline and give it a very original ring, spoilt somehow by *so goldig-rot ein Kirchtumkreuz*—had Rilke not been so unsure of himself, he might have written fine poetry even at that period.

The next development of Rilke's poetry covers roughly the years 1897 to 1900 and his stay in Germany. If the previous period was an eclectic one, this might be called his ornate period. The publications of these years are *Advent* (1898) and *Mir zur Feier* (1899), and the dominating influences Jacobsen and Maeterlinck, influences which, however, mainly affect Rilke's outlook and aesthetic principles, and only indirectly his style. Jacobsen's personality was not unlike Rilke's, and he was very fastidious in the choice of his words.

All the poems contained in the two above-named collections are short and rhymed, hardly any have titles. We note considerable progress in style from one collection to the next; the various conflicting influences are now being rapidly amalgamated and unified, until finally the poet's own melody emerges with clarity. Yet if cleansed and purified, it is still a somewhat thin and brittle melody, dependent to a great extent on an ornamental, superficial use of language, on the exhibition of a skilfully woven word-beauty, on passages like

> Nach einem Glück ist meine Seele lüstern,
> nach einem kurzen dummen Wunderwahn . . .
> Im Quellenquirlen und im Föhrenflüstern
> da hör ichs nahn . . . (I, 154)

Some of the more convincing pieces are still, with considerable virtuosity, modelled on Liliencron:

> Stille rings. Nur ein geblähter
> Frosch hält eine Mückenjagd,
> und ein Käfer schwimmt im Äther,
> ein lebendiger Smaragd. (I, 46)

Gedenkst du noch, wie guter Dinge
wir wallten durch das Nusler Tal;
zwei kleine, blaue Schmetterlinge
verflatterten im Abendstrahl. (I, 59)

But with increasing frequency, we now encounter passages which in their mature, quiet assurance already contain germs of Rilke's later art:

Schau, wie die Zypressen schwärzer werden
In den weiten Wiesen. Und auf wen
Die Gestalten mit den Steingebärden
Warten in den wachsenden Alleen?

This is the original version, which the poet later (1909) revised to read:

Schau, wie die Zypressen schwärzer werden
in den Wiesengründen, und auf wen
in den unbetretbaren Alleen
die Gestalten mit den Steingebärden
weiterwarten, die uns übersehn. (I, 290)

Here, enjambment is conspicuous in Rilke's typical manner, occurring at each of three line endings; rather as an expression of the natural cadence particular to his melody than as a consciously employed artistic device. Still more graphic, compelling in its broad, massive simplicity, is a passage like this:

Weiss-weiter Weg, der sich in Licht verlor,
Und Sonnenwucht auf allem Weingelände,
Und dann auf einmal, wie ein Traum — ein Tor,
Breit eingebaut in unsichtbare Wände.

This, again, is the original version, later amended to:

Blendender Weg, der sich vor Licht verlor,
Sonnengewicht auf allem Weingelände,
und dann auf einmal, wie im Traum: ein Tor,
breit eingebaut in unsichtbare Wände. (I, 292)

The effect produced by such lines is no longer based on decorative words with their facile associations, but on a sure mastery over the means of language: there is balance, a right distribution of weight and accents, a firm yet varied rhythm, and the whole is unmistakably original and Rilke's very own style and melody.

Sometimes, we are even distantly reminded of *Neue Gedichte*, as in lines like

Das ist dort, wo die letzten Hütten sind
und neue Häuser, die mit engen Brüsten
sich drängen aus den bangen Baugerüsten
und wissen wollen, wo das Feld beginnt. (I, 296)

Yet such passages are still in the nature of exceptions among a mass of monotonously mellifluous, uniformly 'beautiful' poems lacking the occasional unevenness and even harshness that mark a more sincere creation.

The first edition of *Buch der Bilder* appeared in 1902. The fact that Rilke, in a lengthy correspondence with his publisher, insisted on a large type, fine paper, a beautiful binding, reveals how much store he set by this collection, which undoubtedly was the most important he had yet given to the public. The edition contains forty-five poems of different length and very unequal merit. Judging historically from Rilke's development, we see in *Buch der Bilder* a product of transition, yet at the time of its publication, it must have been possible, for a critic with a discerning ear, to detect in these poems a great promise, a new and strong melody the like of which had not been heard before on the German Parnassus. *Buch der Bilder* is an ambitious book, a feature that may to some extent spoil it for us to-day; at the moment of its publication, however, the poet's bid for greatness had its justification and weight.

It is, as we said, a work of transition, i.e. the poems come from one plane and move to another; a few, however, will stand at our bidding, a law to themselves, as every good poem should be. Such are *Musik, Aus einer Kindheit, Zum Einschlafen zu sagen, Im welken Walde* (later named '*Bangnis*'), *Gebet, Fortschritt, Ernste Stunde, Srophen, Die heiligen drei Könige, Fragmente aus verlorenen Tagen, Der Lesende, Der Schauende*. These pieces are not without their faults, yet different as they may be from one another and in their intrinsic merit, they have that mysterious quality that makes a poem, gives it character, necessity, the assurance of a thing organically created.

A few passages will illustrate this point:

> Gib ihr ein Schweigen, dass die Seele leise
> heimkehre in das Flutende und Viele,
> darin sie lebte, wachsend, weit und weise,
> eh du sie zwangst in deine zarten Spiele.   (II, 22)

The later Rilke would perhaps have avoided the word *Seele*, but he need not have felt ashamed of the firm ring of these lines, which convincingly compress his thought into few words. We note an early preference for adverbial clauses (three in four lines) and the characteristic participles, one of which, *das Flutende*, is used as a noun, coupled in alliteration with the unusual *das Viele*, the other, *wachsend*, in conjunction with the alliterating adjectives *weit und*

weise. Deine zarten Spiele recalls Stefan George. The lines are
compact without being overloaded, a beginning of the poet's
closely knit later manner. This passage is taken from an otherwise
imperfect poem; another, *Zum Einschlafen zu sagen*, is perfect in
itself, if not quite original, for there are faint reminiscences of
Liliencron as well as Dehmel. By means of a regular rhythm, a
symmetrical rhyming scheme, a sparing and enlightened use of
vowel sounds and alliteration, Rilke has composed a cradle song
vibrating with restrained music. How simply and effectively he
evokes the clocks, in the middle of the poem:

> Die Uhren rufen sich schlagend an,   (II, 40)

with the two long, sonorous '*u*' following each other, and echoing
off into the two '*a*' of different length. Likewise the concluding
line is exquisite with the discreet alliteration of its two nouns, the
last long '*e*' fixing and tranquillizing the preceding vowels, all short
with the exception of an unaccented '*ei*', with three short '*i*' in
sequence in the middle of the line:

> wenn ein Ding sich im Dunkel bewegt.   (II, 40)

Less perfect, if more original, is *Im welken Walde* (II, 48), one of the
few poems where the influence of Maeterlinck is obvious. Slightly
artificial, it is nevertheless powerful in its concentrated endeavour
at giving expression to an intangible feeling. Rilke goes about this
task with heavy repetitions, bringing both *welken Wald* and *Vogelruf*
twice in the first three lines, and *welken Walde* again in the fifth.
The adjectives are simple and graphic: *der runde Vogelruf, breit wie
ein Himmel, der grosse Wind.* There is a dynamic quality, combined
with, or rather attuned to, great subtlety, in this piece, a thing new
in German poetry. It is fully illustrated by the central line,

> Gefügig räumt sich alles in den Schrei,   (II, 48)

which is masterly in its concentration and simplicity; a relative
simplicity, for it is fastidious language used in simple arrangement.

   Gebet is interesting as one of the earliest poems to contain the
word *Ding*, which occurs five times; moreover, we observe Rilke's
manner of posing symmetrical, quietly insisting questions. Among
the passages in *Buch der Bilder* that point to the future are the last
lines of *Fortschritt*:

> mit meinen Sinnen, wie mit Vögeln, reiche
> ich in die windigen Himmel aus der Eiche,
> und in den abgebrochnen Tag der Teiche
> sinkt, wie auf Fischen stehend, mein Gefühl.   (II, 57)

The similes here are very novel, perhaps too much so to be fully
convincing; the felicitous adjective in *windige Himmel* (compare
windiges Licht, III, 83) contributes a fine assonance, and *der abge-
brochne Tag der Teiche* is most original, while the whole is so densely
and harmoniously interwoven that it creates a poetic atmosphere
of its own. *Strophen*, one of the few poems in which Hofmannsthal's
influence can be clearly discerned, is not a perfect poem, but it
moves with a subdued force, and contains the lovely line

still liegend in des Mantels Melodie.   (II, 64)

Die heiligen drei Könige is one of Rilke's few humorous poems;
he calls it *Legende*, and it stands somewhat isolated in *Buch der Bilder*.
For the student of Rilke's style this piece is of special interest, as
it shows what effects he could achieve when he chose to write in a
playful mood that allowed a nonchalantly sovereign use of his
means. The result is a graceful, if slight, little virtuoso piece in
which rhythm, rhyme, diction, alliteration and all the other arts
are skilfully blended to produce a colourful and sparkling effect:

und der zu seiner Rechten ging,
der war ein goldner Mann;
und der zu seiner Linken fing
mit Schwung und Schwing
und Klang und Kling
aus einem runden Silberding,
das wiegend und in Ringen hing,
ganz blau zu rauchen an.   (II, 75)

Nouns and adjectives contribute to the pattern: *Rex, tumb, Funkel-
fürst, Heidenscheich, Magenkraft*. This poem is an early specimen of
the supreme technical mastery Rilke was capable of, although he
rarely employed it in this unserious vein.

A proportion of length is a basic premise of good poetry: one
of the qualities of the perfect poem is that, among all possible
lengths, it finds the delicate balance of its optimum length. Rilke
still fails conspicuously in this respect in *Buch der Bilder*: many of
its longer poems are too long, and moreover, he has not yet discovered that a long poem does not require variation, especially
not of metre, but uniformity. It is a curious phenomenon that,
while the short poem seems to gain by a certain amount of variation,
the longer poem loses by it, or to be more precise, the longer poem
tolerates very delicate, subdued variation only, to be exercised
within the framework of a seemingly rigid outward uniformity.
The variations by which Rilke seeks to enliven the longer pieces

in *Buch der Bilder* are not of this subtle kind, being mainly concerned with length of line and with metre, changes more appropriate within the short poem, and felt as a disturbance in the even flow of the longer one. He also frequently divides these longer poems into several sections, thus destroying their balance.

Summing up, we find that in the first edition of *Buch der Bilder* Rilke's style begins to outgrow the monotonous decorative beauty of his previous production, and is gaining in originality and firmness. It is now wider of range, more versatile, not content, as before, with a single minor key. At the same time, it lacks assurance, is wavering between short, middle and long forms, between simple statement or description and ornate periphrasis. Rilke's style of this period, as also that of his previous collections, is conditioned by his sojourn in Germany and the somewhat provincial outlook of his milieu there. Schmargendorf, although near Berlin, was painfully suburban, and Worpswede and Westerwede were colonies of second-rate artists. The style resulting from such surroundings is narrow and intense, often precious and affected; it lacks that sureness of touch that a great tradition or an established society give its followers or members. Due to general intellectual conditions in Germany, few German artists of that period, poets as well as painters or sculptors, were entirely free from a somewhat cramped artificiality. The artist was not borne along on a great tradition, he had to be a pioneer and create his own atmosphere, his own style, with all the struggles and sacrifices that implied. Rilke had to go abroad to find himself and to forge the instrument for his art.

Stundenbuch

The *Stundenbuch*, written between 1899 and 1903, lies across Rilke's last German and first Paris period, yet unlike *Buch der Bilder*, it cannot be called a work of transition. It is the sum of the poet's intentions, struggles and insights, a final effort of expression beyond which, at that period, he could not proceed in that direction. When analysing Rilke's verse forms, we found that the *Stundenbuch* is a whole formed by single poems of unequal length and metre, all rhymed, linked together more by the motive that makes one proceed from the foregoing than by any formal connection. Without the strong underlying current of forward-driving poetic thought, the *Stundenbuch* would fall to pieces. This flow is something it has in common with the epic, yet the *Stundenbuch*, in spite of a few episodes of a narrative character, is purely lyrical poetry.

Rilke did perhaps not plan this work as a whole from the beginning; when he had started on it he informed Lou Andreas Salomé[1] that he was writing *Gebete*, prayers, but the division into three books and their final union under the title *Stundenbuch* must have come about naturally, for there is nothing forced or artificial about it. The *Stundenbuch* is not a more or less loosely assembled group of poems on one theme, but a poetic outburst with an *élan* that presses on and on till it has exhausted its force. The experience nourishing that outburst had come from Russia: it was there that Rilke had felt, like a revelation, the great breadth and width of life, a real life that freed him from the sentimentally overstressed artificiality of his 'artistic' surroundings in Germany. The two short trips to Russia had helped in breaking down the walls of that milieu, they had truly liberated the poet and released a creative force that had lain suppressed and dormant. The Russian experience was then followed by intense suffering in Paris, a suffering that became the background to the last of the three books that compose the *Stundenbuch*. Thus, although written during several years and at different places, the *Stundenbuch* is after all a unity, expressing and summarizing an important period of Rilke's slowly maturing personality.

Rilke is lavish in the *Stundenbuch* with the three main elements of his formal equipment: rhyme, alliteration and vowelling, to which rhythm must be added as a fourth. Sometimes one, sometimes another of these elements appear to prevail, but on the whole they interact to form a texture of great density and a somewhat heavy beauty. The rhymes are pure, varied, often original in their novelty, if at times too insistent with the frequency of their recurring echoes. The same reproach of a slight too-much might be levied against alliteration and vowel sounds, but more often than not, the wealth of sound they contribute is necessary to what the poet wishes to express. Take this passage as an example:

> Da wachsen Kinder auf an Fensterstufen,
> die immer in demselben Schatten sind,
> und wissen nicht, dass draussen Blumen rufen
> zu einem Tag voll Weite, Glück und Wind, —
> und müssen Kind sein und sind traurig Kind.   (II, 271)

The loud sonority of *draussen Blumen rufen* is really like a call, and how fine is the combination of expressive vowel sounds with moderate alliteration in *zu einem Tag voll Weite, Glück und Wind*!

[1] Lou Andreas Salomé, *Rainer Maria Rilke*, 1929, p. 33.

In the *Stundenbuch* Rilke's style has acquired spaciousness and
with it greatness, due no doubt to his Russian experience. In a
poem of this length we cannot, of course, expect an equal intensity
throughout. There must be subdued interludes, quieter passages,
transitions from one part to another, and summits where the thought
leaps out into a vivid flame of heat and light. From the wealth of
such passages we will give two in full, while indicating others:

> Erneue ihn mit einer reinen Speise,
> mit Tau, mit ungetötetem Gericht,
> mit jenem Leben, das wie Andacht leise
> und warm wie Atem aus den Feldern bricht.   (II, 276)
> Hat denn für sie die Erde keinen Raum?
> Wen sucht der Wind? Wer trinkt des Baches Helle?
> Ist in der Teiche tiefem Ufertraum
> kein Spiegelbild mehr frei für Tür und Schwelle?
> Sie brauchen ja nur eine kleine Stelle,
> auf der sie alles haben wie ein Baum.   (II, 288)

Other such concentrated passages are:

> Ich finde dich in allen diesen Dingen . . .   (II, 189)
> Wie der Wächter in den Weingeländen . . .   (II, 217)
> Wer lebt es denn? Sind das die Dinge . . .   (II, 242)
> Man wird dich fühlen: dass ein Duften ginge . . .   (II, 255)
> Bei Tag bist du das Hörensagen . . .   (II, 258)
> Nicht wie die Herren deiner Hirtenvölker . . .   (II, 280)
> Und sieh, wie ihrer Füsse Leben geht . . .   (II, 285)

Much of the subject-matter in the *Stundenbuch* is new, and it is
interesting to study how Rilke succeeds, with the varied means
now at his disposal, in expressing some of his original thoughts
and more unusual emotions:

> Wenn etwas mir vom Fenster fällt
> (und wenn es auch das Kleinste wäre),
> wie stürzt sich das Gesetz der Schwere
> gewaltig wie ein Wind vom Meere
> auf jeden Ball und jede Beere
> und trägt sie in den Kern der Welt.
> Ein jedes Ding ist überwacht
> von einer flugbereiten Güte
> wie jeder Stein und jede Blüte
> und jedes kleine Kind bei Nacht.   (II, 245)

The law of gravity has hardly before been the subject of lyrical
poetry; Rilke's language is capable of dealing with this theme in a
way that is not only persuasive, but even elegant: *flugbereite Güte*
is as original as it is immediately convincing, and the whole passage

is inspired by that strong poetic breath capable of transforming everything into poetry. Here is another instance of that force:

> Das Erz hat Heimweh. Und verlassen
> will es die Münzen und die Räder,
> die es ein kleines Leben lehren.
> Und aus Fabriken und aus Kassen
> wird es zurück in das Geäder
> der aufgetanen Berge kehren,
> die sich verschliessen hinter ihm.   (II, 254)

Erz is a poetic word in the traditional sense; Rilke links it most naturally with *Fabriken* and *Kassen* without causing a break in his language. This embracing unity of style, which we encounter throughout the book, is a considerable achievement.

Finally, a passage that is neither complex nor new in thought, but typical of the great simple strokes with which the artist is painting:

> Alles wird wieder gross sein und gewaltig,
> die Lande einfach und die Wasser faltig,
> die Bäume riesig und sehr klein die Mauern;
> und in den Tälern, stark und vielgestaltig,
> ein Volk von Hirten und von Ackerbauern.   (II, 254-5)

None of the adjectives here is redundant or ornamental; the lines flow along with a fine, natural rhythm, graphically and with great economy expressing the thought.

As may be seen from this quotation, which may stand for many, the last vestiges of Rilke's over-polished ornateness are now disappearing; his style, no longer provincial or affected, is intense and at the same time clear and limpid. Rilke has acquired a considerable word power, he has become eloquent, able to express a wealth of emotion and new thought in a language quite his own. At times, it is true, he is over-eloquent, overwhelming us with a flow of images and beautiful melody; but this is the exuberance of youth, of a young poet testing the full power of his means. There is much in this newly acquired mastery of language that will be of good use to him later on.

Buch der Bilder, second edition

In 1906, Rilke published the second, much enlarged, edition of *Buch der Bilder*, in which he included thirty-seven new poems, while one was withdrawn. These newly added poems are in the majority much superior to those composing the first edition, but for this very reason the collection as such suffered by their inclusion.

N

If the book had been a somewhat motley collection before, it now became a watershed where the streams divide in opposite directions, some flowing towards the past, others towards the future: the reader might be pardoned who thought that *Mondnacht* and *Ritter* were not by the same poet as *Stimmen* or *Pont du Carrousel*. It is difficult to understand why in 1906, when he had written the *Stundenbuch* and quite a number of his *Neue Gedichte*, Rilke did not throw out some of the very bad poems from his revision of *Buch der Bilder*, things like *Mondnacht*, the last lines of which may be quoted here:

> und dann ein Rauschen und ein Ruf der Ronde,
> und eine Weile bleibt das Schweigen leer;
> und eine Geige dann (Gott weiss woher)
> erwacht und sagt ganz langsam:
>
> Eine Blonde . . .   (II, 11)

The student of Rilke's style will encounter, in this second edition, a group of poems evolutionally belonging to *Frühe Gedichte*, another forming a period of transition, still another in the manner of the *Stundenbuch* and finally one much akin to *Neue Gedichte*, while the cycle *Die Stimmen* cannot be classed with any of these groups. The transition poems are perhaps the most interesting; they include *Kindheit, Der Knabe, Einsamkeit, Der Nachbar, Herbsttag, Abend in Skåne*. Measured by Rilke's later achievements, most of these poems fall short, but in spite of this inferiority they also assert themselves: criticism is unable to demolish them completely, they rebound into a position which they hold. Thus *Kindheit*, weighed down by a heavy sentimentality which manifests itself in a certain verbosity, a plethora of epithets and interjections, in the end withstands the test of re-reading and is a poem not easily forgotten. The flaws of the other poems are not strong enough to destroy their virtues. If *Der Knabe* impresses us, on the whole, as dated, it yet contains powerful and original language:

> die Häuser fallen hinter uns ins Knie,
> die Gassen biegen sich uns schief entgegen,
> die Plätze weichen aus . . .   (II, 32)

The later Rilke would have compressed *Die Konfirmanden* into something like half its length, but it is sufficient to quote the last lines to show what limpid beauty was now at his command:

> Es war, als ob die Dinge sich bekränzten,
> sie standen licht, unendlich leicht besonnt;
> ein Fühlen war in jeder Häuserfront,
> und viele Fenster gingen auf und glänzten.   (II, 33)

Einsamkeit marks a great advance in condensed and graphic expression, and the final modulation of the rhyme-sound from *hassen* to *müssen*, combined with the somewhat sudden break in the rhythmical line, is a technical master-stroke:

> und wenn die Menschen, die einander hassen,
> in einem Bett zusammen schlafen müssen:
> dann geht die Einsamkeit mit den Flüssen . . .   (II, 50)

The greatest discord is brought into the collection by the inclusion of the two cycles *Die Zaren* and *Die Stimmen*. The former is in Rilke's best ornate manner, somewhat akin to the eloquence deployed in the *Stundenbuch*:

> Noch immer schauen in den Silberplatten
> wie tiefe Frauenaugen die Saphire,
> Goldranken schlingen sich wie schlanke Tiere,
> die sich im Glanze ihrer Brünste gatten,
> und sanfte Perlen warten in den Schatten
> wilder Gebilde, dass ein Schimmer ihre
> stillen Gesichter finde und verliere.   (II, 104)

It is one of those poems composed of too many highlights, and of uncertain, unconvincing length. *Die Stimmen*, on the other hand, is in the nature of a severe experiment, never repeated by Rilke with such strict consistency; it forms a blind alley in his work, pointing in a direction he later did not follow up. A strong influence was at work, and improbable though it may seem, there can be little doubt it was that of Frank Wedekind. In its austere concentration, this cycle is the greatest imaginable contrast to decorative verbosity; its terse, forceful language, composed of many monosyllables, interspersed with expressive and ugly familiar words that often border on slang, is acute and strident; the jerky rhythms, the end-lines brutally cut into by enjambment, the unadorned directness, the stark bareness, all tend towards a style that might be called expressionistic. This cycle is undoubtedly the outcome of a conscious stylistic effort:

> Ihr rührt euch und rückt und bildet euch ein,
> anders zu klingen als Stein auf Stein,
> aber ihr irrt euch: ich allein
> lebe und leide und lärme.
> In mir ist ein endloses Schrein,
> und ich weiss nicht, schreit mir mein
> Herz oder meine Gedärme.   (II, 123)

The experiment seems, at a first glance, successful: these poems express in a genuinely original manner what the poet wished to convey. But is it Rilke's manner? For once, his Slav melody is totally suppressed. We feel a tremendous effort of self-restraint, and Rilke must have considered the price too high, for he abandoned this path, and *Die Stimmen* stand in his work like an erratic block.

One group of poems in the new edition of *Buch der Bilder*, mostly those written during his first stay in Paris, point to the future, among them *Die Liebende, Die Heilige, Die Konfirmanden, Das Abendmahl, Pont du Carrousel, Die Aschanti, Abend*. Different as they are, they have in common Rilke's new attitude of seemingly impersonal engrossment with his subject. The poet spins a fine web of language, to catch his subject, as it were, in the meshes of this densely woven net. A few of these poems, as *Das Abendmahl, Die Konfirmanden*, are still in the experimental stage; others, as *Die Liebende, Pont du Carrousel, Abend*, might almost belong to *Neue Gedichte*.

> und lassen dich, zu keinem ganz gehörend,
> nicht ganz so dunkel wie das Haus, das schweigt,
> nicht ganz so sicher Ewiges beschwörend
> wie das, was Stern wird jede Nacht und steigt;
>
> und lassen dir (unsäglich zu entwirrn)
> dein Leben, bang und riesenhaft und reifend,
> so dass es, bald begrenzt und bald begreifend,
> abwechselnd Stein in dir wird und Gestirn.   (II, 62)

These two stanzas, from *Abend*, clearly show Rilke's new style, as later developed and perfected in *Neue Gedichte*: the deliberateness of the heavily moving construction with its many clauses (five participle, two relative, one adverbial); the parenthesis and the unornamental, but quietly effective, alliteration. The result gives the impression of a remarkable fullness and concentration; it is as if the language had sucked up the thought until it has become penetrated with it as a sponge with water. This manner is different from anything Rilke had done before.

Neue Gedichte

With *Neue Gedichte* and *Der Neuen Gedichte Anderer Teil*, published in 1907 and 1908, Rilke enters upon a new and most important period in the development of his style, a period relative to which most of his earlier poems, with the exception only of the *Stundenbuch*, appear, in perspective, as immature and groping efforts.

The creation of *Neue Gedichte* is inseparably connected with Paris. Rilke has left Germany behind; he is now no longer stifled by the narrowness of his former German surroundings. Instead of aspiring and dreaming, he creates; for the first time, he stands securely on his own feet, master of his means which he wields with ease and assurance. This assurance, which had often been a pose in his earlier work, has now become a reality and a characteristic that distinguishes him not only from his previous production, but also from that of most of his German contemporaries. Rilke's mature style is sound, there is nothing tentative or experimental about it; we may probe it where we like, we shall always find the structure and quality of good craftsmanship.

His art had now reached a stage where he was able to express everything he had to say (and that meant many new things) in his own very original language. For by now Rilke's style had almost developed into an idiom: more and more elements of the language were embraced by the steady search for accurate expression of his own world, until in the end they were arranged in a definite system centred in his poetic personality.

But why was Rilke not able to adapt the traditional language of German poetry, which a poet like Hofmannsthal could take over and use for his own ends? Perhaps because so much of Rilke's poetic thought was new and had never before found expression in poetry. And not his material only was new; his very personality was strange and had developed away from the ordinary human being, with whom the poet was losing contact. But while Rilke was in need of a vehicle for his thought, his nature shrank from anything that smacked of reform, from any proclaimed new style in the manner of Whitman, G. M. Hopkins or Arno Holz. Hopkins found himself compelled to defend the startling innovations introduced by him against the objections of his friends; Rilke avoided a situation that would have demanded such an attitude. He conquered the language from within, by gradual permeation; a slow process requiring much perseverance, patience, as well as a certain hardness. Rilke himself testifies to this hard quality required of the poet in the words he addresses, in his second Requiem, to Wolf Graf von Kalckreuth:

> O alter Fluch der Dichter,
> die sich beklagen, wo sie sagen sollten,
> die immer urteiln über ihr Gefühl,
> statt es zu bilden; die noch immer meinen,

was traurig ist in ihnen oder froh,
das wüssten sie und dürftens im Gedicht
bedauern oder rühmen. Wie die Kranken
gebrauchen sie die Sprache voller Wehleid,
um zu beschreiben, wo es ihnen wehtut,
statt hart sich in die Worte zu verwandeln,
wie sich der Steinmetz einer Kathedrale
verbissen umsetzt in des Steines Gleichmut.
Dies war die Rettung. Hättest du nur *einmal*
gesehn, wie Schicksal in die Verse eingeht
und nicht zurückkommt, wie es drinnen Bild wird
und nichts als Bild, nicht anders als ein Ahnherr,
der dir im Rahmen, wenn du manchmal aufsiehst,
zu gleichen scheint und wieder nicht zu gleichen — :
du hättest ausgeharrt.   (II, 341–2)

These significant lines aptly describe the break between the Rilke of the early poems (in a wide sense) and the Rilke of *Neue Gedichte*. It was a profound break with the past that was to establish his position as a man and as a poet.

Hardness, which for Stefan George meant, or often became, formal rigidity, was more of a moral quality for Rilke, not incompatible with a very elastic attitude towards form and language. In his struggle with words Rilke rarely uses the frontal attack; he wins, by pliable methods and with infinite patience, position after position, until in the end he is master and the language at his command. The various devices we analysed one by one are, at the period of *Neue Gedichte*, integrated into a unified system in Rilke's poetry. This co-ordination, together with a purifying condensation of Rilke's poetic material, leads to a compressed intensity ('the pressure of innumerable atmospheres') and gives the poems in *Neue Gedichte* a density and weight otherwise unknown in German poetry. The various technical devices act as connecting links, and together they form a net so fine and at the same time so firm that it is capable of catching the poet's most delicate and fleeting visions. Rilke resembles Hölderlin in that he combines softness with an unexpected firmness: both poets, who often seem to be at the mercy of their sensations, surprise us again and again by the firmness with which they master them in the end. His early poems clearly reveal Rilke's danger: to melt away in the wake of his sensibility. This sensibility was unique, often morbid; yet after the break in his development brought about by his stay in Paris, he would no longer abandon himself to it; his triumph consists in harnessing this sensitiveness to his ends, which were a poet's ends.

The use and full exploitation of a great number of technical devices, together with a certain disregard for traditional and established forms, is the main characteristic of Rilke's new style, and moreover one that distinguishes it from that of most other German poets. Such devices have, of course, always been used, consciously or unconsciously; but German poets, unlike their French counterparts in this respect, instead of stressing the more formal aspects of their art, have rather tended to keep them in the background. For such prominent lyrical poets as Goethe, Heine, Mörike, form had not the same importance as, e.g., for Gautier, Baudelaire or Verlaine. Other German poets, to name only Platen, Rückert, George, were more formally inclined. Rilke differs from them in two important respects: his form was not rigid, a scheme to be followed, but elastic, a scheme to be adapted and modified in each individual case. The second point of difference is that not only the number of various devices regularly used by Rilke is infinitely greater than theirs, but that the interaction, complexity, subtlety of such devices is of an altogether different order. Just as, after Chopin and Liszt, piano technique has become much more complex and subtle than that of their predecessors, so poetical technique as used by George, Hofmannsthal and Rilke is more complex and subtle than that of the nineteenth-century poets who preceded them, and Rilke's technique, again, is the most complex of all. It will be interesting to hear the poet himself in a few of the rare observations he made on poetical technique:

Heute, da eine ganz andere Fertigkeit des métiers allgemein geworden ist, käme kaum ein junger Mensch in die Lage, so Minderwertiges zur Geltung bringen zu wollen: man dichtet, banal gesprochen, ob man will oder nicht, auf einem andern niveau. Das Ausserordentliche ist immer noch Sache der Gnade und der Überlegenheit, aber das einfach Ordentliche und an sich Schätzbare, das Anständige . . . ist zahlreich, ist zahllos.

And again:

Wer von uns müsste nicht *dies* vor allem erstreben: in seinem Können sicher zu werden, um gegen das von Aussen kommende Urteil jeweils die rechten Gegengewichte im eignen Gewissen zu besitzen.[1]

These quotations show that Rilke was very conscious of technique, and also that the possession of a firm, reliable technique was for him not an end, but a starting point only, the condition *sine qua non* for writing poetry. The introduction of conscience in this

[1] *Briefe aus Muzot*, 19, pp. 391 and 233.

connection further stresses the moral background to what Rilke called his *métier*.

Es ist mir später oft aufgefallen, wie sehr die Kunst eine Sache des Gewissens ist. Nichts braucht man so sehr in künstlerischer Arbeit wie das Gewissen: es ist der einzige Masstab. (Die Kritik ist keiner . . .) Darum ist es sehr wichtig, . . . nicht hart zu werden an der Stelle, auf der es liegt. Es muss leicht bleiben bei allem . . . Den leisesten Druck aber, der von ihm ausgeht, muss man beachten, sonst verliert die Waage, auf der man später jedes zu schreibende Vers-Wort wird prüfen müssen, ihre äusserste Beweglichkeit.[1]

There was no doubt, in Rilke's mind, about the legitimacy of the use of various technical devices, and he would not have understood, much less sanctioned, a statement like the one by Percival Gurrey quoted earlier, that alliteration and vowel cadence are two of the less important resources of language. There could be no question of greater or smaller importance in this respect: since poetry is the translation into sound and pattern of the poet's vision, any device that helps to realize this aim is necessary and indispensable.

Rilke's diction had by now become so varied and rich, and the devices used by him so numerous, that they required careful coordination. In order to yield a maximum of penetration and mutual assimilation, they had to be assembled with subtle understanding, and the poet's art in handling them may be likened to a musician's skill in orchestration. Rilke can mass words and isolate them, contrast them by sound as well as by meaning, underline their particular quality by rhythm or enjambment, evoke and exhaust their inherent sound music and significance to the fullest and finest effect they are capable of yielding. He was conscious of the poet's art and responsibility when he wrote to the countess Sizzo:[2]

Schreiben zu können ist, weiss Gott, nicht minder 'schweres Handwerk', um so mehr, als das Material der anderen Künste von vornherein von dem täglichen Gebrauch abgerückt ist, während des Dichters Aufgabe sich steigert um die seltsame Verpflichtung, *sein* Wort von den Worten des blossen Umgamgs und der Verständigung gründlich, wesentlich zu unterscheiden. *Kein* Wort im Gedicht (ich meine hier jedes 'und' oder 'der', 'die', 'das') ist identisch mit dem gleichlautenden Gebrauchs- und Konversations-Worte; die reinere Gesetzmässigkeit, das grosse Verhältnis, die Konstellation, die es im Vers oder in künstlerischer Prosa einnimmt, verändert es bis in den Kern seiner Natur, macht es nutzlos, unbrauchbar für den blossen Umgang, unberührbar und bleibend: eine Verwandlung wie sie sich, unerhört herrlich, zuweilen bei Goethe (Harzreise im Winter), oft bei George vollzieht.

[1] *Briefe*, I, 1897–1914. Brief 85, p. 213. Oct., 1907.
[2] *Briefe*, II, 1914–26, 1950, pp. 339–40.

Earlier Rilke had written in a similar vein concerning the style of *Neue Gedichte*:

Wesentlicher scheint mir, dass ich Ihnen, was jene neueren Bücher angeht [i.e. *Neue Gedichte*], mein gutes, klares Gewissen zusichern kann: jedes Wort, jeder Wortzwischenraum in jenen Gedichten ist mit äusserster Notwendigkeit entstanden, unter dem Bewusstsein jener endgültigen Verantwortlichkeit, unter deren innerem Gericht meine Arbeit sich vollzieht.[1]

Again the 'conscience' is invoked, and the importance of the weight and place of each word stressed, even of the interval between each word and the next. What can Rilke have in mind concerning these intervals? In poetry there is not, as in music, a notation to fix the length of intervals. The tempo of a line will somehow have an influence on intervals, making them longer or shorter; enjambment has a similar effect, and lastly punctuation may play a part—these are somewhat indeterminate means of fixing word intervals, but it is difficult to imagine any others in this connection.

Rilke has also developed an incredibly fine sense for the relationship of words with each other and their reactions on each other, a feeling for values, for the effects one could produce by bringing together the colourless and the conspicuous word, that with a wealth of associations and that which tells us one thing only. A close system of association of meaning and sound connects his language, each word supporting, reflecting, explaining the other; his predilection for alliteration and vowelling, which began in a more superficial way, now permeates his poetry with an interplay of deep meaning.

Far from offering an apology for his extensive use of 'devices', which really are nothing but instruments for the penetration of sound and meaning, Rilke is conscious of thereby leading his poetry towards the goal of all poetry. A philologist defines language thus: 'The natural sounds have been completely transmuted into conventional sound symbols. *This is what constitutes language....*'[2] In assimilating again sound and meaning by means of rhyme, vowel music, alliteration and all the other arts, poetry marches in the opposite direction, back to the very beginnings of language, when sound and meaning were one. Poetry ever strives to recreate this primitive condition on a higher plane, and Rilke's contribution to this goal is of a high order.

The various devices, especially alliteration and vowelling, have a

[1] *Briefe*, I, 1897–1914, 1950, p. 213.
[2] R. A. Wilson, *The miraculous Birth of Language*, 1942, p. 64.

similar function in his poems to that of colour in a painting. Colour may be superficial, a decorative addition, as it were, from the outside; on the other hand, instead of being merely laid on, it may be intimately, inseparably united with the object depicted, express its very soul. Rilke's sound technique in his central period is of that order, and he may even have been, in this respect, directly influenced by his study and admiration of Cézanne, about whom he writes:[1]

Wie sehr das Malen unter den Farben vor sich geht, wie man sie ganz allein lassen muss, damit sie sich gegenseitig auseinandersetzen. Ihr Verkehr untereinander: das ist die ganze Malerei.

If in a painting the colours 'set each other off', words do the same in poetry, especially in poetry as understood by Rilke.

It is interesting to observe how close Rilke is, in this respect, to the English poet G. M. Hopkins, of whose poetry he could not, in 1907, have had any knowledge. The very unconventional use both poets make of alliteration, vowelling and often of enjambment, is amazingly parallel. Hopkins goes even further than Rilke, for his accumulations, by their explosive intensity, tend to blow up the structure of his poems. Although of remarkable soundness, this structure cannot always withstand the pounding and blasting of the clotted masses of alliteration and vowel affinities:

I caught this morning morning's minion, king-
　　dom of daylight's dauphin, dapple-dawn-drawn Falcon, in his riding
Of the rolling level underneath him steady air, and striding
High there, how he rung upon the rein of a wimpling wing
In his ecstasy!

These are the first lines of a sonnet, the structure of which all but disappears under the weight of sound accumulation and word association it has to carry (even the rhymes are hardly heard), while Rilke's sonnets, though not as regularly built and conventional in form as Hopkins', but less weighted, retain a much clearer outline:

Was aber hindert uns zu glauben, dass
(so wie wir hingestellt sind und verteilt)
nicht eine kleine Zeit nur Drang und Hass
und dies Verwirrende in uns verweilt,

wie einst in dem verzierten Sarkophag
bei Ringen, Götterbildern, Gläsern, Bändern,
in langsam sich verzehrenden Gewändern
ein langsam Aufgelöstes lag —　　　　　　　　(III, 50)

Manifold were the influences and experiences that helped to

---

[1] *Briefe*, I, 1897–1914, 1950. Brief 86, p. 214.

bring about the achievement of Rilke's mature style. He lived, for a number of years, in close proximity to Rodin, and the great sculptor, more perhaps by example than by precept, taught him close, patient observation. We may also assume that the daily intercourse with a sculptor's works has left a distinctive mark, if hard to define, on Rilke's production, best to be judged perhaps by the clear-cut contours of the poems in *Neue Gedichte*, each of which stands for itself, in unconnected isolation, like a work of sculpture. Rodin also confirmed the poet's attraction towards 'the things', which Rilke had discovered and begun cherishing some time before on his own account. We need not go here into the deep psychological motives for this affinity, which arose from a necessity for objectivation. This led to a type of poem which Kurt Oppert, with a characteristic, if not wholly felicitous, term, has called '*Dinggedicht*'.[1] Oppert even attempts to trace the model for this type of poetry to Mörike and C. F. Meyer, but in spite of the fact that these poets have written one or two poems that might, by stretching a point, be included in the appellation, their main production has little or nothing to do with this type, and besides their psychological premises were totally different from Rilke's. Moreover, the character of Rilke's '*Dinggedichte*' is not that they treat of things, but rather that they deal with all subjects, including persons, as if they were things. Let us listen to what the poet himself has to say regarding his *Neue Gedichte*:

Connaissant ces quelques goûts de ma vie nomade, les 'Neue Gedichte' vous semblent-ils encore tant impersonnels? Voyez-vous, pour pouvoir dire ce qui m'arrive, il m'a fallu non tant un instrument sentimental, mais de l'argile; sans le vouloir j'ai prétendu me servir de la poésie, dite lyrique, pour former, non des sentiments, mais *des choses que j'avais senties*; tout l'événement de la vie a dû trouver place dans cette formation, indépendamment de la souffrance ou du plaisir qu'il m'avait d'abord procuré. Cette formation eût été sans valeur si elle n'allait pas jusqu'à la *trans*-formation de tout détail passager, il fallait aboutir à l'essence.

'Form-Dichter', je ne sais pas ce que c'est . . . Aussi je n'ai nul besoin d'être éclairé sur mes écrits, toute mon action intérieure, depuis que je suis en possession de mes moyens, se tient, et aucune voix . . . ne pourrait influencer la justesse et le tort de ma balance intime.[2]

This revealing passage defines the character of the poems in *Neue Gedichte*, that is to say of the so-called '*Dinggedicht*', as 'not emotions, but *things* I have felt'. The mention of '*argile*' (clay), the sculptor's

---

[1] *Deutsche Vierteljahrsschrift für Literaturwissenschaft und Geistesgeschichte*, 1926, Heft. 4, 'Das Dinggedicht'.
[2] *Briefe*, II, 1914–26, 1950, pp. 389–90.

material, is most characteristic in this connection, and finally, the passage is interesting for the statement: ' "*Form-dichter*", I do not know what that is', and for the lofty independence expressed in the last sentence: here is a poet 'in possession of his means', impermeable to any voice or influence from outside, assured in his 'intimate balance'.

Rilke is unique in that, for his central period, this '*Dinggedicht*' was practically the only vehicle of his poetic expression: it enabled him to be a poet without being insincere. Sincerity, it is true, is not by itself an aesthetic quality, but it is one of the prerequisites to poetry: without it, no poetry is convincing. The '*Dinggedicht*' allowed Rilke to be sincere by objectivation, i.e. by projecting his personality into objects, thus eliminating the disturbing element of acute self-consciousness that used to block the purity of his expression.

Another important influence was exercised by French poetry, especially by that of Baudelaire and Verlaine. What Rilke learnt from them was not so much any manner or device, not even the general tone of any particular poem—although there are many similarities in this respect—but rather the precise and elegant rounding off of every poem. Such cool assurance, such urbane elegance in the mastery of poetic means, was not a general characteristic of German lyric poetry. Hofmannsthal, it is true, was a master of natural, unstudied perfection; his poetry, although—or should we say because?—it was derived from various sources, was a genuinely Austrian, more precisely Viennese, product. Very unlike Rilke's poetry, it was perfect from the start, the result of a happy but brief period of youthful inspiration, not subject to a process of maturing. Like certain paintings of the Venetian school, especially Giorgione's, Hofmannsthal's poems are without blemish, created in an atmosphere of intuitive perfection. The other poet to undergo an influence similar to Rilke's was Stefan George, who consciously modelled his style on Romance prototypes; but his imperious personality often prevented him from giving his poems the uniformly high perfection attained by Rilke: they plainly fall into two groups, successes and failures, and even the former are sometimes characterized by a certain frail brittleness. Excepting these poets, elegance, i.e. the conscious will to perfection of style and the real or apparent ease in attaining it, was not, and had rarely been, the ambition of German poets, whose custom was rather to write with a fresh, immediate *élan* that often makes them so endearing to us.

Rilke's elegance was of a particular kind, not simply an outward polish applied to his poems; it had deep roots in his personality. An inborn fastidiousness had always distinguished him, an almost feminine love of order and punctilio, that might have become pedantry with a less sensitive and imaginative man. His letters are models of carefully elaborated literary essays, even those addressed to Lou Andreas Salomé, that sometimes are cries of despair from the bottom of his heart. He could not write an informal note without making it 'formal' by the way he rounded it off. The very beautiful handwriting, with its even flow, so firm and neat and at the same time revealing genius in many signs, testifies to this inbred quality. His rooms, if bare, were always scrupulously clean, tidy and cared for, and an aesthetically pleasing arrangement of his surroundings was at all times a necessity to him; the same fastidiousness was expressed in his dress and in all his personal belongings. It is small wonder, therefore, that Rilke's style shows the imprint of this trait of his personality; only that in the elegance of Rilke's writings, the personal trait has been generalized and spiritualized into a quality of great artistic importance.

French influence, in this connection, only confirmed a tendency deep within his nature; he was a perfectionist in things small as in things great, not content until each of his poems was the ideal expression of his vision, as perfect as he could make it. Rilke's elegance is not laboured, however; it is the happy result of a marriage of his searching intensity with his inborn love of order and beauty of form. His orderly and lonely mode of life favoured such creation and made it possible for him to focus his creative powers, free from diversions, on the work in hand.

From the French poets Rilke acquired a sure taste which had been conspicuously lacking in his previous production. The influence of Paris as well as of French poetry and art (besides Rodin, mainly modern French painting), modified his provincial outlook in a remarkably short time, and provided the one element that had been lacking in the wealth of his technical resources: an urbane assurance, based on taste, in assembling them. It is a long way from the painters of the Worpswede school to Cézanne: these two poles aptly express the way Rilke had to go in order to free himself from mawkish sentimentality and his narrow provincial outlook. He would have looked in vain to German poetry for taste as a guiding and selective principle; the standard of each individual poet varies a great deal,

but even so fastidious an artist as C. F. Meyer has left a vast production of poems from which the best stand out like rare gold amid
much chaff. Rilke is perhaps, next to Hofmannsthal, the first
German poet of note to attain in his production an almost uniformly
high standard of excellency based on sound craftsmanship; he was
justified in asserting the assurance of his inner balance. *Neue
Gedichte* occupy an exceptional place as a collection in which every
poem conforms to such a high standard.

The two volumes of *Neue Gedichte* are outstanding in German
lyrical poetry for their quality of artistry; the density of style in
the individual poem has its counterpart in the impression of density
conveyed by the collection as a whole. In German collections of
poetry, we are used to much inequality, to flatland and dreary
valleys to be endured in compensation for high peaks. Some
collections are hasty and untidy, some monotonous, others solemn
and exacting. *Neue Gedichte*, with all their wealth of highly polished
jewels, are balanced; there are no strident inequalities, hardly any
really weak poems, no difficult adjustments from high to low
tension; the exceptionally high intellectual and emotional level has
found perfect expression in the careful gemlike workmanship of
each poem, while few poems are felt as precious or overwrought.
And there is no monotony either; the subjects vary as do the moods,
each poem is a little world in itself, rounded, complete, perfect,
an accomplished work of art. Two qualities come together in
these poems that seem to exclude each other, intensity (*Innerlichkeit*),
and elegance of form, a synthesis almost unique in German lyrical
poetry.

Rilke's cosmopolitan attitude, his complete lack of national
prejudice were helpful to him in absorbing the French influences.
No German poet, not even Heine, was so devoid of a certain
bias in favour of Germany and things German. Rilke does not
pronounce the name of Dürer with greater solemnity than that of
Fragonard, the Hallig island does not make his heart beat faster
than the lagoon. He displays the same impartiality, with no apparent
predilection except perhaps for some favourite personal words, in
the choice of his vocabulary. The variety of words used in *Neue
Gedichte* is remarkable; common and unusual, pale and colourful,
homely and foreign, he chooses and assembles them, without bias,
for the tone-colour, the sound qualities, the shades of meaning they
yield. His word power, remarkable already in the *Stundenbuch*, has

since extended considerably, and is far from being confined, as is sometimes assumed, to the sphere of the gentle and the delicate. Just as the subjects in *Neue Gedichte* range from the beautiful to the grotesque, from the mild to the gruesome, so the expressive power of the poet embraces all these contrasts and extremes. His language testifies to the hardness Rilke advocated and practised, and it is a straightforward, uncramped hardness:

> Und das was war, das wäre irre und
> raste in dir herum, den lieben Mund,
> der niemals lachte, schäumend von Gelächter.   (III, 43)

> Er ging wie Hagel nieder über Halmen.
> Was wollt ihr Gott versprechen? Ungezählt
> stehn um euch Götter, wartend, dass ihr wählt.
> Doch wenn ihr wählt, wird euch der Herr zermalmen.
> (III, 23)

Most of the poems dealing with subjects from the Old Testament might be quoted as examples of Rilke's word power in this respect, and many others besides, of which we will name a few only: *Morgue, Der Marmorkarren, Alkestis, Totentanz, Die Versuchung, Leichenwäsche, Ein Doge, Corrida.*

From Verlaine Rilke also learned a certain intimacy, the light and sure touch with which he handled his subject and makes the reader familiar with it, as well as the soft musical undertone ringing through many of his poems. Lines like these might not have been written without the model of Verlaine:

> Oh, dass ihr stille bliebt,
> wenn euch das Herz verjährt;
> dass keine Mutter erfährt,
> dass es das gibt.
> Oben hob sich der Mond,
> wo sich die Zweige entzwein,
> und, wie von euch bewohnt,
> bleibt er allein.   (III, 166–7)

Baudelaire, besides supplying some of Rilke's subjects, or at least demonstrating that they were capable of poetic treatment (*Les petites vieilles, Le chat, Le balcon*, etc.), was Rilke's master above all in the art of presenting a poem as a rounded and complete work of art with a studied relationship of all its parts, a suggestive beginning and end. We have already dealt with Rilke's concise beginnings: the last lines of almost every poem in *Neue Gedichte* might be quoted as models in the art of bringing a poem to its effective and convincing conclusion. There had hardly been anything like this in German poetry before:

> es trug ihn in den Strom wie in sein Schloss.   (III, 74)
>
> . . . während hoch
> die Sternennächte eines süssen Landes
> in Himmel wuchsen, die sich nirgends schlossen.   (III, 98)
>
> Nun liegt es sorglos in den offnen Rosen.   (III, 113)
>
> und wurde wirklich Schwan in ihrem Schooss.   (III, 120)
>
> und sie hatte Gott noch kaum gekannt,   (III, 162)

and a hundred others.

In comparing *Neue Gedichte* with *Les Fleurs du Mal*, however, we must not be misled by the resemblances, for the dissimilarities are perhaps greater; just because subject and treatment are so parallel in many cases, the fundamentally different character of the two sets of poems is felt the more strongly: they are the products of diverging artistic temperaments. Nevertheless, the two books have something in common, they resemble each other, in their high standard of uniform excellency, as much as such complex things as collections can resemble each other.

The character of *Neue Gedichte* involves a good deal of poetic description, we might even say that, with few exceptions, every poem in the collection is in some way descriptive. There is, of course, an abundance of German verse that is descriptive in a general way, but hardly any description of the minute and tenuous accuracy as practised by Rilke, painting stroke by stroke, using, as the Symbolists do, the precise term, not the most beautiful or the nearest at hand. We do not only mean that Rilke's descriptions are more faithful, more patient: his description is profound since it embraces, from the start, a view from within and from without, and thus transcends the graphic or colourful description hitherto encountered in German poetry. Its precision, if often coldly observant, is never realistic, let alone photographic. We have to do with a new kind of poetic description which seeks to catch and retain the poet's vision, based on a most intense observation, with the same fleeting firmness with which a painter might attempt to hold his 'impression'. Intensity is the magic power that enables Rilke to use description synthetically as a poet: his vision being firmly centred, he can assemble, for its projection, what is near and what is far, the minute and the general, the fact and the sensation. As in a Chinese brush drawing, few strokes of the utmost precision are required, and the things omitted are almost as important as those fixed. Rilke's art, since he was an '*Augenmensch*', may well be compared to a painter's, yet we must not forget that a true poet's vision is far from being two-dimensional; the ideas and associations conceived together with the vision of the object form part of the fixation in this complex process, which is further distinguished from the painter's art by its freedom in time. The novel element in Rilke's art is the combination, in his descriptions, of very precise visual observation with all the other elements that go to make poetic description. The objects of such description might be concrete 'things' as well as sensations. In *Blaue Hortensie* it is a most fleeting thing, the colour of a flower:

> So wie das letzte Grün in Farbentiegeln
> sind diese Blätter, trocken, stumpf und rauh,
> hinter den Blütendolden, die ein Blau
> nicht auf sich tragen, nur von ferne spiegeln.
> Sie spiegeln es verweint und ungenau,
> als wollten sie es wiederum verlieren,
> und wie in alten blauen Briefpapieren
> ist Gelb in ihnen, Violett und Grau;
> Verwaschnes wie an einer Kinderschürze,
> Nichtmehrgetragnes, dem nichts mehr geschieht...
>
> (III, 65)

Precision can hardly be carried farther; in order to convey his impression, the poet assembles all the objects that recall the peculiar faded and indistinct colouring of the blue hydrangea, and the accumulation of these images creates, by a cumulative effect, his vision. Rilke would not speak of 'green colour in paint-jars', but of 'the *last* green'; not of 'old note-paper', but of 'old *blue* note-paper'. Yet not objects alone are being assembled; with a passage like '*verweint und ungenau*', and '*dem nichts mehr geschieht*', the poet transcends the visual plane and enters upon the emotional. It is above all this subtle blending of spheres that makes Rilke's descriptive style so original and attractive.

The novel feature of many of the poems in *Neue Gedichte* is that they are as much pure poetry as pure description, an achievement for which there is some analogy in the poetry of Valéry. We think of *Blaue Hortensie, Schlafmohn, Corrida, Der Marmorkarren, Römische Fontäne, Vor-Ostern, Der Balkon, Papageienpark, Hetären-gräber, Geburt der Venus, Die Rosenschale, Bildnis meines Vaters, Selbstbildnis*. Other poems are a blending of description with associative vision, as *Die Gazelle, Früher Apoll, Flamingos, Kretische*

o

Artemis, Das Karussell, Delphine, Bildnis, Venezianischer Morgen, Die Laute, Persisches Heliotrop, Der Käferstein, Der Ball. In *Rosa Hortensie* it is not, as in its counterpart, a colour that is being described, not even a fading colour, but the process of fading, of delicate dissolution itself. Consequently, the emotional images predominate over the visual ones:

> Dass sie für solches Rosa nichts verlangen,
> bleibt es für sie und lächelt aus der Luft?
> Sind Engel da, es zärtlich zu empfangen,
> wenn es vergeht, grossmütig wie ein Duft?   (III, 242)

Such poems translate a wholly visionary sensation into words; they do not, as *Blaue Hortensie*, describe or delineate an object, as, e.g., in the sonnet *Die Gazelle*. Poetic description of this nature is not confined to static objects; in many poems of *Neue Gedichte* it is concerned with action. Here is an example of this kind, showing what subtle expressiveness Rilke's mature style is capable of:

> Der Beine elfenbeinernes Gestell
> bewegte sich in leichten Gleichgewichten,
> ein weisser Glanz glitt selig durch das Fell,
> und auf der Tierstirn, auf der stillen, lichten,
> stand, wie ein Turm im Mond, das Horn so hell,
> und jeder Schritt geschah, es aufzurichten.   (III, 46)

Yet the magnificent craftsmanship of Rilke's mature style was not achieved without some sacrifice: the price he had to pay for perfection is the remoteness of his language, at times so far removed from the source of all poetry, ordinary human speech, as to become slightly artificial. Lines like

> so sehr
> warf sich das Erglühende der Früchte
> immer wieder an das blaue Meer,   (III, 186)

precise, rich, glowing as they are, are nevertheless written in a kind of over-sensitized studio-language that marks the extreme limit of what is possible in this direction. Occasionally, very occasionally, a word is not fully assimilated even in this highly involved language:

> in jenen kleinen Städten kannst du sehn,
> wie sehr entwachsen ihrem Umgangskreis
> die Kathedralen waren . . .   (III, 33)

Wie sehr entwachsen ihrem Umgangskreis die Kathedralen waren is a prose sentence within a poem, where the word *Umgangskreis* has

not been incorporated, while in the following quotation *Zwangidee*
has a slightly alien ring:

> aus dem Wollen, aus den Gären
> ihres Willens; aus der Zwangidee,
> dass ein Erz ist über allen Erzen.   (III, 153)

In many cases, the balance is precarious, and words and clauses
just succeed in supporting each other in a system of highly specialized
language:

> — so gehn die Gurten
> der Wölbung aus dem wirren Kapitäl
> und lassen drin, gedrängt und rätselhaft
> verschlungen, flügelschlagende Geschöpfe:
> ihr Zögern und das Plötzliche der Köpfe
> und jene starken Blätter, deren Saft
> wie Jähzorn steigt, sich schliesslich überschlagend
> in einer schnellen Geste, die sich ballt
> und sich heraushält: alles aufwärtsjagend,
> was immer wieder mit dem Dunkel kalt
> herunterfällt, wie Regen Sorge tragend
> für dieses alten Wachstums Unterhalt.   (III, 39)

such a passage, as magnificent as it is extreme, poses the question
of Rilke's mannerism.

As soon as consciousness enters into it, style is in danger of becoming mannerism; it is then either imitation of an alien style, or deliberate, by an effort of will
enhanced manipulation of an author's proved own stylistic means.[1]

If, in this connection, we think of the quotations from several of
Rilke's letters in this chapter, one thing strikes us very forcibly:
the extreme firmness and determination in them. Too extreme,
perhaps? No word in a poem, Rilke asserts, is identical with the
like-sounding word in everyday speech, including even every
'and' or 'the'. And again: every word, every word-interval in
these poems originated under the utmost necessity; or: this formation had to be carried on to the transformation of every fleeting
detail. To say that every particle of speech, including words like
'and' or 'the', are in no way identical with their counterparts in
common speech, is an obvious over-statement; Rilke, not content
with creating a poetic atmosphere for every one of his poems,
evidently wanted his poetic language to be lifted right out of the
sphere of common speech. But was he not cutting the roots from

[1] J. Petersen, *Die Wissenschaft von der Dichtung*, 2 Aufl., 1944, p. 196.

under his tree? This over-consciousness, this firm will, this super-hardness are responsible for the traces of mannerism we encounter in *Neue Gedichte*: 'As soon as consciousness enters into it, style is in danger of becoming mannerism'. Traces only; fortunately, the unconscious creative force within the poet was strong enough to balance and overcome his radical theories. We must read the passages quoted from his letters with a true understanding of what lay behind this somewhat extreme radicalism: if before Rilke had abandoned himself to his fulsome emotionalism, he now very forcibly pulled himself together in order to attain that hardness so necessary to the true poet. No easy matter in Rilke's case! He had already made a false start with the cycle *Die Stimmen* in *Buch der Bilder*—it led nowhere, for he cut the trunk with the overhanging branches. He could not reduce his poetry to such bareness without mutilating it out of existence. Hardness, in *Die Stimmen*, became brutality. In *Neue Gedichte*, Rilke found a more constructive way of overcoming his peculiar problem, though a more difficult and complex one.

The somewhat precarious balance achieved in *Neue Gedichte* is one of the attractions of Rilke's style: there is a constant tension, a struggle and ranging of words under the surface, something like the tumultuous passages that enliven a piece of music until in the end they find their harmonious solution; in the whole collection there is not a flat or lifeless passage—a memorable achievement for a collection of almost two hundred poems.

Moreover, we must not forget that in *Neue Gedichte* each poem has its own atmosphere and to a degree its own language, sometimes a very simple language:

> Das ist mein Fenster. Eben
> bin ich so sanft erwacht.
> Ich dachte, ich würde schweben.
> Bis wohin reicht mein Leben,
> und wo beginnt die Nacht?   (III, 223)

> Ich finde Dich nicht mehr. Nicht in mir, nein.
> Nicht in den andern. Nicht in diesem Stein.
> Ich finde Dich nicht mehr. Ich bin allein.   (III, 26)

The gentle, convincing simplicity of such lines is on a different plane from the studied and barren simplicity of *Die Stimmen*. Such contrasts in simple and highly complex language contribute to the wealth of *Neue Gedichte*. If at times conscious effort carried Rilke

too far, it remains for us to admire the supreme achievement of
this original, closely-knit, always graphically expressive style.

Das Marien-Leben

In 1913, Rilke published a slight volume of fifteen poems under
the title *Das Marien-Leben*. The motive for this production was
incidental: an old friend, the painter Heinrich Vogeler, had expressed
a wish to illustrate some of Rilke's poems with his drawings. Rilke,
who in principle strongly objected to any illustration of his works,
and moreover found Vogeler's drawings particularly inadequate,
persuaded him to desist from his intention, but in order to placate
the artist, he dedicated to him a collection of poems gathered and
completed for this very purpose. These poems are quite irrelevant
to Rilke's main work and would not warrant mentioning here
if they did not afford the opportunity of studying the poet's style,
as it were, *in vacuo*, i.e. detached from a subject on which he had
centred his powers. What remains is more or less a collection of
clever artifices deprived of necessity and inner meaning, resulting
in a mild mannerism. The technical devices we know so well are
all there, but since they do not gravitate towards a centre that gives
them order and direction, they remain suspended in mid-air.

In a way, *Das Marien-Leben* demonstrates how tenuous and perish-
able Rilke's style is, how dependent on the artist's intensity and
sincerity. If the dangers inherent in it are not checked by the
magnetic force of a firm centre, it becomes volatile, artificial, even
affected. The explanation for this extreme vulnerability is that
Rilke's style is not a natural growth, not the instinctive emanation
of a balanced personality, but rather an elaborate instrument
perfected by endeavour and sacrifice. Detached from the *Dinggedicht* and its relatives, to which it is admirably fitted, it becomes
thin and brittle: the rhymes ring hollow, the enjambment seems
stilted, the delicate interplay of sounds can become sickly sweet.
Rilke further falsified the style of his *Marien-Leben* by attempting
to marry his complex language to an old legend manner for which
it is not suited. The poet's ear, in this collection, is obviously not
as fine and sure as in *Neue Gedichte*, and we note discords which the
dense style is particularly apt to show up:

> denn sowie sie, klein im grossen Land,
> — fast ein Nichts — den starken Tempeln nahten,
> platzten alle Götter wie verraten
> und verloren völlig den Verstand.   (II, 308)

This sounds hardly convincing, even as a legend. Again:

> Doch der andre sah ihn finster an,
> murmelnd nur: Was hat sie so verwandelt?
> Doch da schrie der Engel: Zimmermann,
> merkst du's noch nicht, dass der Herrgott handelt? (II, 303)

We would hardly credit Rilke, five years after *Neue Gedichte*, with such lines, with the clumsy word-order of *murmelnd nur*, the unwarranted stridency of *schrie*, and their general lack of balance and beauty. Often the words do not fit the pattern, as the awkward *Tränendrüsen* in the following passage:

> An dem Tisch voll Früchten und Gemüsen
> freute sie sich mit und sah nicht ein,
> dass das Wasser ihrer Tränendrüsen
> Blut geworden war mit diesem Wein.   (II, 311)

Yet in spite of such lapses and its general weakness, the *Marien-Leben* is not completely devoid of merit, and passages like those quoted above could be balanced by others of great attractiveness. Moreover, if the collection shows up the weakness of Rilke's style, at the same time, paradoxically, it also demonstrates its strength, for it shows how great Rilke's achievement was in using so vulnerable a medium with such assurance and brilliancy in *Neue Gedichte*. Only a great craftsman at the height of his powers could handle this instrument, so complex and difficult to play, with such superb skill, such unerring rightness.

The Duino Elegies

The long barren interval that followed *Neue Gedichte* was not only one of fatigue: Rilke felt he had exhausted the possibilities developed in those poems, and was groping his way towards a new form of expression. It testifies to the deep earnestness with which he felt his mission that he could not go on writing poetry in the highly successful personal style he had just perfected at the cost of great labour. *Neue Gedichte* had closed and sealed a cycle; something new was now darkly calling for expression, and the poet suffered agonies of frustration at not being able to answer the call. At the height of his powers we see Rilke, the accomplished craftsman and master in the use of every technical device, wrestling with a strong resistance that not only poetic form, but even the language itself seemed to offer.

We know that the First Elegy was conceived at Duino as early as 1912, and that many of the others were wholly or partly written before that day in February, 1922, when they were all finished in a storm of inspiration that overtook the poet. But why, we may ask, was such inspiration necessary for their completion? What prevented Rilke from 'making' the *Elegies*, the thought-content of which was ready in his mind, as he must have made many of the pieces in *Neue Gedichte*, by sheer application to the task? The answer is that the material for the *Elegies* is very different from any Rilke had handled before; it was particularly unresponsive and resistant, and the refined and complex style at the poet's command would not help him to give shape to those masses of profound and dark thought that were now clamouring to become poems. Inspiration was needed to melt down, in its fiery flame, these partly shaped poems, to mould them into poetry, whereas before they had been material for poetry only. We need not be surprised at the enthusiastic messages, so unusual for him, which Rilke sent out to his closest friends after the completion of his ten elegies: it was conferred on him as a blessing he had hardly dared to hope for any longer. In releasing his voice and giving him that unifying, lofty and earnest tone that pervades all the elegies and makes them at all possible as poems, these hours of pure inspiration made him a poet once more.

In *Neue Gedichte*, Rilke had been concerned with form, not indeed with the empty form to be filled with a poetic pattern, which in his central period had long ceased to have any importance for him, but with form as the final condensation of his poetic experience into a definite, organic shape. Moreover, the final perfection of this form had a deep significance for the poet as an achievement that gave direction to his inner forces. But it was not sufficient for the material that now demanded to be shaped: in the *Elegies*, the importance of the message transcends everything, and the triumph of their final form is therefore not quite so complete as in *Neue Gedichte*.

There is a real difference between works of art in what we call their scale or size, and though it argues a more powerful mind and a more comprehensively developed art to work on a large scale than on a small one, nevertheless the larger the scale of a work the more dangerously it courts contact with the world outside; the more it seems to be about life the less it seems to be purely about itself.[1]

The *Elegies* are certainly 'about life', being the sum of Rilke's thought and innermost experiences from his childhood to his

[1] H. P. Morgan-Browne: F. Chopin, in *The Heritage of Music*, Second Series, ed. by H. J. Foss, 1934, p. 175.

maturity. The task Rilke has set himself in these poems was, above all, to express what he deemed to be important in life. Thus the *Elegies* contain a philosophy of life, not indeed one arrived at by thinking, or at least not by thinking alone, but a poet's intuitive value-philosophy. Rilke would have disliked the name very much, but there is no getting away from the fact that the *Duino Elegies* are philosophical poems. With a difference, admittedly, for his philosophy was in part experience that could immediately, or in many cases without great stress, enter the sphere of poetry. Yet some of Rilke's experiences were not of this kind, and some of the material in the *Elegies* is not experience in this sense at all, but thoughts about life and death, valuations, judgments, postulations, even speculations. These had to undergo a process of transformation before they could become poetry.

What kind of transformation? The sphere of poetry is the image: this material had, therefore, to become image within the poet. Then his task was to give these images adequate expression, adequate to the greatness of his vision and the importance of his experience. This close relationship of message and form is the reason why the *Elegies* defy purely formal analysis. On the whole, the transformation of experience and thought into poetic image was successful, but if we compare the *Elegies* to the *Sonnets to Orpheus*, we notice how unequal they are formally among themselves, and even within each elegy. There are transitions, seams, even lapses: the reader has to make allowances. On the other hand, this inequality is relative only: what unites the elegies, since they all come from the same deep source, is their tone. This tone is sustained at a lofty level and moulds the elegies into monumental poetry of great significance.

The *Elegies* are a poetic unity, i.e. they were not arbitrarily gathered into a collection, but conceived as the expression of the poet's life-philosophy: none could have been added, none omitted. They had to be long poems, but it is clear that they would be of unequal length, according to their themes, and different too in metre, in regularity, in intensity. The shortest elegy, the Sixth, has 44 lines, the longest, the Tenth, 112; the others range between 71 (Second) and 95 lines (First). The most irregular in length of line is the Fifth, followed by the Ninth and Tenth; the others are fairly regular in this respect. The length of each elegy is, of course, determined by the full expression of its theme or themes; the balance of the collection as a whole suffers somewhat from this irregularity.

The form of the *Elegies* is large, but it is also rugged, strained, at times breathless, a poet's extreme effort to say 'the unsayable' (*das allen Unsägliche*), to save his thought and experience from chaos by finding the poetic form and language that will contain them. Sometimes it only just contains them, and there are instances where thought has not been transformed into poetry. C. M. Bowra, speaking of these poems, says:

There are moments when he seems near to prose. Yet even then it is not argument that appears but thought that has not been quite raised to an imaginative level.[1]

Such passages, without necessarily being metrically different from the rest, read like statements in prose, or near-prose (they have here been printed as prose):

Kaum erlernte Gebräuche nicht mehr zu üben, Rosen, und andern eigens versprechenden Dingen nicht die Bedeutung menschlicher Zukunft zu geben . . .

(III, 262)

Es rauscht jetzt von jenen jungen Toten zu dir.   (III, 262)

Aber Lebendige machen alle den Fehler, dass sie zu stark unterscheiden.

(III, 263)

wo seine kleine Geburt schon überlebt war.   (III, 272)

Even the blank verse of the Eighth Elegy, which might be considered better fitted for the expression of intricate thought than the dactylic metre, is not free from such flat passages:

das offne, das im Tiergesicht so tief ist   (III, 293)

Wäre Bewusstsein unsrer Art in dem sicheren Tier, das uns entgegenzieht in anderer Richtung . . .   (III, 294)

Being long poems, the elegies lack the elegant proportions of Rilke's sonnets and near-sonnets in *Neue Gedichte*. As we saw in the chapters on verse-form and rhythm, a characteristic of the elegies are certain emotional eruptions from the regular movement of their flow, eruptions that sometimes distort their balance. But on the other hand this co-existence of opaque and heavy with poetically glowing passages may even be felt as a certain attraction: resistance, far from always being a negative element, is a salutary thing for the artist able to overcome it. The unevenness is not marked enough to destroy the unity of the elegies, it pervades them all to a different degree and is one of the distinguishing features of their style.

[1] *The Heritage of Symbolism*, 1943, p. 74.

Two main difficulties had to be overcome in these poems: the incorporation of complex thought and the adequate expression of emotion. The first of these difficulties is a general one experienced by all poets: deep thought may be versified, but in order to become poetry it has to be transformed. During his lonely and unattached life, Rilke had accumulated a store of experiences, ideas and beliefs that in part were almost those of an odd person, '*grandes valeurs-pour-un-seul*'; yet within his personality, they were all connected in a system of thought and feeling. The heat of inspiration was needed to make these opaque and almost uncommunicable ideas to some extent transparent. If they sometimes weigh down the *Elegies*, in the end they are not only borne along on the strong current of these poems, they even create this very current. One example may stand for many to show how thought has been transformed in the *Elegies* by the power of poetic image, condensation and intensity:

> Bringt doch der Wanderer auch vom Hange des Bergrands
> nicht eine Hand voll Erde ins Tal, die allen unsägliche, sondern
> ein erworbenes Wort, reines, den gelben und blaun
> Enzian. Sind wir vielleicht *hier*, um zu sagen: Haus,
> Brücke, Brunnen, Tor, Krug, Obstbaum, Fenster, —
> höchstens: Säule, Turm . . . aber zu *sagen*, verstehs,
> o zu sagen *so*, wie selber die Dinge niemals
> innig meinten zu sein.   (III, 298–9)

Success in this respect is of course greatest where the poet's thought-experience was spontaneously conceived as poetry. Thus, Rilke describes how the first lines of the First Elegy came to him during a storm at Duino:

> Wer, wenn ich schriee, hörte mich denn aus der Engel
> Ordnungen?   (III, 259)

This immediate poetic conception is encountered in many other passages of the *Elegies*, though not throughout. Such conception, since it is not based on a logical thought-sequence, accounts for most of the obscurities in the *Elegies*. However, the reader will gladly tolerate these poetic obscurities, which leave scope for imaginative interpretation and understanding, and prefer them to those clearer passages in which thought has been later transformed, however well, into poetry. Most of the intrinsically lyrical outbursts in these poems are not in the nature of purple passages; on the contrary, they are, in their immediacy, the basic element and very foundation of the *Elegies*.

The second great difficulty for Rilke was the expression of personal emotion, so studiously avoided in *Neue Gedichte*, where even an exclamation mark would be felt as wholly out of place, and a line like this one unthinkable:

alle die Sterne: denn wie, wie, wie sie vergessen!   (III, 288)

This difficulty was a personal one, not inherent, like the incorporation of thought, in poetry itself. On the contrary, the expression of emotion has ever been one of the supreme aims of lyrical poetry, and Rilke had only to abandon his, after all, unnatural reticence in this respect and take the plunge in order to experience that he, too, could be borne along on these waves. The novelty of this experience lends not a little attraction to the style of the *Elegies*: it pervades them with a subdued warmth that not infrequently breaks out into open enthusiasm and furnishes the necessary counterpart to the thought-content which otherwise might have over-weighted these poems.

What has become of the close interaction of technical devices that forms the backbone of Rilke's style in *Neue Gedichte*? They have not been totally abandoned in the *Elegies*, but they are often suspended. The density is now supplied by the pressure of thought and experience, a density often so packed that, instead of support, it rather needs relief. But the dense texture is there, at the poet's command, when it is needed to bring certain passages into relief. If this alternation of what may sometimes appear as two distinct styles does not result in disharmony, but in contrast and enlivening variation, it is due to the organic aptness in each passage.

The language of the *Elegies* is difficult to define or describe. Much more than their form, it is the foundation upon which these poems stand or fall. And it carries them: they stand. This language comes from great depths, purified of all dross during its long way up through hardest rock. Those barren years during which Rilke waited for the power to complete the *Elegies* were not lost after all: in them, this new language slowly matured within him, while he tentatively used it here and there in those poems that were later collected as *Späte Gedichte* and *Letzte Gedichte*. It is simple, it is large, yet there is in it also great wealth, even complexity that sometimes comes to the surface and is always felt below the surface. At times it is terse, at others diffuse, sometimes harsh, sometimes sweet; all these contrasts are held together by an inner concentration emanating from a deep assurance and sincerity within the poet.

It can be as simple as this:

> Wollen es werden. Wem es geben? Am liebsten
> alles behalten für immer ... Ach, in den andern Bezug,
> wehe, was nimmt man hinüber?   (III, 298)

or as involved as this:

> Um diesen
> Stampfer, den Stempel, den von dem eignen
> blühenden Staub getroffnen, zur Scheinfrucht
> wieder der Unlust befruchteten, ihrer
> niemals bewussten, — glänzend mit dünnster
> Oberfläche leicht scheinlächelnden Unlust.   (III, 279)

> Weite Speicher der Kraft schafft sich der Zeitgeist, gestaltlos
> wie der spannende Drang, den er aus allem gewinnt.   (III, 290)

The last quotation sounds like a simple statement, very condensed. Yet it is more than that: a visionary experience become poetry. The poet's vision is simple, great and concrete, caught in a convincing image, and his language fully expressive of his vision. *Der spannende Drang*, with its short *a* sounds and tense *n*'s, conveys the meaning to perfection, preceded by the equally expressive *ei*'s in *weite, Speicher, Zeitgeist*. Success in passages of this kind is not always so complete in the *Elegies*:

> Mehr als je
> fallen die Dinge dahin, die erlebbaren, denn,
> was sie verdrängend ersetzt, ist ein Tun ohne Bild.   (III, 299)

Here, a clause like *was sie verdrängend ersetzt*, is neither visionary nor poetic, and the adjective *erlebbaren* purely intellectual; the passage is further marred by the equally intellectual *denn*. The same is true of these lines:

> O, nicht, weil Glück ist,
> dieser voreilige Vorteil eines nahen Verlusts.   (III, 297)

The definition of happiness is apt and original, but its expression is not poetic. If in the first of these passages quoted, the conjunction *denn* is a disturbing element, in the second *weil* is the offender. Throughout the *Elegies*, these slightly prosy conjunctions tend to destroy the lyrical texture:

> Aber Lebendige machen alle den Fehler ...   (III, 263)
> Denn das eigene Herz übersteigt uns ...   (III, 268)
> Und waren doch in unserem Alleingehn mit Dauerndem vergnügt
>   (III, 277)
> Denn auch das Nächste ist weit für die Menschen   (III, 291)
> denn schon das frühe Kind wenden wir um ...   (III, 293)
> Denn ihm auch haftet immer an ...   (III, 294)

Already in the first line of the First Elegy we encounter the pronoun *ich*, so rare in *Neue Gedichte*:

> Wer, wenn ich schriee, hörte mich denn . . .   (III, 259)

It is later often replaced, or alternates with, the discreeter *du*, or *wir*:

> Aber bewältigtest du's?   (III, 260)
> Aber wir, die so grosse Geheimnisse brauchen . . .   (III, 263)

In the Third Elegy, the pronoun is *er*, to express the general validity of a condition not confined to the individual; the same is true of the Sixth Elegy, although the pronoun in the first person is not absent from it. It occurs, with varying frequency, in all the elegies, but sometimes it breaks through in a warmer, more personal note, as in the Ninth:

> Erde, du liebe, ich will . . .
> Namenlos bin ich zu dir entschlossen . . .   (III, 301)

Never before has the man Rilke confessed his ego so freely as in these lines.

Among the most notable purely formal aspects of the *Elegies* are their beginnings and endings, especially the latter. The ending of each elegy is clearly set off, like the coda in a piece of music, from the body of the poem, so that in each case we can lay our finger on the spot where the coda begins; in the First Elegy with the line: *Schliesslich brauchen sie uns nicht mehr. . . .* The corresponding lines for the other elegies are, Second: *Fänden auch wir ein reines, verhaltenes . . .*; Third: *Und du selbst, was weisst du — . . .*; Fourth: *Wer zeigt ein Kind, so wie es steht?*; Fifth: *Engel: es wäre ein Platz . . .*; Sixth: *War er nicht Held in dir schon, Mutter . . .*; Seventh: *Engel, und würb ich dich auch!*; Eighth: *Wer hat uns also umgedreht . . .*; Ninth: *Erde, ist es nicht dies . . .*; Tenth: *Aber erweckten sie uns, die unendlich Toten. . . .*

These endings are in every instance significant; at the same time, they are of great importance formally, bringing the respective elegies to a dignified, graceful, elegant or moving close.

The beginnings of the elegies are not so distinctly marked off, they merge more imperceptibly into the main body of the poem. It was essential to find the right opening words, to envelop the reader from the start in the atmosphere and climate of each elegy. Four begin with questions, those poetically suggestive questions Rilke puts, like *O Bäume Lebens, o wann winterlich?* (Fourth Elegy). The Second Elegy begins with the short sentence: *Jeder Engel ist schrecklich*; the Seventh with the passionate cry: *Werbung nicht mehr, nicht Werbung . . .*; the Tenth like an organ prelude: *Dass ich dereinst . . . Jubel und Ruhm aufsinge. . . .* Only the beginning of the Third Elegy is somewhat less successful, with its contrast more suited perhaps to prose: *Eines ist, die Geliebte zu singen. Ein anderes, wehe. . . .*

A word remains to be said on the formal merit of the individual elegies, which varies a great deal according to the poetical integration the material has been given. The simpler and less varied the thought, the greater is the formal achievement of each elegy. The Third Elegy, e.g., has one theme only: the terror of Libido, the animal passion, deeply felt by the poet; here thought and expression permeate each other in perfect harmony and create an atmosphere of sombre greatness. This elegy is of one piece, because it concentrates on one theme only. Unity of style is remarkable also in the Fifth Elegy, although here it has been achieved at the price of a somewhat looser form. Next in formal merit we might place the short Sixth, and near it the Ninth, closely followed by the Seventh and Fourth. The Tenth Elegy suffers from a break, not wholly bridged, between the first part and that beginning with the allegorical description of the *Leid-Stadt*, and again between that and its last part; this is the only elegy where allegory has taken the place of image. In the Eighth, the very complex thought has not always found perfect formal expression, except perhaps in the beautiful last lines. The First Elegy we would place last in this connection: it is like an overture, where all the main themes of the subsequent work are touched upon (*Stimmen. Stimmen*, the poet says in the middle of this elegy). This evaluation is based on purely formal criteria and does not profess to group the elegies according to their intrinsic merit: their greatness as poetry does not in every case coincide with their formal perfection.

The Sonnets to Orpheus

If the *Elegies* are *Werbung um ein endlich noch Erreichtes*, the *Sonnets to Orpheus* are pure song: *Gesang ist Dasein. Für den Gott ein Leichtes* (III, 315). In German, 'easy' and 'light' are both expressed by the word *leicht*. *Ein Leichtes*—Rilke must have felt like Orpheus, his god of song, when he wrote the *Sonnets*; indeed, it is their lightness that distinguished these poems from any of his earlier productions; the *Sonnets* read as if they had their origin in a state of grace.

The fifty-five poems were written in a few days, during the great wave of inspiration that generated the *Elegies*; but if these had occupied the poet for ten years, there is no record that the *Sonnets* were even planned one day before they were written. This lightness makes their style very different not only from that of the *Elegies*, from which they are clearly distinguished by their form, but also from *Neue Gedichte*. We said earlier that it was not given to Rilke to sing, and indeed the song of the *Sonnets* comes unexpectedly as if a miracle had happened to the poet.

What do we mean by song in this connection? Not the quality described by the word 'cantabile', but a pouring forth of poetry in a steady, uninhibited flow, as in song, a production marked by the immediacy with which poetic thought is translated into elated, vibrating language. *Sonnets to Orpheus* have this immediacy in spite of the great diversity of their material. Apart from this diversity there is, moreover, the inevitable inequality of merit between the individual sonnets which are not uniformly carried and pervaded by the poetic breath that created them: while most of the material has been transformed in the process, some remnants have resisted. We could point to a few passages that are vague, or too intellectual, or occasionally (a thing very rare with Rilke) even flat—but in spite of such minor blemishes, the great unity of breath is there and pervades the *Sonnets* with its airy intoxication.

How has this miracle of lightness found expression in the style of the *Sonnets*? Partly by the disappearance of some of the density (the 'specific weight' of language) with which Rilke formerly made his style deliberately heavy:

> O erst dann, wenn der Flug
> nicht mehr um seinetwillen
> wird in die Himmelsstillen
> steigen, sich selber genug ...   (III, 335)

Here the language is as unconnected as Heine's: there is no alliteration, no vowel music, no assonance (except *Himmelsstillen*) to give these lines density; there is enjambment, but it does not create density either in this connection. In the following passage, we encounter some vowel cadence (*ei* at the end of every line), but it is not marked enough to make the texture heavy:

> Wir sind die Treibenden.
> Aber den Schritt der Zeit,
> nehmt ihn als Kleinigkeit
> im immer Bleibenden.   (III, 334)

On the other hand, the devices creating density are still present in many of the sonnets, though perhaps generally not as massed as before, without destroying their lightness:

> Nähme sie einer ins innige Schlafen und schliefe
> tief mit den Dingen — : o wie käme er leicht,
> anders zum anderen Tag, aus der gemeinsamen Tiefe.
> Oder er bliebe vielleicht; und sie blühten und priesen
> ihn, den Bekehrten, der nun den Ihrigen gleicht,
> allen den stillen Geschwistern im Winde der Wiesen.   (III, 357)

Here we have intimate connections between the different words: *Schlafen* und *schliefe* (meaning and alliteration); *schliefe, tief, Tiefe, bliebe, priesen, Ihrigen, Wiesen* (vowel sound and assonance); *leicht* and *vielleicht* (repetition of syllable, also interior rhyme); *anders, anderen* (meaning and assonance), and in the lovely last line, all attuned on *i*, the alliterating *w* in *Geschwistern, Winde, Wiesen*.

> Zu dem gebrauchten sowohl, wie zum dumpfen und stummen
> Vorrat der vollen Natur, den unsäglichen Summen,
> zähle dich jubelnd hinzu und vernichte die Zahl.   (III, 356)

This passage, tuned on *u* and *o*, is almost as closely connected as the preceding one; it contains ten *u*, four *o*, the assonance of *dumpfen* and *stummen*, alliteration in *unsäglichen Summen*, in *zähle* and *Zahl*. David I. Masson has very closely analysed Sonnet No. 9 of Part I: *Nur wer die Leier schon hob . . .*, and shown an infinite number of close connections.[1] Yet notwithstanding such associations, the language is rendered light and transparent by a force that lifts the words up and thus counteracts their associative heaviness, and the result is a happy serenity quite unknown to Rilke's earlier productions. There is also a certain hardness in the style of the *Sonnets*, emanating from the supernatural clarity of the poet's vision. We might have expected that the extraordinary condensation of thought in the *Sonnets* would render them heavy, but somehow the contrary has resulted: to such heights has the poet's thought been projected, and with such lightning speed and directness, that it crystallized into something at once light, hard and transparent, like pure, clear glass.

Some of this newly-acquired lightness must be credited to the influence of Valéry. We have seen that the short-lined sonnet occurs several times in his *Poésies*, but it is not this form alone

---

[1] In the *Modern Language Review*, vol. 66, 1951, p. 419.

that contributed to Rilke's style in the *Sonnets*; it is the spirit of
Valéry's language as well as of the French language, a kind of
intellectual, rational ecstasy we discern in the exalted, lucid language
of the *Sonnets*:

> Toute feuille me présente
> Une source complaisante
> Où je bois ce frêle bruit . . .
> Tout m'est pulpe, tout amande,
> Tout calice me demande
> Que j'attende pour son fruit.   (Valéry, *Aurore*)

In spite of their immediacy, the *Sonnets* retain a certain reticence.
The pronoun *ich* occurs in only nine of them, *du* and *wir* more often.
Their diversity is strongly felt, but the leitmotiv Orpheus, the singer,
and Song, hold them together, and still more so their origin in the
poet's liberated voice. Moreover, through all the differences and
contrasts of content, intensity, tone and language, Rilke has strictly
adhered to the fourteen-line sonnet-form. The way he has varied it
by length of line, transparency or density, heaviness or lightness of
tone, gives each sonnet its individual note and setting.

The *Sonnets to Orpheus* are a combination of clear thought (or
of thought too profound to be quite clear) with deep feeling,
professed with a certain elated urgency; their style, a serene beauty
of form, is as unique in Rilke's production as it is in German poetry.
It is undoubtedly the highest achievement Rilke's art was capable
of. Its main source was a state perhaps best described as poetic
intoxication reached by the poet during his unique experience of
inspiration. An early letter will perhaps shed some light on the
unconscious processes involved in such inspiration:

Der Maler dürfte nicht zum Bewusstsein seiner Einsichten kommen (wie der
Künstler überhaupt); ohne den Umweg durch seine Reflexion zu nehmen,
müssen seine Fortschritte, ihm selber rätselhaft, so rasch in die Arbeit eintreten,
dass er sie in dem Moment ihres Übertritts nicht zu erkennen vermag.[1]

Something of this nature must have happened to Rilke when he
wrote the *Elegies* and *Sonnets*. It is clear, from the passage quoted,
that inspiration does not create the 'progress' mentioned, which is
achieved over long periods of struggle for knowledge as well as
form; inspiration, in a flash, draws the sum of these labours, speedily
(*so rasch*) lifts them up in an unconscious act of creation (*ihm selber*

---

[1] *Briefe*, I, 1897–1914, 1950. Brief 86, Oct. 21, 1907.

P

rätselhaft). Rilke was outside himself when the voice pierced him and the intricate mass of thought and feeling that had accumulated within him was taken up and poured out in pure, transparent song.

Letzte Gedichte

Rilke's development as an artist culminates in the *Sonnets to Orpheus*. A survey of his style would, however, be incomplete without a consideration of the poems contained in the collection included in *Gesammelte Werke* under the title *Letzte Gedichte und Fragmentarisches* (1927), and of a separate volume, containing in part the same material, called *Späte Gedichte* (1934). Both collections were compiled after the poet's death, and the material united in them dates from different periods of his development, but most of it comes from the barren years between 1912 and 1922. These were the years of frustration, of mental and emotional despair, when the poet felt the ground give under his feet. There is, therefore, no spiritual unity in these poems, they resemble fragments, broken bits and pieces; E. M. Butler even says, with some exaggeration: 'They have the extra-aesthetic glamour of ruins and relics'.[1]

Yet in spite of their lack of unity and of their unequal merit, the poems of this period have a marked style of their own, a *de profundis* quality stamped upon them by their common origin from the dark depths; or rather a style in the making, the elements of which are being assembled under our eyes. The cloud under which Rilke lived cast its shadow over his poetry and transformed much of it into a baroque tragic landscape, bathed in a sombre and sullen darkness, occasionally lit up by flashes of glaring light. The despair at the back of many of these disjointed pieces, often expressed in powerful concentration, endows them with an unmistakable greatness. For Rilke, although erring in the wilderness, had not lost his great power as an artist, and his faculty of expression was not entirely crippled by the fact that it was a power in search of a centre. *Letzte Gedichte* are indeed tortuous, torn by conflicting tendencies: on the one side an ever-increasing intellectuality tending towards the abstract, on the other the pressing need for readmitting personal emotion that had so successfully (too successfully?) been banned from *Neue Gedichte*. The following passage, as indeed the

---

[1] *R. M. Rilke*, 1941, p. 399.

whole poem from which it is quoted, is typical of the overbalancing
intellectuality so often encountered in these pieces:

> Schon kehrt der Saft aus jener Allgemeinheit,
> die dunkel in den Wurzeln sich erneut,
> zurück ans Licht und speist die grüne Reinheit,
> die unter Rinden noch die Winde scheut.
> Die Innenseite der Natur belebt sich,
> verheimlichend ein neues Freuet euch ...   (S.G., 162)

And again:

> Raum greift aus uns und übersetzt die Dinge:
> dass dir das Dasein eines Baums gelinge,
> wirf Innenraum um ihn, aus jenem Raum,
> der in dir west.   (S.G., 150)

Characteristic, too, are turns of speech like these:

> Nun sollen wir versagte Tage lange
> ertragen in des Widerstandes Rinde   (III, 400)
> der Gipfel reine Verweigerung   (III, 420)
> Gestillte Form der angefüllten Spende.   (III, 410)

And here, as a contrast, is the new call of emotion:

> Leuchte, leuchte! Mach mich angeschauter
> bei den Sternen. Denn ich schwinde hin.   (III, 450)
>   O hab ich keine Haine
> in der Brust? keine Wehen? keine
> Stille, atemleicht und frühlinglich?   (S.G., 23)
> Wem willst du klagen, Herz? Immer gemiedener
> ringt sich dein Weg durch die unbegreiflichen
> Menschen.   (III, 412)
> Ach die Pein der Liebesmöglichkeiten
> hab ich Tag und Nächte hingespürt:
> zueinander flüchtend, sich entgleiten,
> keines hat zur Freudigkeit geführt.   (S.G., 140)

A line like the last: *keines hat zur Freudigkeit* (*!*) *geführt*, quite un-
Rilkean in its clumsy naïvety, is characteristic for the poet's pre-
dicament at this period. His despair finds its most tragic expression
in poems of the confession type, a thing very unusual for Rilke,
whose development had carried him in the opposite direction, away
from any direct expression of the ego in his poems. He felt he had
gone too far in his quest for objectivation, and landed himself and
his art in a blind alley. The poems we have in mind (*Waldteich*,
S.G., 21, *Klage*, III, 412, *Ausgesetzt auf den Bergen des Herzens*, III,
420, and *Wendung*, III, 460), reveal a sense of loss and the struggle
that was going on within the poet during those years. The short

poems *Klage* and *Ausgesetzt auf den Bergen* . . . are moving in their
direct and simple appeal; the other two, if less successful as poems,
are more interesting and revealing: they are a rendering of account,
a poet's desperate monologue, but Rilke's powers at that time were
not strong enough to shape these monologues into poems—they
remain confessions in verse. In *Ausgesetzt* . . . the anxiety of his
heart blends with the peculiar intellectual quality of his suffering
in a new manner:

> Hier blüht wohl
> einiges auf; aus stummem Absturz
> blüht ein unwissendes Kraut singend hervor.
> Aber der Wissende? Ach, der zu wissen begann,
> und schweigt nun, ausgesetzt auf den Bergen des Herzens.
> Da geht wohl, heilen Bewusstseins,
> manches umher, manches gesicherte Bergtier,
> wechselt und weilt. (III, 420)

If we analyse this poem, so simple in appearance, we find that
the compressed sadness so forcibly expressed in it is in part the result
of rhythmical repetition: *auf den Bergen des Herzens* occurs four times
at regular intervals, in the first, fifth, tenth and fifteenth (last) line.
Other words repeated are: *siehe, wie klein, blüht, manches*; moreover,
there is a relation between *unwissendes, wissende, wissen*; *geborgenes,
ungeborgen*; *hier blüht wohl, da geht wohl*. Alliteration, vowelling,
assonance are discreet, but most effective (*wechselt und weilt, der
grosse geborgene Vogel*). The poem leaves the impression of a great,
new simplicity. *Klage* contains similar repetitions.

There are other poems in these collections where Rilke's expressive
power attains greatness by unorthodox means, concentrates of the
new style and language that were maturing within him. We need
not be surprised or shocked if at times we find an artificial ring in
this language: there is a similar artificiality in much of the experimental contemporary music and painting, and Rilke was strongly
influenced by such painting, especially by Cézanne and later, among
others, by Picasso, whose picture 'Les Saltimbanques' inspired his
Fifth Elegy. Here is an illustrative passage of this style from *Christi
Höllenfahrt*:

> Er, Kenner der Martern, hörte die Hölle
> herheulend, begehrend Bewusstsein
> seiner vollendeten Not: dass über dem Ende der seinen
> (unendlichen) ihre, währende Pein erschrecke, ahne.
> Und er stürzte, der Geist, mit der völligen Schwere
> seiner Erschöpfung herein . . . (III, 385)

There are many new elements in this poem: the strange juxtaposition of two participles in succession (*herheulend, begehrend*); unexpected combinations of nouns and adjectives (*dunkle ruhlose Luft, die starken wachsamen Tiere, der Dinge nächtliches Dastehn, trauriger Raum, die völlige Schwere*); the dropping of an article (*begehrend Bewusstsein*); new or obsolete words (*Leidung, rufte*); the accent on an accumulation of active verbs:

> Und er stürzte ... schritt ...
> hob zu Adam den Aufblick, eilig,
> eilte hinab, schwand, schien und verging ...

(The abruptness of the last passage may be compared to that of Hölderlin in *Patmos*:

> Denn alles ist gut. Drauf starb er. Vieles wäre
> Zu sagen davon. Und es sahn ihn, wie er siegend blickte,
> Den Freudigsten, die Freunde noch zuletzt.)

All these elements combine in creating a strong, new atmosphere that we might venture to call expressionistic: beauty resulting from harmony has been sacrificed in an effort of pressing the words into an arrangement yielding a maximum of expressive energy. This, coming after *Neue Gedichte*, is indeed a new style and language, and Rilke himself felt strongly that this poem marked a new beginning in his production.

Similar tendencies are discernible in *Der Tod Mosis* with its many repetitions (*rückwärts, aufwärts, Berg*—three times—*genug*; *alt, Alter*—six times). It is a great poem, one of the finest in the collection; in it occurs the monumental line, arresting in its simple strength:

> Und sein Auge war rein bis zum Grunde der Kräfte.   (III, 404)

As an example from the many startling images that occur in *Letzte Gedichte*, we may quote one from *Witwe*:

> Sie griff sich mit den klammen
> zehrenden Händen Höhlen in das Haupt.
> Wär sie ein Stein im Freien, flösse dort zusammen
> der grosse Regen, reiner als man glaubt,
> und Vögel tränken ...   (III, 408)

The diversity encountered in these collections is very great; besides much experimental novelty, of the kind analysed in some detail, we find Rilke using Catullus' classical forms, only modified by rhymes, in *Tränenkrüglein* and *Ex Voto*; writing his most regular sonnets, some free verse and 'pure poetry' influenced by Mallarmé and Valéry, as *Die Tauben*, *Das Füllhorn* and similar pieces. We can only mention this side by side as another characteristic aspect of Rilke's style at this moment, without being able to enter upon a detailed appreciation of tendencies which are too divergent, at this period of transition, to allow of anything like unity of style. The important fact is that the *Dinggedicht* with its dense and, as it were, closed style is being abandoned and that new elements enter into the poet's style: rhythmical repetition, an increased tendency towards abstraction, the admission of personal emotion as shown in the use of interjections and exclamation marks, the frequent coining of new words, the accent on expression at the expense of structural or verbal harmony. The resulting productions cannot always be called poems, often they are experiments only, attempts at poems. We do not know how many of them, and which, Rilke intended to publish.

THE EFFECT OF RILKE'S STYLE ON
CONTEMPORARY LANGUAGE AND
LITERATURE

IT will be abundantly clear, from the foregoing, that Rilke did not leave the language as he found it: by perfecting his style, he considerably extended the range of language, its possibilities of expression. Perhaps no poet before him had employed and mastered such a wealth of poetic devices to such effect, none had attended with such care to the *art* of poetry. This care was pure: it never seeks effect for its own sake, but always in the interest of sincere poetic expression. Moreover, Rilke's astounding mastery of technique, his wealth of means, is combined with strict economy: if an effect is to be obtained by sparing means, he will not use more than necessary; if, on the other hand, he feels it can only be expressed by the full orchestra, he will not shrink from using all the instruments at his disposal. His compressed thought stands out in clear relief in the sometimes extreme condensation of his language. All padding, even that largely tolerated in poetry, has been suppressed. In addition, Rilke's style is characterized by its shadings, those delicate overtones for which German poetry before did not possess the means of expression: from his exceptionally wide and quite unbiased vocabulary, the poet supplies the exact, i.e., the profound and poetically fitting word, and strengthens its effectiveness by surrounding it with significant affinities of association and sound, and by two specifically musical devices: contrast and repetition. The resulting compact mass of word texture moves along in an apparently natural, though in fact carefully regulated, rhythm, imperceptibly changing with every line, the lifts and dips occurring in obedience to musical necessity, and at the same time helping to express the meaning by their accurately distributed stresses. There is, in this movement, a supple, elastic quality that is new not only to German lyrical poetry, but to the language as well. Another art very peculiar to Rilke is his modulation, those subtly devised transitions from word to word, line to line, vowel-group to vowel-group. To these achievements must be added the colourfulness of Rilke's style, based in part on a vocabulary that admirably expresses the freshness of his vision, in part on a skilful combination of words that reflect each other in various brilliant facets of sound and meaning.

If he was not a reformer like Stefan George, Rilke was a very able remodeller of language as well as poetic technique, as important in this respect for his country as Swinburne was for England. George is more one-sided, he sometimes appears to us as the conqueror with vanquished language at his feet, while Rilke penetrates it and lets himself in turn be penetrated by it. Both poets, at times, almost lost touch with the spoken and emotionally intelligible language of their period, yet Rilke, at least in his later works, found the road back to it.

No poetry, of course, is ever exactly the same speech that the poet talks and hears: but it has to be in such a relation to the speech of his time that the listener and reader can say, 'that is how I should talk if I could talk poetry'. This is the reason why the best contemporary poetry can give us a feeling of excitement and a sense of fulfilment different from any sentiment aroused by even very much greater poetry of a past age.[1]

Rilke's poetry gives us 'this feeling of excitement and sense of fulfilment'; more than that of many a poet living in a great city of his own country, at the centre of life and in constant touch with its major currents, the style of Rilke, the solitary exile, strikes us as contemporary in the sense that it is of our time as well as of the future. His exceptional sensibility did not need close contact with everyday life, since his rare intuition anticipated, as if by second sight, and often without actual experience, the deeper currents of the contemporary mind, while he ignored most of what agitates the surface of our lives.

Rilke's contemporariness is vividly felt when looking at Picasso's 'Les Saltimbanques', a reproduction of which is given as a frontispiece to the English translation of the *Duino Elegies* by J. B. Leishman and Stephen Spender: this picture inspired, as we know, the Fifth Elegy, but it is equally true to say that the observation and experience of acrobats inspired both artists to their respective creations. But while they speak in the different languages of painting and poetry, they speak as contemporaries: it is their period that unites these otherwise incomparable works of art. Just as we feel a painting by Fragonard and a sonata by Mozart as contemporary, it is the style of Picasso's painting and Rilke's elegy, more even than the similarity of the subject, that gives us this sensation of nearness.

[1] T. S. Eliot, *The Music of Poetry*, 1942, pp. 16–17.

In the painted figures as well as in the poet's words we feel the beat of our own time, and moreover, still hidden and not yet entirely intelligible, something that belongs to the future. As we ourselves are continuously extracting new meanings from great works of past ages, and discovering new beauties in them, so we sense that there is much concealed, for the discovery of future generations, in those great works of our own age.

In a way it is odd that Rilke's poetry should strike us as so contemporary, for his style is the closest expression of a thought remote from most of the currents of his period, a thought often in active opposition to the machine age into which he was born. Much of it is, moreover, of such an individual and even private nature that it does not seem to belong to any definite period at all. What is it, then, that makes us feel his poetry as so much of our time? There is, at first, a negative element: Rilke's style never recalls the past; unlike that of other modern poets (we need only think of Hofmannsthal, who so often reminds us of Goethe), Rilke's mature style is so imbued with his personality that it calls no other poetry to mind: it makes us think of Rilke only. To a large extent poetry, as all the other arts, must rely for its effect on tradition, upon which each individual artist in turn builds his personal contribution. Without such traditional basis, art would be neither intelligible nor enjoyable. But at certain intervals this tradition is interrupted and a shock is felt when an artist, without altogether discarding the old forms, handles them in so novel a manner as to produce effects quite foreign to those we were accustomed to. A case in point is the poetry of G. M. Hopkins, who uses the traditional forms of poetry, such as rhyme, metre, the sonnet form and others, in short, with the exception of his sprung rhythm, almost everything that is familiar to us, but in such a startling way that we hardly recognize the old devices and forms, and feel the impact of a wholly new style. We have to learn Hopkins' new language before we are able to understand and enjoy his poetry. Rilke's case is somewhat different: there is no shock, the bridges that lead to the past are still visible in the background, but they lead away from tradition into a new landscape. The deeper we enter into it, the stranger it becomes, and parts of the *Duino Elegies* as well as of the *Sonnets to Orpheus* demand the learning of a new idiom just as Hopkins' poems do. Like him, Rilke makes use of devices generations of poets have been using before, but ever since his central period his poetry does not rely on the effects usually produced by them, but

P*

on entirely new ones. Other poets, it is true, have occasionally drawn new tunes from the old instruments, but Rilke draws new sounds from them, and, moreover, he never plays any of the old tunes. The language he uses is that of German poetry, yet modified in such a subtle manner that we feel the variation more than the continuity; the timbre of his voice, the cachet of his melody are unmistakable in every line, almost in every word. There is, moreover, one important factor Rilke has in common with his time: a certain psychological refinement, a search for the profound, the true relationship of things and ideas, a desire to live near the deep sources of life. The discipline of psycho-analysis may seem far removed from Rilke's intentions and specific emotions, yet it is no coincidence that it was developed during his lifetime. The psychological refinement of his style as expressed in many of its elements, particularly in his use of syntax and the participle, his searching disquiet, the vibrating expression of 'Angst' in all its complexity (especially in the prose work, *Die Aufzeichnungen des Malte Laurids Brigge*), are very much of our time, and of our time alone. To read Rilke's poetry as it appeared was in a sense a revelation: it was the encounter with a new language that made an immediate appeal, especially to young people, while it revealed all the wealth of its complexities and depths only gradually and after patient and loving approach. Rilke, the outsider, has given expression to thoughts and sensations that had never before been expressed in German poetry; he rendered all the half-tones, delicate shades and involved processes that form part of the contemporary mind, because his unique sensibility needed them for its perfect expression. No reader could remain indifferent to the melody that emanated from his poetry, to the cachet of its strong perfume, even repellent at first like the too sweet and heavy scent of some tropical flower. Such repulsion, however, due mainly to the intensity of Rilke's softly insinuating cadence, was generally dispelled as the rich treasure borne on that melody revealed itself. This softly persuasive incantation of the Rilkean cadence might best be described with the poet's own words in *Schlangenbeschwörung*:

> Wenn auf dem Markt, sich wiegend, der Beschwörer
> die Kürbisflöte pfeift, die reizt und lullt,
> so kann es sein, dass er sich einen Hörer
> herüberlockt, der ganz aus dem Tumult
> der Buden eintritt in den Kreis der Pfeife,
> die will und will und will und die erreicht,

> dass das Reptil in seinem Korb sich steife
> und die das steife schmeichlerisch erweicht,
> abwechselnd immer schwindelnder und blinder
> mit dem, was schreckt und streckt, und dem, was löst —;
>
> (III, 179)

Das was streckt und das was löst—it is a characteristic of Rilke's style that it creates a tension which it presently resolves. Enjambment is one of the main agents of this peculiar tension: it is, in a way, a negation of the verse form which, however, continually reasserts itself, mainly through the rhyme; the poem seems to dissolve and is pulled back in a steady rhythm, which accounts for the characteristic breathing pulsation in many of Rilke's poems. The intensity created by this rhythmical movement is then constantly reinforced by all the intricate reactions and relations of the words, knit together in the poem by means of the poet's very individual use of the well-known technical devices.

It is obvious that a style as powerful and original as Rilke's could not fail to exercise influence, and equally clear that the direct influence of so personal a mode of expression could lead to imitation only. If a style of such density is taken over without adaptation—and adaptation in this case is almost impossible—it leaves no opening for personal expression other than its creator's, and Rilke's imitators therefore could not help taking over more than they bargained for. The first of Rilke's works to exercise influence was the *Stundenbuch*, which caused a spate of ephemeral imitations by young, now mostly forgotten, poets. An example which is perhaps more a case of *Einfühlung*, where thought-content as well as form have been taken over, is *Der grosse Abend* by Martin Beheim-Schwarzbach (born 1900):

> Der Efeu wird die Städte überwinden.
> Sie wähnen sich den Zeiten übermächtig,
> doch in den Wäldern sind sie wieder schmächtig
> und in den weissen Dünen nicht zu finden . . .
> Der Wind wird Sturm sein und von Freiheit trächtig,
> und über Türmen, müdgestandnen, schlaffen,
> werden die Wolken wieder gross und prächtig.

This is hardly more than a paraphrase of Rilke's

> Du dunkelnder Grund, geduldig erträgst du die Mauern . . .,
>
> (II, 220)

and his

> Alles wird wieder gross sein und gewaltig,
> die Lande einfach und die Wasser faltig . . .   (II, 254)

Rilke's words and melody are there, but in the long poem, which may stand here for many similar ones, shapeless repetition replaces the graphic conciseness that in the *Stundenbuch*, in spite of a few lengthy passages, so effectively condenses the poet's thought. The influence of the *Stundenbuch* is unmistakable, too, in this poem by Hermann Kesten (born 1900):

> Oh, so verloren sein; wie, wenn es regnet,
> Ein Tropfen wenig ist; so atemlos
> Stets auf der Jagd nach Leben sein; und bloss
> Verlegen sein, wenn wirklich es begegnet;
> So arm sein, so an Träumen reich, so gross
> In der Idee, den Märkten preisgegeben,
> Betrübt sein, doch im Trüben stärker leben . . .
>
> (*Die Lohnfrage*)

The greatest temptation was Rilke's cadence, his long, winding melody, which we meet again in the poetry of many of his contemporaries. Richard Schaukal (born 1874) at one time influenced the young Rilke, later was in turn influenced by him. In his *Kophetua* the cadence sounds somewhat harsher than in the model:

> König Kophetua legte die goldene Krone
> über die eisengerüsteten Knie und harrte
> auf einer der Stufen, bis ihn die traurige, zarte
> Magd erblickte, flehentlich, ohne
> sich umzusehen, wo sein Gefolge war . . .

In Stefan Zweig's (born 1881) *Taj Mahal* the melody is more elegant and supple:

> Im Teiche, wo klarspielend und genau
> Die weissen Formen sich als Bild verkleinern,
> Scheint er ein Spielzeug. Zart und elfenbeinern,
> Wie unter mattem Glas liegt er zur Schau.
> (Man hätte beinah Furcht, ihn zu zerbrechen.)
> Und dann ein Blick: Und sieh, ein Bau!
> Aufragend, blendend, makellos und steinern
> Steigt er empor, löst blinkend seine Flächen
> Von Blättergrün und steigt in immer reinern
> Bewegungen empor ins blanke Blau . . .

This recalls and imitates Rilke in more than one way. The beginning is parallel, in rhythm as well as in thought, to

> In Spiegelbildern wie von Fragonard . . .   (III, 236)

The bracketed line is another reminiscence, and so is the one composed of past participles *Aufragend, blendend, makellos und steinern,*

very similar to Rilke's *erblindend, finster, unbenutzt, verbleit* (III, 89);
the coupling of adjectives *klarspielend und genau* and *zart und elfen-
beinern,* the rhyming of *steinern* with the comparative *reinern,* the
alliteration of *Blättergrün, blinkend, blankes Blau,* are directly dependent on Rilke's style. But we also feel how much the model has
been watered down by bloodless imitation: *wie unter mattem Glas*
is much weaker than Rilke's highly expressive images; the thought-
content of the bracketed line is too banal to be thus emphasized,
and in the line beginning with *aufragend,* the last adjective, instead of
bringing a climax, is the weakest in the sequence. The technique
has been taken over, but not mastered in its all-important details.

A quotation from Paul Zech (born 1881), from the sonnet *Die
fremden Länder,* confirms a similar dependence:

> Die fremden Länder, die ich sah in jenen Jahren,
> als jede Reise Ausfahrt war und Wiederkehr:
> Ich muss sie wohl mit einem anderen Gefühl erfahren
> und aufgenommen haben, denn sie sind nicht mehr
> die riesige Erfahrung, der man lange
> nachsann und immer rühmend davon sprach . . .

The word *mehr,* isolated by enjambment, recalls Rilke's

> die Ferne seiner Väter schien nicht mehr
> für ihn zu gelten . . .,   (III, 74)

and the rhythm of Zech's sonnet reproduces faithfully the Rilkean
cadence.

We find an echo of the long poem *Alkestis* (*Neue Gedichte*),
especially in the images, in *Der Zinsgroschen* by Fritz Diettrich
(born 1902):

> Jetzt standen sie vor ihm. Ein kurzes Warten,
> Das wie ein Wehren gegen seinen Blick war,
> Hielt ihren Gruss und ihre Fragen auf.
> Las dieser Mensch die Worte nicht, die sie
> Wie Messer bei sich trugen, eh sie noch
> Geschliffen von den dünnen Lippen sprangen?
> Hob er die Schalen ihrer klugen Hirne
> Nicht mühlos ab und sah die Schlingen liegen?
> Und klopfte nicht sein Blick an ihre Herzen
> Prüfend, wie eines Arztes Finger klopft?

Franz Josef Graf Matuschka (born 1895), has learnt a good deal
from Rilke's vowelling and alliteration:

> Du zielst und triffst! In blinkem Silbersitze
> Fliegst du mit flinker Klinge zu Gericht,

> Und links und rechts und hier und da den Wicht
> Zitierest du vor deines Degens Spitze.
> Sieh, wie sie zittern! durch der Rüstung Blitze
> Stichst du den Stichel, einen Strahl von Licht: —
> Sie liegen splitterdicht und ganz zunicht
> Und hingesichelt von des Zornes Blitze ...
>
> (*Der Engel Michael*)

This is very ingenious, too much so, with its 33 *i* in eight lines, and the alliteration of *fliegst, flinker, stichst, Stichel, Strahl, Rüstung, Ritze*—talented, but spoilt by excess. The same is true of the following quotation by the same poet:

> Es wolkt der Rauch des Frühlings um die Erde,
> Der Hauch der Hoffnung um die bare, arme:
> Dass sie vom Harm im Arm des Lichts erwarme,
> Tönt schon das ewige Schöpferwort: es werde!
> Die Horde ordnet schon der Hirt zur Herde ...
>
> (*Ewiger Frühling*)

Such lines show very clearly what can become of Rilke's style without his discipline and sense of balance. With him, the devices serve a purpose, here they run wild: the rhyme *arme—erwarme* is not strengthened, but smothered by the interior rhyme *Arm—Harm*, while the ingenious sequence in the last line, *Horde—ordnet—Hirt—Herde* is more ornamental than expressive.

A quotation from a poem by Helmut Bartuschek (born 1905), also shows the influence of *Neue Gedichte*:

> Irrer Hölderlin.
> Er ist besorgt, die Hände wegzutun,
> Weit hinter sich zum Rücken. Im Gebrauche
> Sind sie fast nichts mehr wert. Zum Rosenstrauche
> Zu gehn braucht er die schwachen Füsse nun
> Schon auch nicht mehr ...

The influence is seen in the direct beginning, which is understood from the title; in the way enjambment draws each sentence over into the next line, where it stops somewhere near the middle; in the characteristic use of *fast*, and in the reproduction of Rilke's melody. It is watered down, stripped of its tension and intensity, and ugly accumulations of insignificant words (*fast nichts mehr — nun schon auch nicht mehr*) show a lack of taste.

Instances that reveal the impact of Rilke's later works on young

poets are rarer. Rudolf Bach (born 1901) has strongly felt that of
the *Elegies*:   . . .

> Dem schreckhaft weissen, sich mehrenden Wolkenturm
> Steht er, auf eben noch
> Geltender Sanftmut muldiger Weide,
> Gegenüber. Wie
> Soll er bestehn, hier, er,
> Leichtesten Lebens, unerlittenen
> Herzens und mühloser Stirne?
> Und nichts, was ringsum ist, hilft zum Gleichgewicht:
> Tannen, schweigsame Vielzahl, stehen abgewendet,
> Blumen duften zu zart, der Bach, hell redend,
> Fällt aber seitab zur Tiefe, das Vieh grast fremd.
>
> (*Knabe mit Vater*)

Such lines are impregnated with Rilke's poetry; not only are
language and tone his, but his thought has been taken over together
with its mode of expression. Thus, *eben noch geltende Sanftmut
muldiger Weide* (the rare *muldig* occurs in the Sixth Elegy); the line
Gegenüber. Wie, with its characteristic division in the middle,
enjambment cutting into the rhythm; the verb *bestehn*, often found
with Rilke; a combination like *leichtesten Lebens*, the participle in
unerlittenen Herzens, are all close imitations, almost replicas, of the
language of the *Elegies*. Even the occasional prosiness is there in
the line *Und nichts, was ringsum ist, hilft zum Gleichgewicht. Tannen
stehen abgewendet, Blumen duften zu zart*, strongly calls to mind a
similar passage in the *Sonnets*: *Wagen umrollten uns fremd, vorüberge-
zogen,* / *Häuser umstanden uns stark, aber unwahr* (III, 348). The
adaptation, however, is superficial, for the subject of the poem (the
instinctive leaning of a small boy, overwhelmed by his first experience of a mountain, towards the protective hand of his father)
is too tenuous for the massive style of the *Duino Elegies*. Dependence
on Rilke is even stronger in the next quotation, from the same
poet:

> Oh, wie vieler Opfer bedarf es, unwiderruflicher, bis
> Endlich das junge, schwärmende, träge Herz einmal
> Aufwacht, erschüttert und *weiss*,
> Was es gilt hier im Irdischen! — : Nicht
> Sich zu zerstreuen in Vieles, halb, noch Gedämmer
> Eigensüchtigen Traums,
> Sondern gesammeltes Wachsein, unablässig erneuertes,
> Zärtlich, nüchtern und rein wie
> Die ewige Lampe . . .
>
> (*Klage und Lob*)

The language of this poem is so obviously that of the *Elegies* that particular passages hardly need emphasizing; we might only call attention to a parallel passage in the Fifth Elegy:

> längst, wo Boden nie war, nur aneinander
> lehnenden Leitern, bebend, — und *könntens*,
> von den Zuschauern rings . . ., (III, 282–3)

or to the combination *zärtlich, nüchtern und rein*, which might literally stand in one of Rilke's later poems. A passage from a third poem confirms Bach's dependence on Rilke's late style:

> Den wir am Boden fanden, den wir bald wieder verloren
> Der blausamtne Schmetterling, wo kam er her?
> War er noch einmal erwacht? Oder war er zu zeitig geboren?
> Ach, wir liebten den Leidenden sehr.
>
> (*Ein Gedächtnis*)

The quaint word order (anticipation of a relative clause) is typical of Rilke, and so is the string of insinuating questions, as well as a later line:

> Aber trat jemand, wie leis auch, über die Zimmerschwelle,

which echoes Rilke's *wie klein auch* in *Ausgesetzt auf den Bergen des Herzens* (III, 420). Again, we note a certain discrepancy between style and content (the agony of a butterfly).

The author of the next quotation is Jürgen Eggebrecht (born 1898):

> Wuchs und Fülle liebenden Gewirkes
> Aus der Gütigen, der Mutter, Schoss,
> Reife Gabe grösseren Bezirkes
> Und an solchem Masstab selber gross!
>
> In dem Schwunge seiner Flächen hebt es
> Früher Schöpfung die Natur und Lust;
> Alle Steine und noch Ungelebtes
> Wären Puls der ahnungsvollsten Brust.
>
> (*Landschaft*)

We need only confront this with the first two stanzas of Rilke's *Füllhorn* (III, 436), to note an influence that borders on plagiarism:

> Schwung und Form des gebendsten Gefässes,
> an der Göttin Schulter angelehnt;
> unsrer Fassung immer ungemässes,
> doch von unsrem Sehnen ausgedehnt — :
>
> in der Tiefe seiner Windung fasst es
> aller Reife die Gestalt und Wucht,
> und das Herz des allerreinsten Gastes
> wäre Form dem Ausguss solcher Frucht.

Even the number of stanzas (five in each poem), is identical.
Finally, an example to show the influence of the *Sonnets*:

> Ist das Erfüllung? Sie wär es
> seligern Wesen, als wir sind.
> Ganzes Genügen, entbehr es
> willig, solange wir hier sind.
> Blumen erleben Vollendung
> selig in Duft und Vergehn,
> und des Vogelflugs Wendung
> *kann* in den Räumen bestehn.

(*Tanzmusik! Immer erneute* . . ., by Erika Mitterer, born 1906)

Here we have the short lines of the *Sonnets*, their rhythm and rhymes,
the stress on one word (*kann*), even individual words, like *Räume*,
bestehn. The poem, light and graceful, is Rilkean in spirit as well
as in form, which is not surprising, since the author was in personal
contact with the poet.

Such examples from more or less secondary poets could be
multiplied. What was Rilke's influence on greater, less eclectic
figures? George, Rilke's senior by seven years, was too old and
much too independent to be influenced by anyone. Werfel, although
younger, was too different in outlook and temperament to be able
to accept much from Rilke. Other poets, to name only Hermann
Hesse, Georg Heym, Else Lasker-Schüler, Georg Trakl, move in
orbits Rilke does not touch.

The question arises if literary influence from a poet such as Rilke
is really possible at all, or if it must be limited to the imitation of
external characteristics only. The influences Rilke himself under-
went as a young man gradually disappeared as his outlook broadened
and his style matured; what he took over later, mostly from Baudelaire, Verlaine and Valéry, was assimilated, but it permanently
enriched his style. Indirect influences, from Rodin's personality
and from the paintings of Cézanne, although very strong, cannot
be counted here. At this moment, the last word about Rilke's
influence on German lyric poetry cannot be said. His *Elegies* and
Sonnets were published in 1923, and did not immediately become
widely known; besides, it took some time for them to be understood
and fully appreciated. Then, in 1933, German cultural life was
suddenly darkened and almost obliterated, so that these poems
have had hardly a decade, and a very troubled decade at that, to
exercise any influence. They certainly point to the future more
than to the past or the present. It will, accordingly, be in the

future only that their influence may be profoundly felt, whenever that may be.

If he succeeds, the poet achieves a thought capable of taking on a new aspect for every generation—he enriches humanity with a capital sum which is not spent at once, but goes on earning interest indefinitely.[1]

What is true of the poet's thought is equally so of his way of expressing it, of his style. The immediate influence of Rilke's style, as we could observe from the examples quoted, was not promising: what was firmly centred in the original became scattered and peripheral with the imitators. Subsequent influences may not be so easy to recognize, because they will not be so obvious. Beethoven's symphonies exercised a steady influence for more than a century, although the symphonic form, when he wrote them, had been fully established. What his followers took over was his way of filling this form with personal experience, with the expression of struggle, defeat and victory. They could do this without a close imitation of Beethoven's more individual stylistic characteristics. Similarly, after three hundred years, the style of the 'metaphysical' poets is exercising an influence on contemporary English poetry. Thus we can imagine that one day the monumental form of the *Elegies*, their character as vehicles of deeply felt very personal experience, will become a general model, or that the 'abbreviations' of the *Sonnets* will make their impact felt as an accepted language of poetry.

[1] Herbert Read, 'The Nature of Poetry,' in *Collected Essays in Literary Criticism*, 1938, p. 95.

INDEX OF NAMES